Governance of the Petroleum Sector in an Emerging Developing Economy

This book is dedicated to the citizens of Ghana and people of Africa

Governance of the Petroleum Sector in an Emerging Developing Economy

Edited by
KWAKU APPIAH-ADU

Routledge
Taylor & Francis Group

LONDON AND NEW YORK

First published in paperback 2024

First published 2013 by Gower Publishing

Published 2016 by Routledge
4 Park Square, Milton Park, Abingdon, Oxon OX14 4RN

and by Routledge
605 Third Avenue, New York, NY 10158

Routledge is an imprint of the Taylor & Francis Group, an informa business

British Library Cataloguing in Publication Data
Governance of the petroleum sector in an emerging developing economy.
  1. Petroleum industry and trade--Ghana. 2. Petroleum
  industry and trade--Economic aspects--Ghana. 3. Revenue
  management--Ghana. 4. Petroleum law and legislation--
  Ghana. 5. Petroleum industry and trade--Developing
  countries. 6. Petroleum industry and trade--Norway.
  I. Appiah-Adu, Kwaku.
  338.2'7282'09667-dc23

Library of Congress Cataloging-in-Publication Data
Appiah-Adu, Kwaku.
  Governance of the petroleum sector in an emerging developing economy / by Kwaku Appiah-Adu.
    pages cm
  Includes bibliographical references and index.
  ISBN 978-1-4094-6307-8 (hbk. : alk. paper) -- ISBN 978-1-4094-6308-5
(ebk.) -- ISBN 978-1-4094-6309-2 (epub) 1. Petroleum industry and
trade--Ghana. 2. Petroleum industry and trade--Developing countries. I.
Title.
  HD9577.G42A66 2013
  338.2'72809667--dc23
                                         2012045377

ISBN: 978-1-4094-6307-8 (hbk)
ISBN: 978-1-03-283748-2 (pbk)
ISBN: 978-1-315-58550-5 (ebk)

DOI: 10.4324/9781315585505

Contents

List of Figures

List of Tables

Foreword

Congratulations to Professor Kwaku Appiah-Adu for conceiving this project and for his tenacity and perseverance in seeing it through successfully. I call his achievement 'a project' simply because it was conceived and accomplished as a compendium of well-selected and mutually complementary contributions from several authors across five countries – Ghana, Trinidad and Tobago, Norway, Canada and the USA. The focus of the compendium is on the challenges facing emerging countries that are keen on securing sustainable economic growth. I also wish to extend my congratulations to the authors, who are all recognized experts in their respective fields, for making the project a success.

The special attraction of this book lies in combining descriptive analysis, empirical studies and practical policy recommendations. Thought provoking and instructive in every respect, the content is presented in a captivating and easily digestible style, covering a range of carefully selected subjects that an emerging oil-producing country cannot afford to ignore if it is to manage its petroleum resources effectively.

This compendium could not have come about at a better time. Over several decades, the petroleum sector has grown increasingly in importance within the context of industrial activity, national economies, global economy and geopolitics. In spite of the quest for new ways to meet the world's energy demands over the last decades, petroleum still remains pivotal in ensuring that the global energy demand is met. Escalation in energy needs and the emergence of new demand patterns across the world accentuate the need for old and new petroleum-producing nations to try and meet global requirements in an adequate and timely manner.

However, the proper management of natural resources has for decades been the subject of extensive studies and comments by scholars. While the abundance of natural resources in a country is expected to result in economic blessings for its citizens, the experiences of many developing countries with natural resources are nothing to write home about. Sadly, many of these nations suffer from the 'resource curse' or the 'paradox of plenty'. The ailment makes countries with abundance in natural resources – specifically non-renewable resources like minerals and petroleum resources – have lower, and in many cases negative economic growth, less democratic governments, and consequently worse development outcomes than countries less endowed with natural resources.

After decades of oil exploration, Ghana, a role model for Africa in many ways, has finally discovered oil in commercial quantities and is about to become an oil-exporting nation. The question is: can Ghana really be a trailblazer from which other African oil-producing nations can learn how to manage their petroleum resources effectively? Over the last few years I have had the privilege of sharing my experiences with Ghana in its preparation for the oil era. Many economic, political and social well-wishers of the developing world will join me in hoping that Ghana succeeds in delivering the expected benefits to its citizens and thus become a worthy example for other African oil-producing nations to emulate.

For countries that aspire to achieve the noble goal of soundly managing their petroleum resources, this book highlights a number of thematic areas that must be successfully handled. Firstly, the country should have a well considered and clear legislation based on a fundamental petroleum policy that receives wide support in the country from the beginning. Secondly, the sector must be governed effectively so that the interests of stakeholders are well aligned and justly reconciled when the need arises. Thirdly, the petroleum-producing nation must ensure that transparency and stakeholders' participation are entrenched in the decision-making process. Fourthly, the country should manage operations and the petroleum revenue so as to turn its resource wealth into sustainable and equitable development. Fifthly, it is critical for the host nation to safeguard security as well as prevent any harmful impact from petroleum operations on the environment, the economy and way of life. While each petroleum-producing nation has to develop an approach that best fits its particular social aspirations and economic objectives, there are always lessons that can be learned from the experiences of other countries that have succeeded in making the resource a blessing. In this context, the approaches of Trinidad and Tobago (an emerging economy) and Norway (an industrialized economy) are used as case studies from which Ghana and other African oil producers can learn.

The chapters of this book address several important aspects of the issues mentioned above. In doing so, the book deals with a range of factors that are critical to the success of managing petroleum resources and hence require close attention by emerging petroleum-producing nations. By inviting several authors with different backgrounds to delve into the various issues in breadth and depth, this book makes a significant contribution to the literature on oil and gas, particularly with respect to developing economies. Interestingly, the style of the text makes it of value to a wide spectrum of readers. These include personnel involved in the petroleum industry, particularly technical staff involved in policy-making in both oil companies and government agencies. Additionally, the book is strongly recommended to readers who wish to acquaint themselves with the dynamics of the petroleum industry. I also believe that scholars in business schools as well as engineering institutions, business executives, consultants and policy-makers will find the contents of this book instructive and an invaluable reference material.

I am delighted to note that Ghana with this book has embarked on its own literature on petroleum resource management. I look forward to seeing the evolution of the Ghanaian approach being documented and analyzed in future literature.

Farouk Al-Kasim
Chief Executive
Petroteam AS
Norway

Preface

The discovery of petroleum resources in commercial quantities has been the dream of many a country, particularly those in developing economies that perceive access to and exploitation of this resource as well as reaping of new wealth from the resource as a solution to all their problems.

Following decades of oil exploration dating back to the late nineteenth century, during which Ghana made a few non-commercial discoveries, a major find in commercial quantities was made in 2007. The national oil company, the Ghana National Petroleum Corporation (GNPC) and its partners Tullow Ghana Ltd and Kosmos Energy announced the discovery of oil in significant quantities in the Jubilee Field, offshore the Western Region of Ghana. This find, which is approximately 65km from the nearest coastal town, spawned a great deal of excitement within Ghana. Since this discovery was announced there has been heightened interest in exploration in Ghana's waters, which was hitherto not the case.

As a result of the pioneering role Ghana plays in African politics, as well as social and economic emancipation, the events in Ghana have attracted attention from political, social and economic commentators. Some of the questions asked are: will this oil discovery and its development be a blessing or curse to Ghana? Will Ghana be able to serve as a role model to other African oil-producing countries in the area of good petroleum governance? What should Ghana do to avoid the resource curse? How should Ghana develop its petroleum revenue management strategies such that the oil proceeds benefit both current and future generations? What role should civil society play in ensuring accountability and transparency in the petroleum sector? How best should Ghana approach the exploitation of the resource? What should be the ingredients of the legal and fiscal regime? Are there approaches (or models) of other countries that Ghana can learn from in the governance and management of its oil resources? What are some of security issues as well as health, safety, environment and community relations issues that should concern Ghana?

This book makes an effort to answer the aforementioned questions through the contributions of a set of internationally renowned authors with expertise in the various areas identified. Its contents constitute an indispensable collection covering a range of significant subjects on oil and gas that everyone seeking to gain knowledge in the sector needs to be conversant with. Scholars, business executives and policy-makers would do well to have copies of this book in their libraries.

Kwaku Appiah-Adu (Prof.)
Central University & Centre for Advanced Strategy Analysis, Ghana

Acknowledgments

The editor wishes to express his profound gratitude to the authors who spent several precious hours of their time contributing to the chapters of this project and ensuring that the book saw the light of day: Anthony E. Paul; Prof. Joe Amoako-Tuffour; Dr Inge Amundsen; Samuel Aning; Nana Kegya Appiah-Adu (Mrs); Ama Jantuah Banful (Mrs); Kerston Coombs; Mangowa Ghanney (Mrs); Dr Stephen Donyinah; Patrick Heller and Francis M. Sasraku.

The same goes for my mentor in the oil and gas field, considered the greatest ever value creator of Norway, Farouk Al-Kasim, who wrote the foreword as well as a chapter, and also provided invaluable insights into various aspects of this project and inspired me to make excellent decisions along the way.

Thanks goes to my wife Nana Kegya, a co-author, and our children, Afua, Kwaku and Akua, who gave me the time and breathing space to complete this project on schedule. Words cannot express my appreciation for your prayers, patience and encouragement which were more than adequate to propel me to higher levels of motivation when the going got tough.

On my behalf and on behalf of the whole team, I wish to thank the following eminent citizens who inspired the team by demonstrating their confidence in the project: H.E. John Agyekum Kufuor; Prof. E.H. Amonoo-Neizer; Dr Mary Chinery-Hesse; Prof. Martin Tsamenyi; Most Rev. Prof. Emmanuel Asante; Rev. Dr Joyce Rosalind Aryee; Stephen Sekyere-Abankwa and Mrs Bertha Amonoo-Neizer.

Finally to all others that time and space would not permit me to list, I say a big thank you for the diverse roles you played in making this project a success.

About the Contributors

Farouk Al-Kasim has spent 54 years in private and government positions within the petroleum industry. With a background in petroleum geology, he worked for 12 years with the Iraq Petroleum Company in exploration, reservoir geology and field development planning. He then moved to Norway as advisor to the Ministry of Industry (1968–1973) where he was instrumental in establishing the Norwegian approach to managing the petroleum sector. He played a key role in developing the Norwegian Petroleum Directorate (NPD) where he was Director of Resource Management (1973–1990), responsible for the planning and supervision of all petroleum operations on the Norwegian Continental Shelf from reconnaissance, to exploration, development, production, tail-end production and decommissioning of fields. He has served on several public committees in Norway on energy and petroleum research and development (R&D), field development and gas development strategies. His long and varied experience in technical management and petroleum administration has given him valuable understanding of multi-disciplinary and cross-institutional teamwork where effective communication and role appreciation are the key to sound cooperation. After leaving the NPD in 1991, Mr Al-Kasim has devoted most of his time to international consultancy work. For the last 21 years, through his consultancy firm Petroteam AS, he has advised developing countries in Africa, Asia and South America on good governance of the petroleum sector and how to secure optimal resource exploitation that helps achieve lasting benefits to the nation from the operations and the generated petroleum revenue.

Joe Amoako-Tuffour (PhD) received both his BA and MA in Economics from Simon Fraser University, Canada and holds a PhD in Economics from the University of Alberta, Canada. He was a Professor of Economics at Saint Francis Xavier University in Canada where he taught from 1990 to 2012. When not teaching at the University, he spends his time in Ghana. Between 1994 and 1998 he served as a Summer Visiting Research Fellow at Centre for Economic Policy Analysis (CEPA) in Accra. In 2001–2003, he served as technical advisor at the Ministry of Finance and Economic Planning, and was instrumental in developing Ghana's Poverty Reduction Strategy and the associated Multi Donor Budget Support framework. Subsequently, he played a lead role in setting up the Tax Policy Unit at the Ministry of Finance and in 2008-2010 was appointed the lead technical advisor in the design of Ghana's Petroleum Revenue Management Law. He has been published in international journals on the demand for public goods, recreational demand analysis, fiscal deficits and public debt. In 2008, he published a book on *Poverty Reduction Strategies in Action: Lessons and Perspectives from Ghana*. He has also been published in the *American Journal of Agricultural Economics, the Review of Economics and Statistics, the Journal of African Economies, Environmental Management, Tourism Economics, Journal of Environmental Management, Water Resources Research, and Journal of Applied Economics*. He is also a member of the Natural Resource Charter Technical Advisory Group based at Oxford University. He currently holds the position of Senior Advisor at the African Centre for Economic Transformation (ACET), Ghana.

Inge Amundsen (PhD) is a Senior Researcher at the Chr. Michelsen Institute (CMI) in Bergen, Norway. He is a political scientist focusing on democratic institutionalization, parliaments, political parties, political corruption, and natural resources (petroleum revenue management). His main study area is francophone West Africa, Ghana, Angola, Tanzania, Nigeria, and Bangladesh. Amundsen obtained his PhD in Comparative African Studies at the University of Tromsoe, 1997. He was Research Director at CMI from 2000-2003 and Director of the U4 Anti-Corruption Resource Centre from 2002-2006. He has also coordinated three CMI institutional cooperation programmes. Amundsen teaches extensively on corruption prevention and good governance in the petroleum sector.

Samuel Aning is a Fellow of the Centre for Advanced Strategic Analysis. He holds a BA (Social Sciences) and an LLM, London School of Economics and Political Science, University of London specializing in Natural Resources, Environment, Law of the Sea and International Protection of Human rights. Sam was the Deputy Chair of the Oil and Gas Technical team that was set up to develop policies and a master plan for the petroleum sector when Ghana discovered oil in commercial quantities in 2007. He currently lectures in contemporary issues covering areas such oil and gas, climate change, human rights, HIV-AIDS, gender issues, good governance, policy analysis, monitoring and evaluation. Sam has undertaken assignments for both public and private sectors spanning the areas of organizational development, human resource management, as well as development and delivery of training, monitoring and evaluation and oil and gas. He has supported different teams and provided business advice to Small and Medium Enterprises in the areas of Strategic Planning, Market Research and Surveys, Organizational Restructuring, Strategic Plan Development and Project Appraisals. Sam has made significant inputs in the area of Public Sector Reforms, especially diagnostic studies and made recommendations for commercializing the operations of key public sector institutions. His country experiences span Europe, America, Asia and Africa and he has publications to his credit in leading academic and professional journals.

Kwaku Appiah-Adu (PhD) is a Professor of Business Management at Central University and Chairman of the Centre for Advanced Strategic Analysis, Ghana. He is also the Vice-Dean of the Central University Business School. Previously, he worked at the Office of the President, Ghana, where he was Head of Policy Coordination, Monitoring and Evaluation, Chairman of the Oil and Gas Technical Committee, Director of Ghana's Central Governance Project and member of the Advisory Board for the UN Initiative on Continental Shelf Delineation. Kwaku served as a member of the President's Investors' Advisory Council. Prior to that he worked as a Consultant with PricewaterhouseCoopers (PwC) and lectured at the Universities of Cardiff and Portsmouth. An author of six books and over 65 publications in reputable scholarly and professional journals, Kwaku has presented at several international forums dedicated to business and policy management. He has been elected to the ANBAR Hall of Excellence for his *'Outstanding Contribution to the Literature and Body of Knowledge'*. Kwaku is a director of a number of blue-chip companies.

Nana Kegya Appiah-Adu (Mrs) is a lawyer by profession. She holds a Bachelor of Law Degree (LLB) and a Master of Law Degree (LLM), both from the University of Wales, Cardiff. She started her legal career at the Bank of Ghana where her duties involved staff training and advising the bank on agreements and guarantees. She joined the academic staff of the Ghana School of Law in 2003 and initially taught law of contract. At present she teaches banking law. She has undertaken research in the area of electronic banking in Ghana and is currently conducting research into credit reporting in Ghana. Furthermore, she has a keen interest in human rights law and is involved in prison outreach work at one of the prisons in Ghana.

Ama Jantuah Banful is a Chief State Attorney and has worked with the Attorney-General's Office for 33 years. She obtained her LLB Degree from the University of Ghana and Barrister-at-Law (BL) from the Ghana Law School. Ama also holds an LLM in Oil and Gas from the Robert Gordon University of Aberdeen, Postgraduate Diploma in Human Rights and Humanitarian Law from the University of Lund, Sweden and a Postgraduate Certificate in Legislative Drafting. She is currently a member of the Tariff and Trade Advisory Board. Ama began her career in the Prosecutions Division of the Attorney-General's

Department where she was a Prosecutor for 19 years and then moved to the Civil Department where she is currently responsible for energy and oil and gas related matters among others.

Kerston Coombs is the Chief Executive Officer of Entech Consulting and a senior consultant with the Association of Caribbean Energy Specialists (ACES). Previously, he was the Plant and Production Manager at Federation Chemicals (now Yara Trinidad Ltd)/Trinidad Nitrogen Limited, Technical and Engineering Manager at the National Energy Corporation (NEC) and CEO of Clico Energy Company Limited. Mr. Coombs holds a BSc in Chemical Engineering from the University of London and a Diploma in Management from the University of the West Indies. He has participated as a presenter in many conferences on fertilizer, methanol and energy matters both locally and internationally. He has also been a member of the board of several companies and chairman of the Trinidad Nitrogen Company (Tringen). He is a past secretary of the Methanol Institute (based in the USA) and past president of the Trinidad and Tobago Chamber of Industry and Commerce. More recently he has been a member of the Boards of Methanol Holdings (Trinidad) Ltd. and the C.L. Financial Group and Chairman of Ventrin Petroleum Company Ltd., Caribbean Business Services Limited, and Information Support Services Ltd. (Carsearch). Mr. Coombs is a member of the Energy Committee of the Trinidad and Tobago Chamber of Industry and Commerce.

Stephen K. Donyinah (PhD) is currently a lecturer in the Department of Petroleum Engineering. He holds a PhD in Environmental Science and Engineering from the China University of Geosciences, Wuhan, (2004) and received a Masters degree in Petroleum Geology, Exploration, and Engineering from the same university in 1996. He obtained his BSc degree in Geological Engineering in 1990 from the Kwame Nkrumah University of Science and Technology. He was listed in the 'Who's Who' in the 21st century, 2001 edition of the Biographical Centre of the United Kingdom. His research interests lie in environmental pollutants and toxic wastes in water bodies as well as energy-related issues. He is an associate member of the American Association of Petroleum Geologists (AAPG) and an associate member of the Ghana Institution of Engineers.

Mangowa A. Ghanney (Mrs) is the Deputy Director of the Legal Affairs Division at the Ministry of Finance and Economic Planning. She holds a Bachelor of Law Degree (LLB) from the University of Ghana and a Master of Law Degree (LLM) from Temple University, Pennsylvania, USA. A member of the Ghana Bar Association since 1981, she was also licensed to practice law in the State of New York, USA until September 2011, when she retired from law practice in the NY State. Mangowa has several years of experience as a company lawyer, legal consultant and in regulatory compliance management in consumer and mortgage financing in the US. Over the years she has become an expert in contracts law and has developed adept skills in contract development and drafting, reviewing and analyzing contracts, and in contract negotiations. In 2007 when oil and gas were discovered in commercial quantities in Ghana, she served as the Minister's representative on the Presidential Technical Committee on Oil and Gas and was part of the team that planned and hosted the first international conference in Africa on oil and gas, and which also developed the first Framework National Petroleum Policy. She was the lead legal advisor in the development and enactment of Ghana's Petroleum Revenue Management Act of 2011, and has been actively engaged in its aftermath, to ensure effective implementation of the Law and the development of supporting Regulations. She is currently actively involved in the development of Ghana's new Extractive Industry Transparency Initiative legislation. She currently serves on the Board of Directors of the Public Procurement Authority and of the Financial Intelligence Centre, and has served on several governmental committees including the committee for the development of a Public Private Partnership (PPP) Policy, the committee to review and advise the Minister for Finance on Ghana's contracts with Mining Companies in Ghana, and the committee to develop a National Strategy for Anti-Money-Laundering and Combating Terrorist Financing (AML/CFT).

Patrick R. P. Heller is a Senior Legal Advisor at the Revenue Watch Institute, where he conducts research and offers policy analysis on legal and contractual regimes governing oil and mineral revenue. He has worked in the developing world for ten years, for organizations including the U.S. State Department, United States Agency for International Development (USAID), the Asian Development Bank, and the International Centre for Transitional Justice. At Revenue Watch, Patrick focuses on governance and oversight of oil sectors, the role of National Oil Companies, transparency, and the promotion of government-citizen dialogue. He has worked and conducted research in more than fifteen developing countries, including Afghanistan, Angola, Ghana, Lebanon, Nigeria, Sierra Leone and Peru. He has worked extensively with the Program on Energy and Sustainable Development at Stanford University, where he is a contributing author of an upcoming book on the strategy and performance of National Oil Companies. He holds a Law degree from Stanford University and a Masters degree from the Johns Hopkins School of Advanced International Studies.

Anthony E. Paul is the Managing Director of the Association of Caribbean Energy Specialists (ACES) Ltd., a leading Caribbean oil, gas and power advisory firm. He has spent over 30 years in the oil and natural gas business, in several technical, commercial and leadership roles, in Government and State and Private companies. He has led exploration programmes for the Trinidad and Tobago Ministry of Energy, Petrotrin and BP Trinidad and Tobago (BPTT). As a consultant, he provides analytical inputs on the energy industry, covering policy, regulatory, strategy, technical, commercial and business development issues. Recently, his advice has focused on extracting value from the full natural gas chain, as an advocate of local content and value-added, deepening of local participation and sustainable development from the sector. He has been supporting governments, companies and NGOs in several countries in Africa (including Angola, Equatorial Guinea, Ghana, Liberia, Nigeria, Mozambique, Tanzania and Uganda), Latin America (Bolivia, Peru and Suriname), Iraq, and East Timor. He has served on the Boards of major Caribbean companies in finance, IT and engineering, as well as in public institutions and business associations and is a member of the Advisory Board of the Revenue Watch Institute (New York, USA) and the Technical Advisory Group of the Natural Resources Charter (Oxford, UK.). Mr. Paul holds a BSc in Geology from The Imperial College of Science & Technology, University of London, UK and an MS in Exploration Geophysics from the University of Houston, Texas, USA.

Francis Mensah Sasraku is the Chief Executive of the Energy Finance Group, Ghana and head of the business development and consultancy division of the National Banking College in Ghana. He is an economist, a certified chartered accountant, management accountant and a chartered banker. He holds an MBA (Oxford Brookes University), an LLM in Oil and Gas Policy (Dundee University) where he obtained a distinction and is currently pursuing a PhD with a specialization in Petroleum Finance and Economics.

1

Introduction

Kwaku Appiah-Adu

The purpose of this book is to examine governance issues relating to Ghana's petroleum sector. Against the backdrop of global developments and experiences as well as within the national context, measures that are critical to the realization of optimal benefits to Ghana's economy are proposed. The book covers a number of pertinent themes considered by petroleum sector experts to be essential in assessing the appropriateness of policies and strategies as well as the effectiveness of their implementation. Five broad themes are addressed.

Thematic Areas

- turning oil and gas (O&G) wealth into sustainable and equitable development;

- entrenching transparency and stakeholder engagement;

- effective management of the O&G sector;

- safeguarding security and the environment;

- country-specific models and lessons for Ghana and other African oil-producing nations.

Turning Oil and Gas Wealth into Sustainable and Equitable Development

This theme is covered in chapters 2, 3, 4 and 5 and provides the opportunity to consider the contribution of O&G to economic growth in terms of Ghana's development based on strategies and experiences (positive and negative) across the globe. It reviews approaches necessary to achieve this both in terms of principles of sound management of public finances (revenue and expenditure) and specific instruments including petroleum revenue funds that have been developed to support this. The basic essentials of petroleum resource management are explored. Clearly, the operation and management of O&G resources in a company or government organization is no doubt a difficult and sophisticated undertaking. It usually entails a myriad of factors, uncertainties and risks. Decision-makers' options are contingent on the various conditions and limitations covering local–global, technical, commercial and social issues. Moreover, approaches necessary to achieve sound management of public finances (revenue and expenditure) and particular instruments that have been developed to support this, including petroleum revenue funds, are presented. At the nascent phase of the O&G industry, Ghana's petroleum reserves are expected to be modest by international standards. However as the industry grows and more oil is discovered, the impact of petroleum activities on the economic development of the country will depend on how transparently and efficiently oil revenues are managed. To ensure sound and prudent revenue management, Ghana's parliament has passed a Petroleum Revenue Management Act. An assessment of the nature and the eventual impact of public participation in the formulation of the law is undertaken to address the revenue management challenges, and explain why the law potentially represents an important step towards effective management of Ghana's petroleum resources. Furthermore, owing to the growing importance of gas as a source of power in Ghana, an effort is made to examine risks associated with gas-power project financing.

Entrenching Transparency and Stakeholder Engagement

This theme is covered in chapters 6, 7 and 8 and examines the role of transparency, accountability and stakeholder engagement in developing and implementing good extractive industry policy, using examples from Ghana and elsewhere. The respective roles of parliament, the judiciary, electorate, special agencies and the media in ensuring transparency and accountability are thoroughly investigated. A specific chapter focuses attention on the influence of civil society on the evolution of norms and procedures for oil sector management, both at a national and international level, and identifies emerging issues and tactics that civil society groups are beginning to utilize as their approaches continue to grow more nuanced. Additionally, the standards and processes that would ensure peaceful coexistence with various communities cannot be overemphasized, and in this respect, the roles of government as well as international and national oil companies in establishing stakeholder engagement are thoroughly explored. The main findings are presented for the key players and stakeholders so they can work together efficiently to ensure that the petroleum sector functions effectively to the benefit of all parties involved. Furthermore, an exhaustive analysis of how Ghana can avoid the resource curse is undertaken to guide policy makers and stakeholders from 'catching' the Dutch disease which so many oil-producing developing countries have grappled with.

Effective Management of the Oil and Gas Sector

Details revolving around this theme can be found in chapters 9, 10, 11 and 12 where the laws, contracts and regulatory institutions examined can be used to provide effective management of O&G exploration and production in order to achieve maximum benefits for Ghana. This includes discussions of licensing and negotiations, fiscal terms and the roles of the regulator and national oil company, using examples from Ghana's own recent experiences with regulatory reform and examples from around the world. Detailed analyses of fiscal regimes for the O&G sector in Ghana are undertaken with a discussion of the subject of petroleum economics, focusing on Ghana's petroleum tax regime and its strategic implications for the effective management of the O&G sector. Furthermore, the review assesses local content and its building blocks, participation aspirations, policies and strategies for the O&G sector. The role of government in creating a level playing field is highlighted alongside pitfalls to be avoided by host countries. Within the context of value addition, the utilization of natural gas as a source for downstream industrial development is addressed. Gas-based petrochemical projects for both in-country use and exports are explored, along with a clarification of gas contract terms and their associated arrangements. The concept of gas project management is investigated in cases where there is need for a major petrochemical project to pass several tests in order to secure project financing. To this end, the importance of a sound, credible, feasibility report that underpins the financial/economic viability of the project is underscored. In the same vein, various funding sources are presented against the backdrop today's credit squeeze in the financial markets. Also discussed is project insurance, an interesting adjunct that is usually provided through multilateral insurance schemes. Finally, for large gas projects, light is shed on provisions to guarantee specific performance criteria, covering areas such as managerial, operational and financial performance.

Safeguarding Security and the Environment

The penultimate theme is covered in chapters 13 and 14 and explores best practice experience to ensure thorough examination of both security and environmental issues relating to the O&G industry and appropriate safeguard measures suited to Ghana and the best means for their implementation. While Ghana may have adequate experience in designing the necessary environmental policies that are expected to guarantee safety from activities that may be hazardous to the environment, the current activities regarding oil discovery transcend the environment. There are other issues of health and safety standards as well as community engagement and expectations and how to manage all this in a manner that engenders added benefits that petroleum brings to a developing country. Concerning security, the dynamics in Ghana are changing with increasing influx of people and growing crime. Moreover, the Gulf of Guinea is registering increasing piracy activities, the use of the region as transit point for the transfer of illicit substances and other emerging threats. Also of equal concern is the insecurity in some of the countries in the region and the likely spillover effects if the security agencies are unable to cope. It is proposed that all actors be engaged with early warning systems designed to ensure the safety and security of personnel and installations of oil companies, safety of communities and engagement with all whose livelihood can be lost in the event of an oil spill. More importantly, it is suggested that Ghana would need to develop excellent relations between the various security sector institutions and local communities for effective response to emergencies should they occur.

Country-specific Models and Lessons for Ghana and Other African Oil-producing Nations

The final theme is captured in chapters 15, 16 and 17. Under this theme, two country models (approaches) and the pertinent lessons that Africa can learn from their experiences are discussed. One of these countries discussed in this book is Trinidad and Tobago (T&T). It is considered that to a large extent, what the world sees in the T&T Model and wants from it is the outcome. But not just that – how did T&T do it, what are the pieces of the energy eco-system that T&T built, what were T&T's successes and failures, what lessons can African host nations learn from T&T's experiences and, can T&T hold their hands in this process? The other country is a highly developed economy with well-established and effectively functioning national and petroleum sector institutions, namely, Norway, which is hailed as a country that has managed its petroleum resources with distinction and whose approach to governing the sector is worthy of emulation.

In the case of T&T, the model and best practice examples for Ghana and other African oil-producing countries are explored. It is intriguing to see how T&T's focus in the energy sector has evolved over the last four decades. In the 1970s a deliberate decision was made to convert some of the windfall from oil production and high prices to development of the natural gas industry. As the gas industry grew and prospered in the 1990s and beyond, another calculated strategy was implemented to build human capacity. In the 2000s, as the world has moved on from an industrial society to a knowledge society, T&T has shifted its focus to one of exporting energy expertise.

With respect to the Norwegian Approach, one chapter provides the essential elements of the model and a different chapter focuses on the lessons that Ghana and other host nations could learn from Norway's experience. Together, the contributions highlight areas where Ghana and other African oil-producing countries would do well to apply specific lessons in their quest to ensure that petroleum resources become a blessing and not a curse. A variety of subjects are covered including legislation, national participation, petroleum administration, licensing, petroleum agreements, the fiscal regime, transparency and accountability, national skills development, health, safety and environment, community relations, oil recovery and natural gas utilization.

In order to obtain in-depth analyses of the thematic areas presented above, specific chapters were written by global experts in their respective fields. In effect, the book is presented as a compendium of works that would serve as reference material for business practitioners, policy-makers, scholars, students and all persons interested in gaining insight into the O&G sector, particularly as it pertains to Ghana and other African petroleum-producing nations, with lessons drawn from the global arena and international best practice.

PART I

Turning Oil and Gas Wealth into Sustainable and Equitable Development

Managing the Extractive Resource

Stephen K. Donyinah

Abstract

Ghana is endowed with abundant natural resources; from minerals to raw materials from forest and agricultural products, and has mined gold for centuries, but is still grappling with prudent management of resources. While we can highlight 'the Norwegian Model' in the case of oil and gas (O&G), nothing can be said about the Ghanaian model in the management of resources. Sadly, despite an abundance of natural resources, Ghana has nothing to show in terms of development as a result of the improper management of the income generated from the sales of raw materials. For example, there is a lack of value added to commodities before sale and Ghana is still practising the old ways of merely selling raw materials to traditional partners without the additional value that can generate extra income. It is the aim of this chapter to outline the effective ways of managing Ghana's natural resources prudently in order to obtain optimal value from its natural resources. It is believed that if Ghana's natural resources are well managed, its economy will improve and great development will be realized. The issue of resource management is critical at this point in the country's history, given that it is now counted among petroleum-producing countries. Ghana cannot afford to make mistakes in this sector as witnessed in other commodities over the years. This chapter recounts the history of resource exploitation in Ghana, issues that were not properly managed, and subsequently discusses the way forward. The Norwegian Model for managing petroleum resources, which has a successful story worthy of emulation as far as petroleum production is concerned, is presented and the key points elucidated. Advice on the prudent management of Ghana's natural resources and the concluding remarks with regards to the benefits to be derived from the abundant raw materials are finally presented.

Introduction

Given Ghana's endowment with a wide array of abundant resources, the country would have been prosperous and would have attained a high level of development if there had been proper management of its natural resources. The need for an effective management of its resources is therefore important, especially with the advent of the discovery of oil in commercial quantities, and it is the hope of many in the country and across the African continent that Ghana's efforts to manage its O&G resources will be a success. There is therefore the need to develop a model in the management of the natural resources of the country.

This chapter therefore focuses on the ways and means of producing a management model for Ghana's natural resources. This assertion could not have been better put than the Financial Times's (FT) prediction that Ghana's economy will be the best on the African continent if the petroleum resources of the country are managed prudently. In a special edition dedicated to Ghana, the FT expressed the view that Ghana had the potential to become 'an emerging black power, rather than an aid-dependent African reformer, collecting World Bank stars' (*Financial Times*, 2011).

Despite centuries of gold mining and other mineral extraction in Ghana, it is perceived that the prospects of these mineral resources have not left any identifiable blueprint for ensuring sustainable development and poverty alleviation. Though mining constitutes the largest source of foreign direct investment (FDI) and minerals are the leading export earner, the sector has not helped to reduce poverty and tackle other development challenges. With the influx of multinational mining companies, the result has been development that largely benefits these companies to the neglect of people and the economy at large. Despite a boom in the demand and prices of minerals, the woes of people and countries on the African continent, particularly Ghana, keeps deepening with no end in sight. The searching question to pose is – what operational shortfalls in the mining industry bring about the untold hardship of citizens within countries whose natural resources are exploited?

Natural Resources of Ghana

The natural resources of Ghana include gold, industrial diamonds, bauxite, manganese, fish, hydropower, petroleum, silver, salt and limestone. Agricultural products include cocoa, timber rubber, coconuts, coffee, pineapples, cashews, pepper and other food crops. Ghana's industries are dominated by mining, timber and processing, light manufacturing, fishing, aluminium production and tourism (CIA World Fact Book, 2011). The country has a long history of gold mining and exploration. Gold represents Ghana's major export commodity, providing approximately 50 per cent of gross domestic product (GDP). Ghana is the world's tenth and Africa's second largest producer of gold, with current production estimated in excess of 2.4 million ounces (Moz) per annum. High gold prices have resulted in a recent significant increase in expenditure on gold exploration in the country. Ghana is also the third largest African producer of aluminium metal and manganese ore, and a significant producer of bauxite and diamond. In addition, Ghana has produced a number of industrial minerals, which include kaolin, limestone, salt, sand and gravel, and silica sand on a small scale.

Discoveries of More Minerals

The interesting thing is that more new and precious minerals are discovered from time to time in addition to the already known ones. According to the Government (Ministry of Lands and Natural Resources), Ghana has made more discoveries of mineral deposits which are expected to boost the country's economy and development. The deposits include copper, phosphate, nickel, chromium and uranium. The Ministry made this assertion at the opening of the third West African Mining Summit (www.ghanaweb.com, November, 2010). The Government has, therefore, invited the investor community to partner it to develop the country's enormous natural resources in an efficient, economic and environmentally sustainable manner that will ensure the sustainable development of the country. The Government of Ghana (Ministry of Lands and Natural Resources) stated that there are bright prospects for mining in Ghana.

History of Gold Mining in Ghana

From the prehistoric times to the present, one commodity that has been mined over the years is gold. In fact, this single commodity is what attracted the early Europeans to this region -particularly the Portuguese followed by the Danes, and finally, the English who eventually colonized and named the country the land of Gold and later the Gold Coast. Prehistoric accounts also indicate that Ghana's ancestors could virtually pick up gold nuggets on the streets after rainfall and strangely enough did not have immediate use of the commodity at that time. They only regarded the gold as family wealth, which was then kept safe as a 'sacred treasure' by the Abusua Panyin, the head of the family. This person was expected to provide protective custody of the gold and was obliged to hand it over to the next of kin to follow this tradition. This practice went on for years until the advent of European industrialization, which rekindled the quest of minerals to support the emerging industry, and the era of colonialism which was sweeping across Africa. The eventual exploitation of the commodity began with underground mining across the southern parts of Ghana. Consequently, infrastructural development such as roads and railways were confined to this area alone, thus serving only the interests of the colonial powers.

Ghana has been a producer of gold since the sixteenth century and today boasts of one of the largest and richest reserves of gold in the world. Ghana's gold-mining industry is a *relative* success story in the Government's attempts to turn the fledgling economy around. The gold sector followed the country's general trend of economic stagnation during the 1970s and, by the early 1980s, was starved of foreign investment to modernize and improve output. However, following the Government's policies of market liberalization aimed at increasing foreign investment, the industry was turned around, and gold output exceeded 2.4 Moz per annum (Noble Minerals Resources Ltd, 2009). Ghana has a long history of mineral production and gold mining has been prominent in the economy of Ghana for about 2,000 years using indigenous methods. Historically, this method of gold mining attracted Arab traders into the country (Botchway, 1995) and from the fourteenth to the nineteenth century, the Gold Coast produced about 14 Moz of gold using indigenous methods. In the nineteenth century, the colonial masters outlawed traditional methods of gold panning to pave the way for modern methods after the colonial masters took over the Ashanti Kingdom (Ayensu, 1997). The development of modern modes of extracting minerals made gold mining an exclusively foreign-run enterprise. For example, the Ashanti Goldfields Corporation (now Anglogold Ashanti), which began operations in 1897, gained a concession of about 160 square kilometres to prospect for gold. A number of the world's largest gold companies are either producing or exploring within the country and several new multimillion-ounce goldmines are currently planned for development, ensuring Ghana's ongoing role as one of Africa's leading gold producers. Mineral extraction has become a great attraction for investment and many developing countries endowed with mineral resources see mining as a development panacea. The question many mineral-endowed countries of the South face is how to translate their country's mineral and oil resources into economic wealth to reduce poverty, protect the environment and uphold social stability. This is a critical and complex question faced by resource-rich countries across the developing world.

Potential from Proper Management of the Mineral Resources

This chapter provides a concise historical account of gold mining in Ghana, from the pre-colonial period, through to the present age. For over 1,000 years, the Ancient Kingdom of Ghana, the former Gold Coast Colony, and present-day Ghana have produced a substantial portion of the world's gold. Initially frequented by Arab traders who had crossed vast stretches of the Sahara, the trading routes of the Ancient Kingdom of Ghana stimulated significant conflict among groups, in particular, the Europeans, who, for centuries, battled for control of the West African gold monopoly. The region's first gold-mining companies were formed shortly after the British established the Gold Coast Colony in 1874, and, following two successive gold rushes in the early 1900s, gold prospecting and extraction were widespread in Obuasi, Tarkwa and Prestea. However, the industry soon entered a period of depressed production, which began after independence in 1957 and ended shortly after the implementation of the country's Economic Recovery Programme (ERP) in 1983. Ghana's gold-mining industry has since grown rapidly, supplanting cocoa cultivation as the country's chief economic activity. In the past 20 years, production increases in the order of 700 per cent have been achieved and today output from resident gold mines account for some 37 per cent of national exports and 97 per cent of mineral exports (Hilson, 2002).

Ghana (Gold Coast) could thus feign an excuse of not having had the monopoly and control of its natural resources until independence. Sadly, not only did Ghana not have the opportunity to manage its resources (including gold and other natural resources), but to make matters worse, the income accruing from these commodities was not used for the development of the country (or benefit of Ghana's citizens) either, but rather managed to the advantage of the colonial masters. For instance, according to Wikipedia (Mining industry in Ghana), under British colonial rule, the Government controlled gold mining to protect the profits of European companies. The colonial government also restricted possession of gold as well as of mercury, essential in recovering gold from the ore in which it is embedded. Following independence, foreign control of the sector was tempered by increasing government involvement under the Nkrumah regime; however, production began to decline in the late 1960s and did not recover for almost 20 years. This was the order of the day until the struggle for independence which witnessed a gush of wind blowing over the African continent, resulting in Ghana becoming the first sub-Saharan country to gain independence on 6 March, 1957.

Post Independence Era

Ghana's 1992 Constitution and the preceding ones in 1964 and 1969 vested the monopoly and control of all natural resources of the country in the president, who became the trustee of these natural resources on behalf of the people of Ghana. What this meant was that no individual or group of persons had authority over the exploitation of the mineral resources of the country. All natural resources belonged to the state and the exploitation and management of these resources could only be capitalized on by the permission of the Government and the people of Ghana. The first republic of Ghana had the responsibility to put in measures for the management of the natural resources to the advantage of the Ghanaian people. State corporations were established and these included all the State Gold Mining Corporations (SGMCs) at Tarkwa, Prestea, Konongo and Dunkwa-on-Offin as well as the Manganese Corporation at Nsuta and the Akwatia Diamond Consolidated Company. Sadly, all these state companies were deemed poorly managed and were later divested by the government of the day, the Provisional National Defence Council (PNDC), as one of the measures of the ERP. In this regard, opportunities were given to private foreign investors to compete with their local partners to take over these assets either by outright purchase of some of these companies or as direct investment into the gold-mining activities through acquisition of concessions from the state for gold prospecting giving them the opportunity to then form their own companies. Mineral development became a major focus of attention for governments in developing countries such as Ghana. In 1984 the Minerals Commission was established by the Government to assume overall responsibility for the orderly promotion and development of all important and exploitable minerals in Ghana. The PNDC Government launched special investment incentives that recognized the unique characteristics of mining. The resulting legislation, the Minerals and Mining Law 1986 (PNDCL153), combines regulation of the mining industry with a special fiscal regime structured to encourage investment and development of mineral resources (www.ghanaweb. com; news article January, 2003).

In fulfilment of the mineral extraction dream for development, the Government (PNDC) launched a neo-liberal ERP in 1983 resulting in a gold boom and massive FDI inflows into the extractive sector. The review of the laws relating to minerals in 1986 paid some dividend to investors in the industry and the country as a whole. In the 1990s the World Bank group catalysed the scramble for Africa's natural resources and granted loans to the tune of $2.75[1] billion to private multinational companies for investments into the extractive sector (Pegg, 2003; Owusu-Koranteng, 2005). During the early 1970s and late 1980s there was a gold boom in the world and, with a favourable investment climate prevailing in Ghana at that time, a number of companies such as Terberebe Gold Mining Company in the Western Region of Ghana, Southern Cross Mining Company in Ashanti and other foreign companies (mostly from the USA and Australia) were attracted to Ghana to invest in the gold-mining companies. This was followed by investments by giant companies like Anglogold in Ashanti Goldfields Mining Company at Obuasi in the Ashanti Region and Newmont at Kenyasi in the Brong Ahafo Region.

The overall legislative framework for the mining sector in Ghana is provided by the Minerals and Mining Law of 1986 (PNDC Law 153), as amended in 1994 and 2005. Under the Law, mining companies must pay royalties and corporate taxes at standard rates. The 1986 mining law had been instrumental in attracting more than $5 billion in foreign investment to Ghana's mining industry between 1986 and 2002. The 1994 amendments reduced the general mining corporate tax rate from 45 per cent to 35 per cent, which is the same as that imposed on other industries. The 2005 amendments included changes to royalty rates and the establishment of the period of duration of a mining lease. The royalty payable by the mining sector to the Government was increased from 3 per cent to 5 per cent in 2010.

Other legislation that affects mining and mineral exploration in Ghana are: the Minerals Commission Law of 1986 (PNDC Law 154); the Small-Scale Gold Mining Law of 1989; the Investment Promotion Act, 1994 (Act 478); the Additional Profits Tax Law, 1985 (PNDC Law 122); the Minerals (Royalties) Regulations, 1987 (LI 1349); the Environmental Protection Agency Act, 1994 (Act 490); and the Environmental Assessment Regulations, 1999, and as amended, 2002.

The question one may ask is how was the income accruing from this gold mining managed and what profits or benefits have been derived from this sector for the development of the country? How long will the country leave its resources in the hands of foreign investors? What are the citizens doing to take

---

1   All references to $ are US$.

control of the country's natural resources to the benefit of themselves? How far has the country been able to manage its resources to date? It could be argued that the exportation of these raw materials from some natural resources could earn the country foreign exchange from trade for development of infrastructure and also position Ghana favourably for external borrowing for development.

In view of the lack of infrastructure immediately after independence, there was the need for accelerated development by the Government of the first republic. Some of these early developments included a harbour, road construction, hospitals, schools and universities as well as the source of energy that led to the construction of the first hydroelectric dam at Akosombo and which later powered all the industrial and domestic energy requirements of the country.

What Went Wrong?

Owing to the lack of a sound model for the management of the country's resources and also lack of people of integrity in positions of trust, mismanagement and corruption set in and the economy of the country began to decline and consequently the rate of state developments also declined. People in authority managing state assets could not run the affairs of their stewardship in an honest, dedicated and committed manner which eventually led to the collapse of most state enterprises. This resulted in military intervention in the affairs of the nation over the period where the order of the day was to use force to manage the affairs of the state. During that era, public sector officials apparently carried out orders and managed affairs in fear under military command without any well laid down procedure or model to follow. This did not augur well for the enhancement in the efficient management of the affairs in all sectors of the economy. Things could not have been better put than the reports by DanWatch and Concord Danmark (2010) that 'if we did a proper cost-benefit-analysis of the mining industry in Ghana, taking into account the environmental and social cost, we'd be getting nothing' (DanWatch and Concord Danmark Report, 2010).

The Oil and Gas Era

Ghana is now counted among the countries of O&G production. This follows the successful discovery of oil in 2007, off Cape Three Points within the South Tano basin, by a consortium of O&G companies. A brief historical account of the O&G activities of the country is given below. The history of exploration for O&G activities in Ghana started in the onshore Western Region of Ghana around the nineteenth century and spanned from then to the present. The Petroleum (Exploration and Production) Law, 1984 (PNDC Law 84), sets out the policy framework and describes the role of the Energy Ministry, which regulates the industry. The Ghana National Petroleum Corporation (GNPC), which is empowered to undertake petroleum exploration and production on behalf of the Government, is authorized to enter joint ventures and production-sharing agreements with commercial organizations; GNPC was established under the GNPC Law of 1983 (PNDC Law 64). The mandate for oil exploration was held by the Technical Directorate of the Ministry of Fuel and Power and the Geological Survey Department prior to the establishment of the corporation. The corporation was created to promote the Government of Ghana's objective of supplying adequate and reliable petroleum for the country and the discovery of crude oil in the country's territories. The corporation was established as a state-owned company with the statutory backing of PNDC Laws 64 and 84. The laws mandated the corporation to engage in exploration, production and disposal of petroleum products. The laws also established the legal structure that informed the corporation in contractual agreements between the Government of Ghana and private oil exploration companies (www.gnpc.com).

History of Oil Exploration

Besides the traditional commodities, from agriculture to mining, there is now the emerging industry of O&G following the country's discovery of oil in commercial quantities in 2007. A brief history of exploration activities is given below.

Phase 1 (1896–1969): onshore exploration activities commenced in the Tano and Keta Basins.

Phase 2 (1970–1984): the first offshore oil well was drilled in the Saltpond basin. Attention began to focus on the prospectivity of the offshore sedimentary basins. Fourteen wells were drilled offshore within two years during this period resulting in two milestone discoveries.

Phase 3 (1985–2000): GNPC commenced operations in 1985, immediately putting in efforts to accelerate the exploration process as the sole statutory body spearheading the search for commercial O&G to meet the country's needs; GNPC pioneered Exploration and Development (E&P) activities. Their initial successes include the establishment of the block system with the hydrocarbon potential regions of Ghana that mostly cover the offshore basins. This was followed by the legal framework (PNDC Law 84) of the then government, the PNDC.

Current Phase (2001 to the present): over the last seven years exploration for commercial hydrocarbons have intensified and GNPC was restructured, downsized and given the directive to focus on its core function of facilitating activities of E&P companies in Ghana to find commercial accumulation of hydrocarbons.

Eleven (11) offshore licenses were granted to the various companies operating them. The companies are Tullow Oil, that held licenses in partnership with others; Kosmos, Hess Corporation, Vitol Upstream, Vanco Energy, Gasop Oil, Lushine Eternett and partner, Afren plc and Oranto petroleum. In June 2007, Kosmos Energy, Tullow Oil, Anadarko and E.O. Group struck a significant (about 312ft net) column of high-grade oil in the Mahogany prospect with the Mahogany 1 well in the deep waters of West Cape Three Points basin. The Hyedua-1 discovery in the Deep Tano Contract area by Tullow constitutes a large accumulation of O&G underlying both blocks. The accumulation was named the Jubilee Field. The discovery opened the floodgates for many reputable companies to apply for open blocks in the offshore and onshore sedimentary basins.

The Norwegian Model

Part V of this book is dedicated to the study of country models including the Norweigian experience that new host nations in Africa could learn from. But in relation to this chapter, relevant aspects of the Norwegian Approach are highlighted for our perusal. From the account presented in the preceding sections of this chapter, Ghana cannot be said to have had any laudable achievements in the management of its natural resources to date. Since Ghana discovered oil in commercial quantities only in mid-2007, followed by the commencement of production in December 2010, it is too early to draw any conclusions on how successfully the country has managed its petroleum resources. How will Ghana perform in the management of this important commodity that could either bring the country great fortune or lead it into turmoil? Ghana cannot afford to fail this time and there is therefore the need to develop an approach that will enable the country to properly manage its O&G industry. Following its non-performance in the management of mineral resources discovered earlier, will Ghana allow this new industry to be mismanaged in the same way the other commodities like gold, manganese, diamond (to mention a few) were, eventually letting control fall into the hands of foreign investors? The answer to this question will indeed be negative and in order to achieve a breakthrough, there is the need to make an effort to learn from others who have managed their resources successfully. This therefore should lead Ghana to adopt the success stories of some of the countries that managed their hydrocarbon resources well. Norway is a primary example of such a country with its successful natural resource management story.

One issue that needs to be addressed by new petroleum-producing countries is the need to develop policies and a legal framework that could form the basis for the proper management of the O&G industry in the nascent stages. Blocking of the areas with hydrocarbon potential, petroleum policies and legal regimes as well as the effective management of petroleum revenue and a taxation regime are critical. Highlights of Norway's example pertinent to this chapter, that Ghana must take note of and draw lessons from in managing the petroleum sector, are as follows:

1. Ownership of natural resources rests with the host nation and there is no reason to believe that this will change in the foreseeable future. However, in its eagerness to cover its energy requirements, the international community will probably pressurize the host countries that are endowed with petroleum resources to make them available for exploration, development and production. Host countries will therefore continue to play a major role in the governance of petroleum operations under their jurisdiction but will be persuaded to contribute to the growing world demand for energy.

2. National oil companies will continue to play a central role, particularly in major petroleum-producing countries, but they will find it prudent to work side by side with international oil companies (IOC) in order to cover a growing need for state-of-the-art technology, operational management and financial resources.

3. Future technological and operational demands related to petroleum exploration and development will increase the need for involving

IOCs. A multitude of such companies, in healthy competition with each other, will be the key to achieving efficiency in exploration, development, extraction and utilization of the remaining petroleum resources.

Judging from the above remarks, Ghana needs to take advantage of the international competitive climate to gain as much as possible from its reserves of O&G. In other words, Ghana needs to cautiously exercise the advantages it has as a result of the natural resources it possesses to the maximum benefit of its people.

According to Al-Kasim(2006), the fundamentals of resource management are the following three cardinal elements: the resource base; the market; and the enterprising capacity. He further indicates that these three sets of factors seem to play a decisive role in defining the boundaries within which we may have a breakdown of choice.

In view of the uncertainties and the risks associated with petroleum reserve, the management of this single commodity requires careful consideration of the country's prerequisites in terms of its resource base, its opportunities for marketing petroleum and its capabilities for participating in petroleum activities. The host country is best served by creating a competitive environment where several oil companies compete to make new discoveries and to develop these in the most efficient manner through cooperation between the authorities and oil companies both on bilateral and joint industry bases, and that such a strategy is key to successful resource management.

Value Creation

It is assumed that the host country has already opted to establish a petroleum regime based on competition among several oil companies. Under such a regime, it is obviously prudent that companies and the authorities cooperate with each other within the framework provided in the legislation and contractual agreement. For this cooperation to function efficiently it is essential that the petroleum administration is fully aware of the process and is willing to exercise its powers to enhance value creation. Equally important, the oil companies must respect and fully comply with the legislation, regulation and contractual obligations. It follows therefore that, within the framework conditions, the interests of both sides are to be reconciled through creative cooperation in all the phases of the petroleum cycle.

In general, a country aspiring to attract oil companies must first convince itself that there are possibilities for petroleum in the country. If there are insufficient thick sedimentary sequences or if the sedimentary rocks have been subjected to intensive magmatic or tectonic activity it is normally difficult for a country to promote itself as a potential petroleum province to attract the attention of the petroleum industry at the very beginning.

Health, Safety and Environmental Protection (HSE)

Health, Safety and Environmental Protection (HSE) should always be a top priority in any country exploiting O&G and there should always be continual cooperation between the authorities and oil companies on how to pursue HSE objectives so as to make petroleum operations viable within reasonable sets of norms and standards. In many cases joint research projects could be initiated to help achieve these objectives.

Drawing from Norway's Model

With regard to this chapter, one pertinent lesson from the Norwegian Model is the high degree of integrity, openness and transparency with which it has governed the petroleum sector. Another issue to critically consider is encouraging the development of national expertise so that it may provide services to petroleum operations (local content participation) in Ghana now.

A critical study of the history of activities of O&G exploration in Norway from the 1960s to the 1990s provides insight into the challenges and struggles the country faced during this period to the final success story of effective management of its petroleum resources. It is quite clear that Ghana will likewise face varying degrees of challenges, similar or different, to those faced by Norway and other countries that have managed their petroleum resources successfully. In this context, the way forward for Ghana, as far as the management of its resources, should include the following:

- ownership of its resources;

- value creation for the resources;

- market for the resources;

- prudent policies for investors.

First and foremost, the fundamental issue to be considered is for Ghana to completely know her resource base and completely take ownership of the resource. Unlike its traditional minerals (that is, gold, diamond, bauxite, manganese and so on), Ghana does not have any worry about the ownership of these commodities since the country's Constitution states that all minerals are owned by the state. The problem may be the undiscovered minerals and other natural resources which need proper and careful plans to ensure that Ghana can take over full management of the resource in order not to lose the right of ownership to foreign domination or individuals. In contrast to these traditional minerals, the resource from agricultural and forest products (cocoa, timber and other cash crops) are within the hands of individuals.

In order to achieve and realize the maximum benefits, there is the need to put in place prudent and favourable policies for both the Government and investors. The policies established in the early 1980s during the gold boom (PNDC Law 83/84) were not the most ideal for the nation since the investor got the upper hand in the areas of tax and profit repatriation of the foreign exchange by the investor to the detriment of the state (PNDC Law 153). This was when the Government was at the crossroads of economic recovery and was compelled to put in those measures to attract FDI into the gold industry. Sadly, even though the purpose for formulating such policies has long been achieved, later investors are still enjoying the leverage of some of the policies, such as taxes, to the disadvantage of the state.

The early days of the O&G industry in Ghana followed the same trend of developing policies that seemed to have the aim of attracting investors (PNDC Law 84). This was still the case when oil was discovered in commercial quantities and, as such, the state has been compelled to 'rush' in some measures and formulate prudent policies that would suit both the state and investor.

Another issue to consider is value creation in order to gain maximum profit from the resource. Ghana has been mining gold for centuries however, apart from the direct export of this unrefined commodity, it does not have much value. Undoubtedly, more profits could be accrued if, instead of the raw material, more value could be added. This added value could come in the form of gold refinery or jewellery for instance. As such, profit would be maximized and overall revenue in this industry increased. Value creation could also be extended to other natural resources such as timber (wood processing) and cocoa (cocoa processing) and the country could realize more profits from the sale of these value-added commodities instead of the raw form of export.

Having added value to the commodities, the next step is a search for markets both internally and externally. Once the commodity has reached premium quality, the government will have to search and insist on good prices for it. This will yield additional income from the sales of these commodities. In a competitive world, there is always a need to have a strong market attraction strategy and earn maximum profit from all commodities. For Ghana, a country that is well endowed with many natural resources, all things being equal reaping the highest profits possible will result in high income and higher levels of development when the inflows generated are appropriately utilized.

Attributes of Effective Resource Management

In order to have effective controls of resource management, there are two key attributes that new petroleum-producing countries need to focus on. Firstly, good governance is at the heart of effective resource management. It creates the right atmosphere for investment and exploitation of the resource, the development of good policies, strong institutions and effective management of funds or income accruing from the resource. Secondly, legislation is also important, however, instead of developing an elaborate and comprehensive legislation at the outset, it is better to do so as and when necessary. This is a better practice for a host nation in the early stages of the exploitation of the resource until it is familiar with the challenges and implications of the resource and industry.

Conclusion

Ghana's abundant natural resources have not been able to transform the economy of the country. This is the result of a lack of proper and prudent resource management. It is about time the country restored the lost glory of the mining sector. Revenues that accrue from the mining sector should be channelled to providing basic services to the poor. In this regard, civil society groups as well as research and advocacy organizations have a responsibility to shed light on revenues and overall operations of mining companies and government in order to set the stage for accountability and prudent management of the people's money. A comprehensive publication of revenue flows will ensure a level playing field that would extirpate unwarranted contentions and suspicions. Certainly, Ghana ought to use the benefits of the sweeping US Congress financial transparency reforms to reverse the unmerited mining blunder. The transparency legislation will clearly provide momentum for sorely-needed changes in the mining sector and even the emerging petroleum sector, and the earlier the order of things is changed the better and faster the prospects of success are.

There is therefore the need for a robust approach to be put in place and executed to enable the country to realize maximum profit and successful management of the resources. Ghana and other African countries who find themselves in a similar situation can only do away with the domination of foreign investors and operators if the host nations can evolve an effective resource management approach which can be a guide to the effective management of their rich and abundant mineral resources. In the case of O&G, the Norwegian Model (which is covered comprehensively in the country experiences section of this book) is a good example for Ghana to draw pertinent lessons from. The lessons gained from Norway's experience could also be translated to the management of other mineral resources and it is hoped that Ghana would eventually develop a reference archetype which could be referred to as 'Ghana model' for others to emulate.

References

Al-Kasim, F. (2006). *Managing Petroleum Resources*. Institute for Energy Studies, Oxford.

Ayensu, E. (1997). *Ashanti Gold: The Legacy of the World's Most Precious Metal*, Marshall Editions Developments Limited, London, p. 66.

Botchway, F. (1995). Pre-Colonial Methods of Gold Mining and Environmental Protection in Ghana. *Journal of Energy and Natural Resources Law* 13(4), 299–311.

Castle Minerals Ltd (2005). *Overview of Ghana Gold Projects*, retrieved from http://www.castleminerals.com/.

CIA World Fact Book (2011). October.

DanWatch and Concord Danmark (2010). Golden Profits on Ghana's Expense – An example of incoherence in EU policy, May.

Financial Times (2011). London, December.

Hilson, G. (2002). Harvesting mineral riches: 1000 years of gold mining in Ghana. *Resources Policy* 28(1&2), 13–26.

Noble Minerals Resources Ltd (2009).

Owusu-Koranteng, D. (2005). Pursuing Development agenda and the use of voluntary Guidelines in Mineral Rich Developing Countries, an International Multi-Stakeholder Round Table Conference on the OECD.

Pegg, S. (2003). Poverty Reduction or Poverty Exacerbation? World Bank Support for Extractive Industries in Africa, Oxfam America, Friends of the Earth-US, Environmental Defence, Catholic Relief Services, Bank Information Centre, Washington, DC.

www.wikipedia.com

www.gnpc.com

www.ghanaweb.com

3

Revenue Management in the Oil and Gas Sector

Kwaku Appiah-Adu and Francis Mensah Sasraku

Abstract

This chapter examines the issues relating to revenue management in the oil and gas (O&G) sector. First, the need for a good governance system is emphasized. This is followed by the argument for an oil-producing country to take such a system seriously because of the potentially significant impact that petroleum revenues can have on its economy. Also addressed are the challenges faced by oil-producing nations and steps taken by some host countries to ensure that proceeds are protected and/or invested for optimal benefits. Next, principles of petroleum revenue management are presented, followed by the concept of petroleum revenue funds for social needs. Finally, a proposal is made for the development of a Ghanaian revenue management approach given the context in which the country currently finds itself.

Introduction

It is widely acknowledged that rising oil prices tend to have a major impact on the world economy as a whole. For high net importing nations and those especially dependent on oil, rising prices should result in a windfall for oil-producing nations including those in developing economies. Nevertheless, the advantages of oil proceeds are yet to be accumulated and employed to the maximum potential for many of these nations. Whether a country is developed or developing, an absence of governance constitutes an unfortunate missed prospect for equity and advancement that has to be tackled.

O&G proceeds in several oil-producing nations in emerging economies represent a sizeable proportion of economic output, gross national product, national budgets, foreign exchange earnings and reserves. Nonetheless, owing to a variety of factors which may be described as governance related, the management of O&G proceeds can only be described as abysmal, at the least.

In some countries, it is estimated that up to 50 per cent of petroleum revenues have been diverted into the hands of rogue beneficiaries, siphoned off by dishonest officials, organizations or governments. In other cases, the revenues have been wasted on unproductive and uneconomical projects. This condition is even more disconcerting given the cyclical windfalls of petroleum revenues that arise from high global prices and the critical necessity for such revenues to support the socio-economic development in many of these impoverished nations.

It is interesting to note that though oil revenues are escalating remarkably, there is no corresponding increase in the per capita gross domestic product (GDP) in many of the oil-producing nations in Africa (Lahn et al., 2007). The good news is that some of these countries are starting to explore policies and strategies that seek to better manage petroleum revenues in an effort to secure the gains of petroleum proceeds for both existing and yet-to-be-born generations.

Countries such as Angola, Equatorial Guinea and Gabon are working towards setting up robust systems to manage oil wealth and enhance investment returns, and also generate much needed funds to finance vital social, economic and technological infrastructural projects. Other countries such as Nigeria, Algeria and Libya are also prolific producers of oil but only a few countries in Africa are able to take care of their resources in a sustainable way.

It is ironic that most nations that have had huge income from natural resources have not had much to show for all the revenues made. It has been stated that nations that earn immense revenues from natural resources have tended to post weaker economic growth relative to comparative countries without similar resources, owing to corruption, maladministration and the absence of a vision for managing in a sustainable manner. The end result of the large inflows from petroleum proceeds are not evidenced in either social investment or per capita income. Nevertheless, paradigms do exist to break this vicious cycle. It is possible to manage the industry in a sustainable manner, administer petroleum proceeds prudently, improve investment in the sector and provide funding for socio-economic change in this situation.

Principles of Revenue Management

Many groups and individuals appear to assume that if a country is blessed with deposits of minerals or petroleum especially then it is incumbent on the nation to exploit such deposits and this will inevitably lead to economic gain (or enhanced welfare) for the nation as a whole. This taxation is only one link in a chain of tasks which all have to be implemented effectively to result in general gain or economic development (Andrew-Speed, 2009).

What cannot be measured cannot be managed. For a country to effectively plan to manage its oil revenue it needs to have a good knowledge of the long-term nature of the oil industry on which it is planning its oil management. There are a number of reasons for such value-adding information.

Firstly, O&G field development is capital intensive initially, and for maximization of economic rent the country should have an understanding of the oil companies' cost of capital and how they impact on the viability of such ventures. Secondly, there are geological and political risks that can influence the degree of exploitation of the oil reserves depending on the way the tax is designed and imposed on the oil companies. Thirdly, taxes designed to fall on 'presence' and 'incomes' of the oil companies tend to discourage development of marginal fields especially where discovery is seen to be moderate as in the case of Ghana.

To effectively raise revenue that sustains long-term development demands that the taxes are designed to fall on profits and at best on economic rent. But that will depend on the country's effective tax administration and existence of experts who understand petroleum operations and its associated dynamics. The contractual design defining the type of relationship between the host country and the petroleum companies will also determine the possible revenue that can be generated. Failure to ensure a proper contractual relationship and fiscal design will result in low revenues and overexploitation of the oil resources to the detriment of the country concerned.

It is therefore important for countries such as Ghana to analyse the discovery process, effectively deal with its disadvantaged position in terms of asymmetric information trade-off and the absorptive capacity of its economy in the design of its fiscal regime. The consideration of these principles in the fiscal systems design is supposed to lead to a systematic generation of optimum economic rent for the oil-producing country in question (Collier, 2010).

The next level of concern is to prevent diversion of rent which accrues to non- government bodies or individuals and dissipation of rent through the inefficient exploitation of resources. Diversion of rent can occur as a result of illegal levies or fees charged by government and non-government agencies, illegal rewards demanded by traditional landowners and high fixed prices for inputs or low fixed prices for outputs (Garnaut & Clunies-Ross 1983). Dissipation of rent occurs if investors are required to exploit the resource in an inefficient manner as a result of government policy or government inaction through layers of bureaucracy and complex procedures for approval. Other factors include a failure to promote unitization of oil operations to prevent duplication of effort and investments (Garnaut & Clunies-Ross 1983).

These two levels need to be analysed and managed at the strategic level by policy makers before one thinks of what to manage.

Petroleum Revenue Funds

The concept of investment funds for social needs have existed for the past three decades. While originators of this notion included Norway and Mexico, the idea of setting aside proceeds and establishing an account devoted to the cultivation of investments and technical support in areas of primary importance is continually being improved (Hensley, 2011).

Various concepts of funds for social needs, varying from funds where proceeds are isolated and directed to social needs assignments by way of technical support and grants (for example, Bolivia, Egypt), to funds where proceeds are efficiently managed for capital gains and a portion devoted to social investments (for example, Kazakhstan, Azerbaijan). In all instances, the advantages of the aforementioned funds can be realized only if at the inception phase some essential principles are adopted. These comprise:

- legislative instruments that clearly identify conflicts of interest between fund management and recipients;

- as much as possible, fund management should encapsulate all representatives of all stakeholder groups;

- unambiguous guidelines on fund operation should be established before disbursements commence;

- explicit rules on eligibility of projects to be set out to ensure that funds are apportioned to key assignments;

- provisions to underlie the plan to realize selected social goals (for instance harnessing local industry technology, improving human resource capacity, productive resource allocation);

- autonomous auditing of programmes and/or projects and procurement processes should be consistent with global benchmarks;

- end of lifespan of resource arrangements should also be in place with various alternatives considered.

Building on the achievements of some countries in the developed world, some developing nations have made efforts to develop petroleum revenue funds drawing on their peculiar socio-economic attributes. While some of these funds concentrate on social investments, others are based on accountability, and still, others focus on transparency that enables the distinct benefits to be achieved and identified.

Besides the transparency, accountability and participation characteristics of the aforementioned, it is also possible to explore how these funds may be configured to include a financing instrument. In devoting a portion of such funds to two purposes: (1) to support social projects; and (2) as a credit enhancement instrument, remarkable gains could be achieved. For instance, if these funds allocated a percentage of their reserves to be applied as a guarantee facility for private sector promoted initiatives, investors would be encouraged to finance projects in areas of the economy that hitherto would not have been financially feasible.

The adoption of this public–private partnership would accentuate long-term access to finance, either equity or debt. It would also make the petroleum revenue management idea a financier of oil proceeds and a stimulant for better utilization of capital, private sector growth and socially responsible investment in nations keen to realize transparency, accountability and capital exploitation as well as social egalitarianism.

Developing a Ghanaian Revenue Management Approach

The general view of how petroleum revenue should be used has generated various views including assumed models which may not suit the peculiarities of the country concerned. Some of the views have focused on a structured approach to saving part of the revenue for future generations for several reasons including the fact that oil is not a renewable resource and its depletion may have some implications on the resource country.

For a developing country like Ghana it is expected that the use of the savings would provide a level playing field for public sector borrowing to be made at the world market rate from domestic or international markets. This process is not easy to achieve and in the short and medium term requires a trade-off between investing in assets that can create alternative economic activities that may or may not be export driven to replace the lost oil resources and saving the money in international banks which will not directly benefit the current generation whose efforts largely influence the very future development of the country.

Interestingly, given the history of lack of institutional framework to ensure the protection of money generated and possible deliberate actions of some governments to circumvent laid down procedures, the application of oil money needs to be seen as something independent from local political games and be stretched to incorporate serious developmental and economic transformational policy and actions which will benefit societies. The focus should be on supporting meta-skills development and not general assets which provide no competitive advantage to Ghana.

This brings to question whether the energy sector will play a leading role as the engine of growth or will play a secondary role in Ghana's development. If Ghana has the objective of using its energy potential as the engine of growth, then it needs to be understood that such an objective demands huge investments in both O&G segments. For example, the World Bank estimated the cost of providing a standardized infrastructure package in a number of African countries, including Ghana. The package is designed to meet foreseeable economic and social demands for the next decade.

Conclusion

In the case of Ghana, the package includes for power, 2,000MW of new generation capacity, and an increase of electrification up to 76 per cent coverage. The doubling of existing capacity to 4,000 MW by 2017 would make it possible to satisfy a domestic demand projected to grow by 7 per cent annually (including a small and constant proportion for exports to neighbouring countries). Additional capacity investment to become a large exporter of electricity in the region could be envisaged with higher gas reserves than currently assessed, among other industrial choices for gas use (World Bank, 2009).

Meeting Ghana's infrastructure needs would cost $1.6 billion per year for the next decade or around 10 per cent of GDP. Almost half of the total spending requirement is associated with the power sector, with investment needs for that sector as high as $600 million per year (World Bank, 2009).

Using oil revenues is a combination of art and science, and as such, policy makers should understand the dynamics of project financing as a driving mechanism to achieve the harnessing of the oil resources. It would be appropriate to use the funds to finance initial engineering, procurement and construction than to keep them in monetary assets. Additionally, it is considered that whereas there is little correlation between keeping oil money in financial assets and economic development, developing the gas sector which can translate into electricity trading, fertilizer, plastics and construction sectors leads to higher economic advancement. More challenging, yet a strategic issue is how the potential in aluminium, which Ghana has huge deposits of, can effectively be harnessed depending on cheap and reliable power supply. The gas-aluminium development strategy can provide a sound basis to eliminate the potential 'Dutch disease' syndrome.

What this approach implies is that a concrete strategic export-driven plan needs to be formulated based on the initial concentration of the oil money into the energy sector itself. Using a stabilization fund approach leaves room for misdirection of funds. The oil out of which these fund management concepts are being developed demands intensive capital injection to optimize its usefulness to the country with sovereign rights over its existence. Therefore short-term management of funds should be distinguished from long-term management because resource availability and usage would be different depending on the time horizon under consideration. Creating sustainable assets with both forward and backward linkages should be the guiding principle.

It appears that the development of many revenue regimes starts from the premise of how to allocate what is finally received and ignores how the monies come in. For example, Ghana has no Gas Law and no Law on Infrastructural Development. The legal and regulatory framework to support the generation of the wealth to be managed should be the focus of the initial allocation of the oil wealth so that the financial packages and commercial structures underlying the oil wealth generation processes are strategically, structurally and continually tilted towards Ghanaian ownership and control. Institutional and comprehensively thought through energy-wide legal and regulatory frameworks should provide the orienting lens in the dynamics of managing the funds.

References

Andrew-Speed, P. (2009). Mineral and petroleum taxation, Distance Learning Manual Unit 10: *Further Issues in Tax Policy.*. Dundee: CEPMLP, 10.5–10.11.

Collier, P. (2010). Principles of Resource Taxation for low income countries. In Daniel P., Keen M., & McPherson, C. (Eds), *The Taxation of Petroleum: Principles, Problems and Practices.* Abingdon: Routledge, 75-87.

Garnaut, R., & Clunies-Ross, A. (1983). *Taxation of Mineral Rents.* Oxford: Clarendon Press.

Hensley, M. (2011). *Avoiding the Curse of Oil: Strategies to Improve Governance and Finance Social Investment in Sub-Saharan Africa.* Virginia: Institute for Public-Private Partnerships.

Lahn, G., Marcel, V., Mitchell, J., Myers, K., & Stevens, P. (2007). *Good Governance of the National Petroleum Sector.* The Chatham House Document, London: Chatham House, 1-63.

World Bank (2009). Economy-wide Impact of Oil Discovery in Ghana. Report No. 47321- GH.

4

Ghana's Petroleum Revenue Management Law: A Social Contract for Good Economic Governance and Possible Challenges

Joe Amoako-Tuffour and Mangowa A. Ghanney

Abstract

Although Ghana's petroleum reserves are modest by international standards, petroleum activities may affect the economic development of the country positively or negatively depending on how oil revenue is managed. To ensure sound and prudent revenue management, Parliament passed the Petroleum Revenue Management Act (PRMA) (Act 815) (PRMA) in April 2011. This chapter looks at the nature and the eventual impact of public participation in the formulation of the law, outlines the essential features of the law, assesses the approach taken by Ghana to address the revenue management challenges, and explains why the law potentially represents an important step towards transparency, accountability and good economic governance. But, will the framework remain robust? Will it be a law for the sake of having it? And what are the possible challenges that Ghana might face in carrying forward its petroleum revenue management law?

Introduction

For economies where poverty alleviation and economic growth remain central challenges of economic management, it is hard to imagine that the discovery of riches buried below ground or sea could generate dysfunctional behaviour such as patronage and rent-seeking, drum up social conflict, deepen poverty and worsen inequalities. Yet, managing windfall petroleum revenues for many oil-producing countries, especially in sub-Sahara Africa, has proven a daunting challenge (Wakeman-Linn, Mathieu & van Selm, 2002; Bell & Faria, 2007) and has delivered just those kinds of undesirable results (for example, Angola, Cameroon, Chad, Congo and Nigeria) in varying degrees. Many of these countries failed to invest sensibly in human and physical infrastructure (Gylfason, 2001) with dismal growth performance.[1] Corruption, patronage politics and rent-seeking behaviour, as well as the breakdown of the state's accountability to citizens, are some of the explanatory channels for the negative outcomes associated with oil-rich economies.

As Ghana joins the ranks of oil-producing economies, adding to its production of cocoa and gold, the question being asked by anxious citizens is: can Ghana avoid the noted dysfunctional behaviour and outcomes, and emulate others such as Norway and Botswana to translate its oil revenues into significant improvements in basic standard of living for its citizens? Confronted with the added challenge of nurturing a young democracy with ethnic political associations, Ghana's transition to a petroleum-producing country represents perhaps one of the most critical tests for the country's economic, social and political development since independence. There are also latent concerns: Ghana is among the top ten exporters of gold in the world, the second largest African exporter after South Africa and the second largest cocoa producer after Ivory Coast. The oil windfall comes at a time when most Ghanaians point to the lack of any visibly positive outcomes of their experience with mining (Acosta & Heuty, 2009). There has been no active management of mining revenues, and all available funds are spent. Weak accountability of mining revenue sharing and weak transparency in the use of available funds give citizens significant cause for concern as Ghana enters into an era of even more volatile and unpredictable revenue flows from oil. Ghanaians are under no illusion that oil and gas (O&G) will mark the end of poverty. But expectations are understandably high that well managed, O&G could create greater opportunities for prosperity for current and future generations.

In July 2007, the National Oil Company, Ghana National Petroleum Corporation (GNPC) and its partners Tullow Oil and Kosmos Energy announced the discovery of light, sweet crude oil and associated gas in commercial quantities in the offshore Western Basin of Ghanaian waters. Preliminary appraisal in 2010 by the International Monetary Fund (IMF) put

---

1   African Development Bank and Africa Union, *Oil and Gas in Africa*, 2011.

the core reserves of oil at about 1.5 billion barrels. The field has substantial associated natural gas reserves estimated at about 120 million cubic meters expected to increase to about 340 million cubic meters with production from Jubilee Phase 1A. Total proven natural gas reserves, in January 2011, was estimated at 22.65 billion cubic meters. The pace of exploration activity has quickened remarkably since 2007.[2]

At $65 and recoverable reserves of 500 million barrels over the production horizon (2011–2029) total revenue for oil production is estimated at $19.8 billion in current value terms (averaging just over $1.0 billion annually) or $16.1 billion in 2010 US$ terms evaluated at 3 per cent. World Bank estimates based on recoverable oil reserves of about 500 million barrels and total field life (2011–2029) generate the following results (World Bank, 2009): (1) an oil price of $75 yields government revenues of $19bn, averaging just over $1bn annually and peaking at $1.8bn in 2016; and (2) an oil price of $50 and $30 result respectively in total government revenues of $8.6bn, averaging just over $0.452bn annually, and $3 billion, averaging about $0.104bn annually.

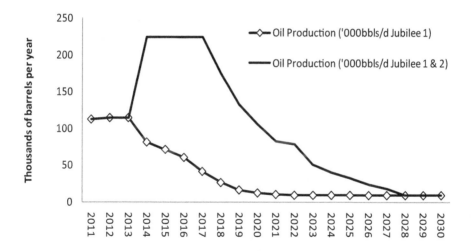

Figure 4.1   Jubilee 1 and 2 Crude Oil Production Profile 2011–2030

---

2   Actual estimates may be higher since the 2010 estimates were based only on initial evaluation of the Jubilee Field. In July 2010, Tullow announced potentially substantial light crude oil discovery in its Owo-1 exploration well in the Deepwater Licence offshore and located 6km east of Tweneboa 1 gas field. In September 2010 Tullow announced potentially 70–500 million barrel of light crude oil in its Owo-1 well in the Deepwater License offshore. Discoveries (but yet to be appraised) in 2011 include Enyera-2A and Banda-1 (Kosmos in March and June), Teak-2 (Tullow in March) and Paradise-1 (Hess Corp in June). The Ministry of Energy puts an upside estimate of 3 billion barrels (Ghana Energy Policy, 2011).

On the basis of its proven reserves, Ghana faces a short but sharp spike in its O&G production trajectory over the next 20 years (Figure 4.1). How it manages the revenue streams is critical for its economic future. Determined to avoid the mistakes of other oil-producing countries, the Government passed a revenue management law in April 2011. The PRMA, 2011 (Act 815) lays down the key parameters for the accounting and collecting of petroleum revenues due to the Government of Ghana. It establishes the limits on the amount of revenues that shall be directed into the annual budget and into savings. It provides for the operation and management of the savings, and ensures that the savings shall be prudently managed. In addition, the law provides clear oversight, auditing, transparency and reporting mechanisms to safeguard the management of petroleum revenues.

This chapter assesses the essential features of the law and the forces that shaped its outcome. Equally important is whether the law provides a defence against wasteful spending of petroleum revenues. What are the instruments of defence? Will the framework remain robust? Will the law exist for the sake of having it but without any real force? What are the risks and challenges that Ghana faces in carrying forward its revenue management law? To shed light on these questions, we begin in the next section with a brief narrative of the consultation process and how the consultation process played a role in shaping the content of the legislation. The following section outlines and assesss the key features of the law and the rationale behind them. The risks and challenges that Ghana may face in carrying forward its revenue management legislation are the subject of the section entitled 'Challenges and Risks in Petroleum Revenue Management'. The final section provides a conclusion.

Survey of Public Preferences

Ghana made public announcements of its oil find in July 2007. The Government immediately initiated steps to ensure that Ghana avoids the pitfalls that other petroleum-rich nations have unfortunately fallen into and thus avoid the 'oil curse' to deliver the best possible future for citizens. Using oil revenues wisely was every politician's slogan leading into the 2008 presidential and parliamentary elections, in part because of the public's expectations of the benefits from oil wealth, and in part in acknowledgement of the strong need to avoid the mistakes of Ghana's giant neighbour, Nigeria.

Public consultations began with the oil forum held in Accra in February 2008 to solicit advice on best practices in institutional design in petroleum sector governance, contracting approaches, regulation and revenue management experiences from the international community. A flood of advice followed with two key conclusions: (1) there was the fundamental need to develop a holistic petroleum policy framework that will guide the development of the sector; and (2) there was need for further consultations on various regulatory frameworks, institutional structures, managing revenue flows and public expectations, human capacity building and development in order to consolidate expanding local content, and infrastructure development.[3] The myriad of advice culminated in a draft Petroleum Policy that was produced in July 2008. The task of developing a comprehensive Master Plan to guide petroleum resource and revenue management was divided among task teams.[4]

With the realization that the development of O&G activities could generate substantial revenues and potentially create a new fiscal environment for the country, and the recognition that how well the revenue streams are managed is crucial to the economic development and well-being or otherwise of the country, the decision was made in early 2008 to separate revenue management issues from the other, equally pertinent, legal and contractual upstream petroleum-related issues. The Ministry of Finance and Economic Planning (MoFEP) was then tasked to develop the fiscal regime as well as the framework documents that would eventually lead to the drafting of a law to guide petroleum revenue management in Ghana. With the debate on the institutional structure of Ghana's petroleum administration ongoing and unclear, the MoFEP stood fast to the policy to develop petroleum revenue management legislation, and a technical team was constituted to see the process through. In order to ensure appropriate representation of government institutions relevant to revenue management, the team comprised MoFEP as leader, Ghana Revenue Authority (GRA), Bank of Ghana (BOG) and GNPC officials.

Public consultation as a source of input to policy making is not new in Ghana. There is precedent in the preparation of the Ghana Poverty Reduction Strategy (GPRS) in 2001–2002. While some may argue that it is hard to tell the impact of the consultations on the content and on the direction of the GPRS,

---

3   The Government of Ghana received advice from outside academics, non-government organizations (NGOs) and official agencies, particularly IMF, World Bank, Commonwealth Secretariat, Government of Norway, Oxfam, Revenue Watch, International Growth Centre of London School of Economics, and Earth Institute to name a few, along the entire spectrum of exploration licensing, development, production and revenue management. There was no broad consultation on the Petroleum Policy document and it is unclear to what extent it was discussed at the Cabinet or Parliamentary level.

4   The six technical teams were Fiscal Regime and Fund Types; Legal Regime; Health, Safety, Environment and Community Issues; Security; Local Content and Capacity Building; Downstream, Natural Gas Utilization and Infrastructure Development.

it is just as hard to conclude that the consultation did not help the content nor the process one way or the other (Amoako-Tuffour, 2008). By all accounts, the consultation was extensive and drew upon a cross-section of stakeholders. It increased stakeholders' understanding and knowledge of the policy directions of Government in the use of debt relief funds. In a small way, a social contract between citizens and Government emerged. The monitoring, evaluation and reporting of poverty reduction expenditures in the budget was unprecedented. It is not surprising therefore that since windfall oil revenues are expected to make long-term contributions to growth and ultimately poverty alleviation, there would be considerable effort to open up the revenue management debate and decision making to public consultation.

The public consultation process began with a review of international practices from Alaska, Alberta, Azerbaijan, Botswana, Chile, East Timor, Nigeria, Norway, Sao Tome and Principe as well as Trinidad and Tobago. Consultative meetings were held with various government, civil society and private sector institutions mostly in the capital city, Accra. Following these meetings, the outline of the building blocks of the petroleum revenue management legislation framework was developed.

After several months of local stakeholder consultations, internal discussions and significant updating of the revenue management framework, the team took its public consultations on the road around the ten regions of the country between mid-February and mid-April, 2010. The team composition reflected the desire to address and respond to a wide range of public concerns and issues regarding petroleum activities and petroleum revenue management. Whilst issues of taxation, fiscal regime and revenue management remained the focus of the public forums, the officials from Ministry of Energy and GNPC presented the facts of Ghana's petroleum exploration and production activities, a proposed local content policy and the avenues for local capacity building to make possible the anticipated local content policy. The BoG officials shed light on the macroeconomic implications of windfall oil revenues and the challenges to exchange rate management. Prior to the road consultations, MoFEP had published the preliminary proposals for the petroleum revenue management law online at the Ministry's website in order to provide civil society groups and citizens the opportunity to review the drafts directly and to enrich the discourse whilst the team was on the road.

The goals of the public consultations were: (1) to ensure that the eventual rules and guidelines of petroleum revenue management would meet the aspirations of the people; and (2) to the extent possible, ensure broad consensus on the most fundamental elements of what would eventually become the law. Five primary areas were identified as critical to good petroleum revenue management, of which ten major issues were captured in the following questions which formed the basis of the survey:

Assessment, Collection and Accounting

    1.   Who should assess and collect the petroleum revenues due to Government?

    2.   Should petroleum revenues be counted as part of general revenues or as special revenues?

Spending–Saving Challenge

    3.   How much revenue should be spent in the national budget and how much should be saved for the benefit of future spending and for future generations?

Budget Allocation Challenge

    4.   For what is to be spent, what should be the priority allocation in the budget and should there be restricted budget uses?

Savings Challenge

    5.   Should we establish savings fund(s)?

    6.   Who should manage the fund(s), and how?

    7.   Who may authorize withdrawals from the fund(s)? How, by how much, and how often?

Accountability, Transparency Challenge

    8.   How do we ensure transparency and accountability?

    9.   What measures are needed to ensure public oversight?

    10.   What other safeguards may be needed if any to protect the revenues from abuses?

These questions highlight a range of critical elements that inform how a country may prudently manage its windfall revenues. The elements are implied in the Generally Accepted Principles and Practices (Santiago Principles) adopted by the International Working Group of Sovereign Wealth Funds in October 2008 and by the precepts of the Oxford-based Natural Resource Charter. The questions address the administrative and operational challenges in assessing revenue due to the state, the inter-generational resource benefits sharing problem, as well as the social contract of accountability and transparency of the state and its citizens.

Providing answers to these questions formed the core of the public consultations. The broad consultations were also an opportunity to educate the public on the many facets of the petroleum resource development, the production horizon and the approximate revenues expected under different scenarios. This education was the first step in managing public expectations, and equally important, in minimizing misinformation and misrepresentation of the magnitude of expected revenues. Indeed, only a well-informed public can truly provide input that will guide the decision-making process. And knowing that their input can shape critical elements of the law can only enhance the public's sense of ownership.

Policy borrowing, learning and diffusion of best practices are common in developing policy, and legal, fiscal and contractual frameworks in extractive resource developments. There is no shortage of answers to the above survey questions and therefore no shortage of models that literally can be copied from one country and pasted to another. But Asfaha (2007) offers helpful counsel that in fashioning out a framework for managing resource funds, each country should undertake its own assessment and come up with the model that best reflects public preferences and fits its political economic reality. Just as countries' institutional, administrative and fiscal management capacity vary so too do the cultural forces that shape public policy.[5]

---

5   Side-by-side with the open town-hall discussions, the team conducted on a regional basis a formal survey of the public's perspectives on O&G revenue management. The survey–questionnaire focused on the above ten questions, answers to which would form the building blocks of the eventual law. The timetable of the regional consultations was published in the national dailies and was also advertised on local radio stations. The questionnaire was distributed to participants on self-selection basis; that is, to those who expressed a preference to participate by show of hands during the town-hall meeting. The survey was also made available online via Ministry of Finance's website. The number of participants in each of the regional town-hall consultations ranged between 300–500 and represented a cross-section of the population, including school children. The number of questionnaires administered in each of the 10 regions was 120. Total completed questionnaires received were 1,147 (out of the possible 1,200) plus 95 online respondents. There were also a number of written submissions

It was evident from the nationwide consultations that Ghanaians were committed to the transparent collection and management of petroleum revenue and its prudent and efficient use for the benefit of all Ghanaians. Whilst existing legislations on petroleum operations had served well in the promotion, licensing and exploration of petroleum in the country, none provided guidelines on how to collect and manage petroleum revenue, how to tackle the dynamic consumption-saving decision, or on the fiscal task of spending smoothening in response to the volatility of petroleum revenues. Moreover, in the town-hall meetings, the lack of active management of mining revenues, the lack of accountability of revenue sharing and the spending of all mining revenues as they become available were oft-repeated concerns to be avoided in the case of the more volatile and unpredictable revenue flows from oil.

Besides, experience worldwide suggests that proper and responsible management of petroleum revenues is essential to deliver the best possible future for citizens. The commonly cited reason is that petroleum revenues are not income in the usual sense because they are derived from the extraction of a resource that is non-renewable and cannot be reproduced. Once depleted, the revenue flows shall cease. As a result, the revenues are different from conventional tax revenues. Treating petroleum revenues as ordinary income often leads to excessive waste, corruption and potential loss of control of public spending.[6]

The Key Features of Act 815

International best practice recommends that the revenue management law should be simple, transparent and flexible. Yet, it should be rules-based with the view to ensure greater discipline in the management of public finances. Further, access to petroleum revenues should not compromise domestic mobilization of non-oil tax revenue through the conventional tax handles. Act

---

(unsolicited and solicited) either directly to the Minister, Parliament, or to the technical team from a cross section of Ghanaians.

6   See the collection of papers in Davis, Ossowoski & Fedelino (2003), See also Stiglitz (2007). Treating resource revenues as ordinary income reduces the problem simply to one of deciding on how to spend now to meet current needs. Savings is a residual to be used in smoothening spending. An income management approach arguably may have no need for a law, other than simple regulations on spending in line with sound public financial management. A wealth management view gives natural resource revenue management a more long-term and strategic perspective.

815 contains these basic elements. We elaborate on the ten-point key features of the law summarized in Box 1 in the rest of this section.

ASSESSMENT, COLLECTION OF PETROLEUM REVENUES

The first central feature of the law is that it provides a framework for the assessment, collection and accounting for the revenue due to the Government.[7] First, it assigns the responsibility foremost to the GRA. Recognizing the complexity of the tasks, section 63 of the law requires the Minister responsible for Finance to provide regulations and guidelines for the determination of the quantity and price for tax purposes. Second, it establishes a Petroleum Holding Fund (PHF) to be held at the BOG to receive and to disburse revenues. To avoid revenue diversions and to further protect the integrity of the system, amounts due are to be transferred directly by the license operators to the PHF and shall be considered paid only when received at the BOG. Third, for further protection,

---

BOX 1: KEY FEATURES OF ACT 815

The Petroleum Revenue Management Act (PRMA) responds to the expectations of Ghanaians through the following provisions:

Establishes the procedural, accountable and transparent mechanisms to guide the assessment, collection and the movement of petroleum receipts from collection to final utilization.

Sets limits on how much of the petroleum revenues may be spent through the budget and at the same time provides room for government to decide on this matter on a year-to-year basis.

Seeks to ensure and secure the efficient planning and proper management of the national budget made possible by the additional petroleum revenue inflows.

Captures the desire of Ghanaians to save, however modest the revenues, as part of their desire to ensure inter-generational equity and fairness, and to allocate a larger portion of what is spent for public investments.

Establishes the Stabilization Fund and Heritage Fund, allocates savings between them – the former as the rainy day fund to support budget implementation, the latter as an endowment for the benefit of current and future generations.

---

7   Petroleum revenues are defined to include direct payments from oil companies engaged in both upstream and midstream activities. Except for corporate taxes, all payroll taxes from O&G activities shall be considered as part of the normal conventional tax revenue pool and shall not be considered for the purposes of this law.

Makes provisions for withdrawals from the Stabilization Fund, but it places clear ceilings on the amount that can be withdrawn.

Sets clear guidelines and assigns responsibilities for the management of the funds.

Places limitations on borrowing against petroleum revenues and savings.

Makes great effort to respond to the needs for accountability and transparency.

Provides clear oversight mechanisms, auditing, transparency and reporting mechanisms to safeguard the management of petroleum revenues.

section 5 of Act 815 stipulates that money in the PHF is not permitted to be used to give credit to any public or private institution

SPENDING LIMITS

All heavily dependent resource economies are faced with the challenge of deciding how much to spend and how much to save from the windfall revenues. One of the centrepieces of the public consultation was reconciling the pressing development infrastructure needs of the country and the desire to save part of the revenues for future generations. The tension between current spending demands and saving for the future was evident. And no less evident was the public's general mistrust of politicians for unrestrained public spending of petroleum revenues. It became quickly evident that the law would have to strike an acceptable balance to ensure that infrastructure needs could be readily and easily accommodated without compromising savings.

Act 815 requires that a maximum amount – Annual Budget Funding Amount (ABFA) – be transferred from the PHF to the budget each year. This amount is based on a Benchmark Revenue determined by a formula, taking into account historic and expected prices and anticipated production levels. The ABFA as a spending limit accomplishes the fiscal task of limiting spending and increasing saving during periods of high oil prices. For the period 2011–2013, the ABFA is set to be no more than 70 per cent of the benchmark revenue. The exact percentage is to be determined on a year-to-year basis and approved by the Parliament of Ghana as part of the annual budget process.

The evidence provided in Figures 4.2 and 4.3 from the public consultations survey provided the basis of the spending–saving split opted for in the law. Survey respondents were presented with the question: 'If you know that oil

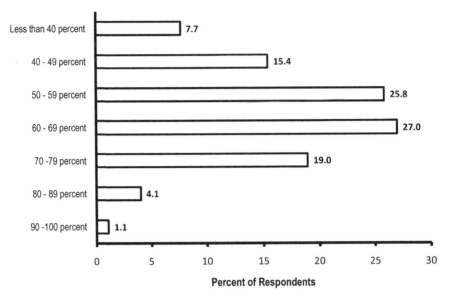

Figure 4.2   How Much of Current Revenue to Spend Now?

production may come to an end about 25–30 years from now, about what proportion of petroleum revenues would you recommend that Government spends every year?' About 27 per cent of respondents favoured spending between 60–69 per cent of current revenues; about 26 per cent were for 50–59 per cent spending; and 19 per cent for between 70–79 per cent spending. On average, about 82 per cent of respondents opted to allocate no more than 70 per cent (53 per cent would allocate between 50–70 per cent) for current budget spending and save at least 30 per cent.

On a Regional basis (Figure 4.3), there was a clear general preference for balance between the needs for current spending and savings as investment and for future generations. The most preferred allocation of 60–69 per cent was the choice of respondents especially in the Northern, Upper, Central, Western and Greater Accra Regions. Most respondents wanted a stable, predictable annual level of budgetary expenditures from petroleum revenues. Rather than directing all revenues into the budget and simply saving the annual budget surplus, the majority of survey respondents preferred that the law be explicit about the share of petroleum revenues to be allocated to annual Government spending for the purpose of achieving development goals.

The law not only reflects this manifest public preference, but goes further to secure it with the provisions in section 18 that the 70 per cent ceiling may be

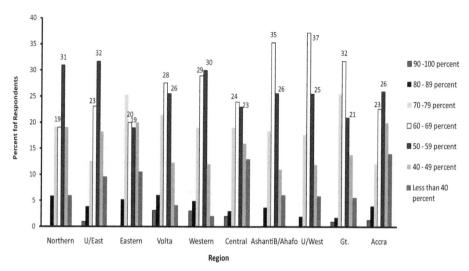

Figure 4.3   How Much Petroleum Revenues Should be Allocated into Government Coffers for Current Spending?

reviewed every three years, and that any proposed changes shall be approved by Parliament by votes of not less than two-thirds majority.

THE BUDGET CHALLENGE

The PRMA recognizes that petroleum revenue is only a means to an end. Transforming petroleum resources in the ground into development outcomes depends on how Ghana organizes and manages the revenue through the budget. The efficient planning and the proper execution of a comprehensive national budget are key to Ghana's transformation into a modernized economy. To this end, 75 per cent of respondents saw the national budget as the single fiscal instrument that ensures that Ghana pursues high, broad-based national sustainable and equitable growth (Figure 4.4).

There are three benefits to directing the petroleum revenues through the budget, all of which the PRMA recognizes and capitalizes on: (1) the revenue side of the national budget will reflect the total (domestic tax, non-tax, petroleum revenues and external) resource envelope; (2) the allocation and spending of oil revenues will more likely reflect national priorities to ensure fair distribution of the benefits to all Ghanaians; and (3) the spending of all oil revenues will be subject to the same procurement and accounting, monitoring and evaluation systems as all other revenues.

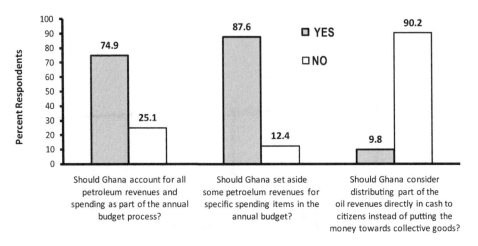

Figure 4.4   General Use and Distribution of Revenues

Direct cash distribution of oil revenues to citizens is a potentially powerful instrument to protect economic gains and a way to strengthen the country's social contract (Moss & Young, 2000). When asked to choose between cash distribution and collective use through national systems, a remarkable 90 per cent of survey respondents rejected direct distribution of revenues to citizens, perhaps not so much because of the logistics of implementing such a scheme, but because of the strong collective desire to use resource revenues – cocoa and gold as precedents – for development through national programmes. The law therefore makes no provision for cash distribution of revenues to individuals. But as Acosta & Heuty (2009) remarked, while this has the advantage of strengthening central government in its plan and use of revenues, it has the potential for escalating demands from regional groups and local governments who may seek a greater share of the oil wealth.

The PRMA stops short of restricting or earmarking revenues for any area of spending, and for that matter, for any specific distributions. It simply prescribes that the budget shall be the primary vehicle for moving forward the country's development agenda and that it will be aligned with a medium-term expenditure framework, which shall also be in line with a long-term national development plan. In this way, Act 815 seeks to encourage the development of a long-term national development plan to underlie and buffer the nation's development agenda. A more detailed allocation of expenditures in a revenue management law may place limitations on government spending that some consider as inconsistent with democratic principles.

The law simply ensures that at least 70 per cent of the share of petroleum revenue directed into the budget goes to support investment spending. It then outlines the general areas of spending priority in the event that a national development plan is not in place. The obvious challenge of ring-fencing petroleum revenues for investment spending is that money is fungible. But the intended discipline can be successful only through transparency in budget process and only if complemented with some discipline which limits the non-oil fiscal deficit. In order to increase transparency in the spending of petroleum revenue, the PRMA imposes a restriction of no more than four prioritized programmes or activities to benefit from petroleum revenues that shall be reviewed every three years, and also imposes strict annual reporting requirements on the Minister responsible for Finance on how petroleum revenue is spent.

SAVINGS POLICY: GHANA HERITAGE FUND AND GHANA STABILIZATION FUND

BOX 2: TO SET UP OR NOT TO SET UP SAVINGS FUNDS

From Figure 4.5, nearly 55 per cent of the respondents favoured setting up two funds from the onset, while nearly half as many, 28 per cent, favoured setting up a single fund for the dual role of smoothening budget spending (stabilization) and savings for future needs. Setting up a single fund now and splitting it later, as was the case in Botswana and Trinidad and Tobago in their early years of resource extraction, was the choice of 13 per cent of the respondents, and even fewer, 5 per cent, supported the idea of treating petroleum savings as part of the general pool of foreign exchange reserves. In short, 55 per cent preferred two funds, 40 per cent a single fund and 5 per cent favoured no special fund. Whilst a two-funds model creates the impression of 'Chinese walls' protection of savings for future generations from savings to insulate government spending from year-to-year fluctuations (stabilization), it is possible to construct a single fund with sub-portfolios to achieve the same objectives and perhaps with greater administrative simplicity. In the end only fiscal discipline can assure the integrity of whatever form the country chooses to hold its savings.

About 40 per cent of those who favoured setting up two separate funds preferred a near equal split of the savings between the two funds. About 28 per cent would set aside between 50–70 per cent of the aggregate savings into the Ghana Heritage Fund. Despite the varying positions in what form to hold the savings and how to invest the savings, the general sentiments of saving part of the petroleum revenue for future generations echoed across the Regional town-hall meetings.

Source: Results of National Survey.

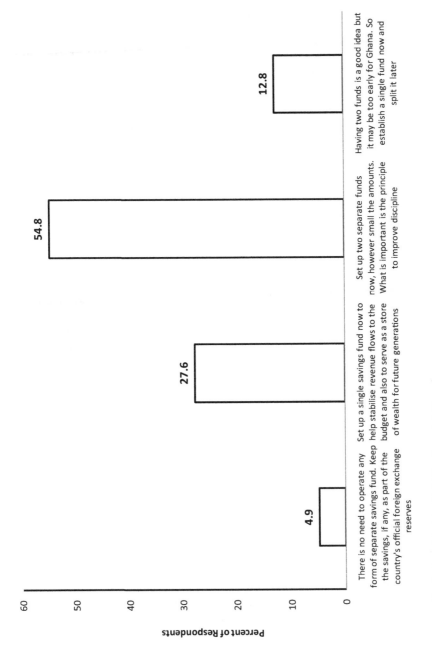

Figure 4.5   To Set or Not to Set Up Special Funds

The next central feature of the law is the establishment of two savings funds: the Ghana Heritage Fund (GHF) and the Ghana Stabilization Fund (GSF). The national survey results are summarized in Figure 4.5 and Box 2. The GSF is a rainy day savings fund intended to cushion the impact of sudden shortfalls in petroleum revenues caused by falling prices or production changes on budget implementation. Ghana's petroleum revenue management strategy is essentially investment led, and therefore it ensures predictability in order to avoid the stop–go spending syndrome that often halt projects, even after making huge irreversible investments. The GSF is therefore a fiscal tool to support budget implementation.

The GHF is an endowment asset to generate an alternative stream of income for the future. But that reason alone would not justify the existence of the Fund. The important and long-term use of the GHF is to build up the country's international reserves to support its external balances and the external value of the cedi, and to demonstrate commitment to inter-generational equity. To safeguard the GSF and GHF from the day-to-day politics, their inflows and outflows are governed by the law. In the long run, the savings also bolster Government's creditworthiness, and consequently enhance its ability to borrow unsecured, from capital markets.

SAVINGS POLICY

In simple terms, Act 815 requires that Ghana opens three accounts held by the MoFEP at the BoG. The PHF is the transit account for all of the Government's share of petroleum revenues. It receives and disburses petroleum revenues to support the budget and into the two savings accounts. In the short to medium term, the GHF and the GSF together shall receive at least 30 per cent of the expected revenues for any fiscal year. The actual amount shall be derived as the excess of the actual revenues over the planned annual budget support. And this excess shall be determined on quarterly basis with reconciliations to take place at the end of the year.

Directing a greater percentage of the expected petroleum revenues into the budget in the early years exposes the budget to the volatility of petroleum revenues often caused by price fluctuations. However it is necessary to do so in order to ensure optimum petroleum revenue budgetary support for rapid public investment in the early years of petroleum revenue inflows. To guard against the recognized vulnerability, the allocation of the excess revenues between the GHF and the GSF places relatively more emphasis on the GSF, especially in the early years. The recommended allocation of the excess revenues is 70 per cent for the GSF and 30 per cent for the GHF.

What is set aside as savings shall be prudently managed by investing in specific qualifying securities abroad. This is important for at least three reasons: (1) to ensure that the savings are invested in safe instruments; (2) to reduce political pressures on the fund's investment policy so far as may be possible; and (3) to boost Ghana's international reserve build-up. In addition, total investment income from the savings shall be retained in the funds in order to preserve the real value of the funds as well as generate additional revenue. For the GSF, the investment income that is ploughed back shall be available to support budget spending if specified withdrawal conditions are met. For the GHF, the total investment income is retained in the fund, and shall not be withdrawn for current spending until petroleum production ceases. However, restrictions on the transfer of the interest income of the GSF is subject to Parliamentary review every 15 years to permit transfers of portions of accrued interest into any of the other two funds if necessary.

The additional requirement that there be an upper limit on the size of the GSF is intended to guard against excessive build-up in the Fund in the event of steady rise in petroleum prices. Setting an optimal Fund size pre-empts the inevitable social and political pressures to spend from the GSF if the balance keeps growing. The law requires that: (1) the Minister responsible for Finance shall recommend the upper limit of the GSF and this shall be reviewed from time to time as determined by macroeconomic conditions; and (2) once the upper limit is attained, any excess shall be directed into the Contingency Fund established under Ghana's Constitution or towards debt repayment approved by Parliament.

WITHDRAWALS FROM GHANA STABILIZATION FUND (GSF)

Safeguarding the savings and sustaining the budget stabilization process requires clear rules. It also means setting ceilings on withdrawals from the GSF. Figure 4.6 presents a schematic outline of the steps both in determining the ABFA, the allocation of savings and the withdrawal provisions as prescribed by the law.

Withdrawals from Ghana Stabilization Fund (GSF)

The withdrawal rules for the GSF are intended first, to support the implementation of the national budget in the event of sudden shortfalls in

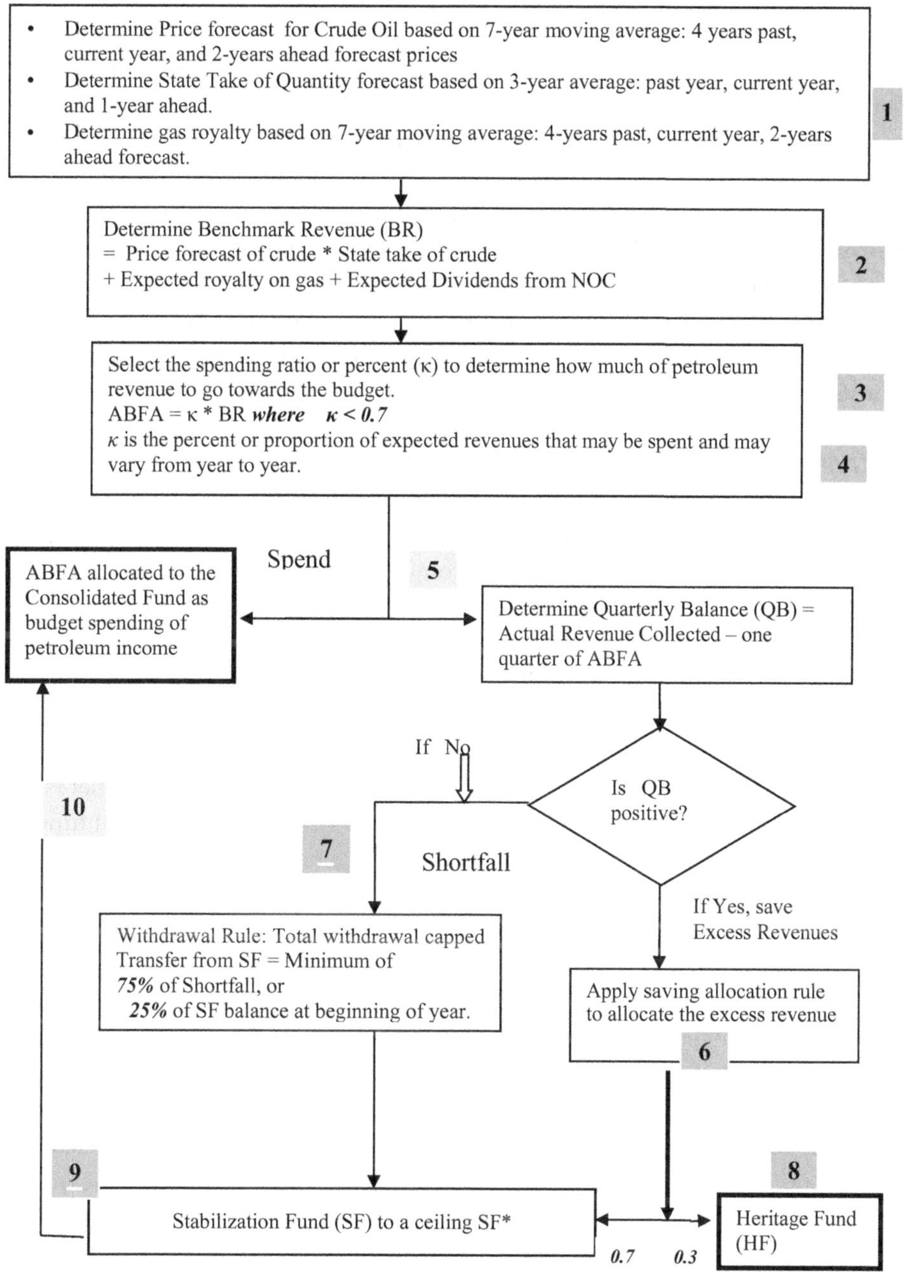

- Determine Price forecast for Crude Oil based on 7-year moving average: 4 years past, current year, and 2-years ahead forecast prices
- Determine State Take of Quantity forecast based on 3-year average: past year, current year, and 1-year ahead.
- Determine gas royalty based on 7-year moving average: 4-years past, current year, 2-years ahead forecast.

1

Determine Benchmark Revenue (BR)
= Price forecast of crude * State take of crude
+ Expected royalty on gas + Expected Dividends from NOC

2

Select the spending ratio or percent (κ) to determine how much of petroleum revenue to go towards the budget.
$ABFA = \kappa * BR$ *where* $\kappa < 0.7$
κ is the percent or proportion of expected revenues that may be spent and may vary from year to year.

3

4

ABFA allocated to the Consolidated Fund as budget spending of petroleum income

Spend **5**

Determine Quarterly Balance (QB) = Actual Revenue Collected – one quarter of ABFA

If No

Is QB positive?

10

7

Shortfall

Withdrawal Rule: Total withdrawal capped
Transfer from SF = Minimum of
75% of Shortfall, or
25% of SF balance at beginning of year.

If Yes, save Excess Revenues

Apply saving allocation rule to allocate the excess revenue

6

9

Stabilization Fund (SF) to a ceiling SF*

0.7   *0.3*

8

Heritage Fund (HF)

Figure 4.6   Steps in Determining Annual Budget Funding Amount (ABFA) and Savings

petroleum revenues and second, to enhance and maintain fiscal discipline. For any fiscal year, withdrawals cannot exceed 75 per cent of petroleum revenue shortfalls as determined by the predetermined ABFA or 25 per cent of the balance of the GSF, whichever is the lesser. By restricting withdrawals to occasions of unanticipated shortfalls in petroleum revenues and by placing a ceiling on the amount of permissible withdrawals from the GSF, Act 815 ensures that petroleum revenues will not be used arbitrarily to offset budgetary shortfalls, especially those stemming from poor non-oil tax revenue mobilization or from excessive expenditure growth. In this way, the law intends to prevent overdependence on petroleum revenue as an alternate or replacement to traditional revenue sources.

Withdrawals from the Ghana Heritage Fund (GHF)

Section 20 of Act 815 stipulates that withdrawal from the GHF is only permitted when petroleum reserves become depleted. At that time, the balance of monies held in both the GSF and GHF shall be consolidated into a single Petroleum Wealth Fund and the separate funds shall cease to exist. From that time onward, the amount of withdrawals from the consolidated fund shall be limited to the real interest income or real returns from the accumulated funds. In other words, the inflation component of the interest income shall be retained in the fund. The withdrawal rule emphasizes the important fact that what is set aside as long-term savings are not to be seen narrowly as 'development funds', but rather as endowment for current and future generations.[8]

MANAGEMENT

The Minister responsible for Finance has the overall responsibility of managing the petroleum revenues and savings. The BoG is responsible for the operational management of the transitory PHF as well as the GHF and the GSF under an Operations Management Agreement with the Minister. An Investment Advisory Committee (IAC) advises the Minister in the design of investment policy and strategies for the management of the savings, develops benchmark portfolio for performance measurement, reviews reports and audits, and generally monitors the performance of the management of the savings.

---

8   It is worth making note of the fact that even when the total returns from the GHF is retained during the production horizon, we have not made allowances for population growth. As a result, savings in terms of the share of each citizen may decline over time adding to the need for caution in making spending–saving decisions during the production horizon. It is therefore misleading to assume that the law locks away far more needed revenues at the expense of current spending.

LIMITATIONS ON BORROWING

An important, yet controversial, provision in the law which is debated extensively in Parliament is that the GSF, the GHF or the future streams of petroleum income shall not be used to or pledged to secure international borrowing.

BOX 3: BORROWING AGAINST PETROLEUM RESERVES

Figure 4.7 focuses on the protection of petroleum revenues and the integrity of savings accumulated out of petroleum revenues, and in so doing avoiding some of the mistakes of other oil-producing countries, including Mexico and Nigeria.

The results suggest an overwhelming preference that neither the savings fund nor the future stream of revenues be used to secure any borrowing. While in principle such borrowing could be used to accelerate human development and the growth of the economy that, according to Jeffrey Sachs, is rarely the experience in many oil producing developing countries.

Source: National Survey.

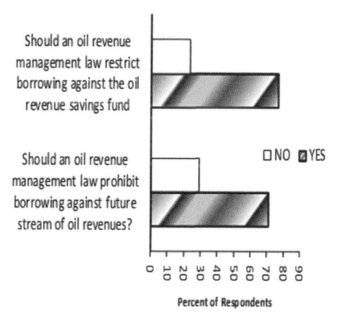

Figure 4.7   Borrowing towards Petroleum Resources

This recommendation followed international best practice intended to curtail excessive spending which will put the savings and the security of future income at risk. It encourages government not to rely excessively on petroleum revenues for its development agenda, but rather to strengthen domestic tax policy and revenue mobilization. Finally, it recognizes that the Ghanaian economy is now ever more vulnerable to commodity price volatility (with cocoa and gold). Excessive borrowing risks macroeconomic instabilities and can only make the economy more dependent on external assistance in the event of unanticipated adverse commodity price shock.

There is another reason to restrain borrowing against a nation's future stream of natural resource rents because it is hardly prudent. In order to manage its strategic development choices wisely, government must protect its freedom to manage its portfolio of revenue inflows now and in the future. Securing loans with government barrels of oil runs the high risk of playing into the hands of predatory lenders, and compromises the nation's ability to manage its own strategic stock of crude oil. Given the enormous uncertainties of oil revenue flows, pledging future barrels of oil to secure loans puts excessive burden of risk on the borrower. All that the restrictions in Act 815 intend to achieve is that while government may borrow to meet capital needs below the budget line, these borrowings should not be tied to the GHF, GSF or to the ABFA. It is a disciplining feature intended to ensure sustainability of public finances in the longer term.

Stating the limitations against borrowing in the law is an important signal to all lenders and a discipline on the managers of the economy. Does this mean government henceforth cannot borrow? Certainly not. Government shall always engage in borrowing but funded by general budgetary revenues or revenues from particular development projects. The provision in the law for the ABFA from petroleum revenues to be used as collateral for loans for the period 2011–2021 (Section 17(7) Act 815) is inconsequential as long as the use of the loan proceeds is guided by the country's medium-term development framework seamlessly aligned with a long-term development plan, is transparent and accountable, and it is integrated with and managed through the normal budgetary process.

ACCOUNTABILITY, AUDITING AND REPORTING

The PHF, GHF and GSF shall be audited in a manner that is consistent with the auditing requirements of similar public funds. There will be quarterly internal audits and annual audits with provisions for special audits where the Auditor-General deems necessary. Best international practice is that periodic special audits may include an investigation of whether the GRA, Ministry of Finance and Economic Planning and the BOG are managing the revenues and the savings from petroleum in accordance with the letter and the intentions of the law.

Moreover, the law makes serious attempts to meet the growing demands for accountability and transparency. The general demand was captured by the following reporting requirements:

- The Minister shall publish quarterly reports of all the inflows into the transitory PHF in the Gazette and in at least two state-owned daily newspapers, and same shall be available on the Ministry's website.

- The BOG shall publish semi-annual reports on the GHF and the GSF each year. Such reports shall also be publicly available on the Bank's website.

- At the end of the first quarter of each year, the Minister is required to reconcile the actual petroleum revenues received with the anticipated receipts of the immediately preceding year and submit a prescribed written report to Parliament. This report also has publication requirements.

- The Auditor-General shall also publish its annual audited financial statements of the PHF, GHF and GSF.

- Finally, the Minister shall submit a comprehensive annual report on the activities and performance of the PHF, the GHF and the GSF as part of the annual budget presentation to Parliament. The specific reporting requirements are spelt out in the law.

OVERSIGHT AND PUBLIC INTEREST ACCOUNTABILITY

Transparency as a fundamental principle is entrenched in the PRMA in a number of ways and in a manner that conforms with Ghana's commitment to abiding by the principles of the Extractive Industry Transparency Initiative (EITI). Act 815 goes a step further with the premise that transparency and accountability should not be assessed only in terms of having representations in the parliamentary process. Rather, it should be seen more generally as having the capacity to enrich understanding of the public and providing assurance of what the Executive and Parliament are doing with petroleum revenues through active engagement and enhanced information availability. To these ends, it is important to have in place a public body with a legitimate and formalized role to oversee and interact with the petroleum industry and with government institutions charged with any petroleum revenue management responsibility under the law.

On one hand, the law responds to the demands of the public expectation of the broad collective vigilance of citizens. It requires that public oversight on the collection, use and management of petroleum revenues be strengthened by setting up an independent Public Interest Accountability Committee (PIAC). The composition of the PIAC is structured to ensure competence, public legitimacy and to encourage and provide active public voice.

On the other hand, it mandates public access to information regarding all aspects of petroleum revenue management. A narrow exception is made for the protection of the Ghana Petroleum Funds. The Minister responsible for Finance is given the prerogative to declare some limited information as confidential and therefore not accessible to the public. Even then the Minister has the burden to demonstrate the proprietary nature of the information to Parliament.

Challenges and Risks in Petroleum Revenue Management

Do the provisions of the Act 815 guarantee that Ghana will use and manage its petroleum revenues prudently, share the benefits fairly and equitably, improve the living standards of current and future generations, and escape the 'resource curse'? Are the accountability, reporting and transparency provisions sufficient defence against wasteful spending? Will they safeguard the social contract between citizens and state for the wise use of the windfall revenues? There are plausible risks that could negate all the good intentions of Act 815, the greatest of them being that civil servants and politicians may renege on the enforcement of the provisions of the law. Other risks lie in the track record of weak public financial management, the recurrent fiscal slippages in election years, the persistent weaknesses in Ghana's budgetary process, and the absence of fiscal responsibility rules or laws. The oil bonanza adds some urgency to addressing these perennial problems.

First, the workings of the law depend on politicians and the bureaucrats in their compliance commitment. The biggest hurdle is in the estimation of the benchmark revenue and hence the ABFA. Overstating the benchmark revenue will undoubtedly undermine the savings prospects. Prudent advice is to resist the political expediency to overstate the expected oil revenues in the course of the annual budget preparation. Another manifestation of weak enforcement or commitment to compliance will be a slow enactment of implementing regulations after the enactment of the law.

Another major point of concern is the absence of a non-partisan long-term national development vision that lays out what the country hopes to achieve and how it proposes and commits to get there regardless of the party in power. Without such a plan, politicians are likely to continue to dream up partisan ad hoc plans on the go with no guarantee of continuity in the execution of those plans in a manner consistent with maximizing the welfare of the majority of citizens in the long term.

In the absence of a commitment to national planning, the World Bank Report (2009) echoes the general sentiment that there are high political incentives for patronage spending with governments readily responding to narrow special interests along labour, regional or ethnic lines. The risk is high that public expenditures will rise, not in favour of judicious provision of public goods, or ostensibly so, but largely as a result of the Executive's response to narrow interest groups through subsidies, energy and utility subsidies as favourite political instruments. It is more urgent now, with the expected inflows of petroleum revenue, to enforce greater fiscal discipline in the provision of energy sector subsidies, especially on petroleum products.

A third area of concern is on matters of institutions and processes. Evidence in the literature suggests that institutional decay is likely to worsen when state institutions are weak prior to the inflow of windfall resource revenues (Amundsen, 2011). Weak institutions are not likely to withstand the increased pressure from various pressure groups (Bartels & Piccinni, 2011). The weaknesses in Ghana's budgetary processes and public financial management are well documented in the IMF (May 2008) study on 'Ghana: Enhancing Fiscal Discipline' and various Public Expenditure Reviews. The operational reality in Ghana's budgeting is that the resource envelope is always based on incremental projections of the current resource base rather than through a strategic analysis of the revenue potential of the economy. Investment appraisal is low.

While many government departments appear to follow a three-year budget framework, the commitment to the process in practice is rather weak and as a result spending plans for the years beyond current budget year carry very little fiscal meaning. The prospects of petroleum revenue inflows diminish considerably the incentives for spending rationalization or prudent selection of projects as budget stakeholders turn into rent-seekers, each seeking to receive higher budget allocations to increase their spending capacities. Spending may also rise as a result of outright huge bureaucracies.

It certainly does not help if there is insufficient coordination between policy, planning and budgeting; if there is weak budget prioritization; if there is a disconnect between capital projects and the recurrent expenditures needed to support the projects; and if there isn't enough time in the budget calendar for budget hearings, for scrutiny by Parliamentary sub-committees, and for thorough debate in Parliament. Windfall petroleum revenues only add to the challenges of the budgetary institutions and the budgetary process. Weak budget prioritization, weak budget execution, and weak spending monitoring and appraisal further undermine the capacity to evaluate how petroleum revenues are being allocated through the budget and ultimately how they are contributing to growth. According to the Economic Governance and Management Report on Ghana prepared under the African Peer Review Mechanism, cost consciousness and ensuring efficient public finance management are by no means revered public sector ethics. The absence of any credible mechanism for discipline weakens incentives for compliance. Most civil servants take no pride in ensuring efficient public financial management in ways that secure welfare for themselves later in their life and for future generations.

Fourth, on structural issues, the ability to manage the budget to achieve government's policy objectives, given competing spending demands, is currently undermined by the large recurrent expenditures including the public sector wage bill and statutory expenditures. Between the years 2000 and 2008, recurrent expenditure by the budget classification equaled or nearly exceeded total domestic tax and non-tax revenue. Payroll management remains perhaps the weakest spot in expenditure control. The public sector wage bill averaged nearly 55 per cent of total tax revenue or 10 per cent of gross domestic product (GDP) for the period 2007–2009. The continued failure of administrative measures to keep the wage bill even within budgeted levels is a strong indication of the weak commitment to fiscal discipline and the noted weakness in the public financial management system. Considering that the average wage level of the public sector is low compared to the private sector, there are already signs of pressing wage demands, much of that in anticipation of additional budgetary resources from oil revenues flows.

Fifth, while Ghana has taken visible steps to improve budgeting and public financial management with the enactment of legislation and the adoption of a Medium-Term Expenditure Framework (MTEF), the actual practice is a far cry from achieving the objective of improving allocation of resources. An important area to stress is the link between the ABFA, the budget, and the MTEF. While Act 815 provides the framework that links the oil revenues spending to the budget and provides some broad guidelines on how the ABFA should be spent in the budget, it only makes a weak link to the MTEF and to the national development plan. The surveillance role of Parliament over the use of the ABFA should be strengthened. Whilst Act 815 charges the PIAC to provide some form of surveillance, PIAC has no investigative powers. It simply reports on the use or potential misuse of the revenues. It is up to Parliament to use PIAC reports as one of its inputs in providing the necessary legislative oversight on the use of petroleum revenues.

Initiating formal pre-budget consultations and strengthening the process of the budget debate are two things Parliament can do to strengthen its oversight responsibilities in the use of oil revenues. It should be possible for Parliament to hold its own pre-budget consultations every year, at least two months before the budget is tabled on the floor. Parliament then presents a bi-partisan report to government to inform the budget preparation. Once presented, Parliament should provide the opportunity for public review of the budget as part of the budget debate. Making this platform possible requires a review of the budget calendar so that there is ample time for preparation heading into the budget debate. In a political economy environment of substantial pressures to increase spending fast, or increase transfers to local governments, it is urgent now to improve the transparency and efficiency of the budget process, carefully prioritizing, controlling and tracking expenditures, especially for capital projects.

Conclusion

Ghana's PRMA, 2011 (Act 815) broadly responds to public preferences and public choices. The basic revenue management strategy is investment led. The law lays down the key parameters for the accounting and collecting of petroleum revenues due the Government. It establishes the limits on the amount of revenues that shall be directed into the annual budget and into savings. The underlying fiscal rule is simple and logical. It provides for cautious spending. Flexibility is part of the fiscal guideline by allowing for the exact spending percentage to be determined on year-to-year basis. A fixed percentage is a straight jacket likely to be stripped off under political pressures. At the same time, for the fiscal guidelines to be credible, there are limits to the flexibility, limits that are to be revisited every three years. It provides for the operation and management of the savings and that the assets of the savings shall be prudently managed.

By providing for clear assignment of institutional responsibilities for the assessment, collection and management of petroleum revenues; by establishing processes and standards for reporting, accountability and auditing; by setting out the clear guidelines for the management of savings and investment policy; by entrenching transparency as a fundamental principle in how Ghana intends to collect, account for and manage its good fortunes from petroleum; and by providing a platform for public interest and accountability, Ghana has taken a step to assure all its stakeholders that the petroleum revenues will be managed wisely for the benefit of the current and future generations.

The clear provisions notwithstanding, there are challenges, not least of them being ensuring the enforcement of the provisions of the law. Will Act 815, to borrow from Schwarte (2008) 'be a law for the sake of having it?' Much depends on the collective vigilance of citizens and on the ability of the PIAC in carrying out its mandate as provided for in the law. The absence of fiscal responsibility rules or laws can easily undermine any restrictions in the law against borrowing. To be effective, the law needs strong complementary provisions that enforce comprehensive government accountability and disclosures in public financial management.

References

Acosta, A.M., & Heuty, A. (2009). Can Ghana Avoid the Oil Curse? Policy Briefing prepared for UK's Department for International Development, May.

African Development Bank & the African Union (2011). *Oil and Gas in Africa.* Oxford: Oxford University Press.

Amoako-Tuffour, J. (2008). Public Consultations, the Role of Civil Servants and Development Partners in Ghana`s Poverty Reduction Strategy. In Amoako-Tuffour, J. & Armah, B. (Eds), *Poverty Reduction Strategies in Action: Lessons and Perspectives from Ghana.* Maryland: Lexington Books: Rowman and Littlefield, 95–118.

Asfaha, S. (2007). National Revenue Funds: Their Efficacy for Fiscal Stability and Intergenerational Equity. Policy Recommendation Paper published by International Institute for Sustainable Development, Winnipeg.

Bartels, F.L., & Piccinni, A. (2011). Is Public Financial Management System in Ghana ready to deal with Petroleum Resources? Policy Briefing Paper, Office of UNIDO, Accra.

Bell, J.C., & Faria, T.M. (2007). Critical Issues for a Revenue Management Law. In Humphreys, M., Sachs J.D., & Stiglitz, J. (Eds), *Escaping the Resource Curse.* New York: Columbia University Press, 287–321.

Bell, J.C., & Faria, T.M. (2005). Sao Tome and Principe Enacts Oil Revenue Law, Sets New Transparency, Accountability, and Governance Standards, *Oil, Gas & Energy Law Intelligence (OGEL),* Vol 3, Issue 1, pp. 1-9, March.

Davis, J.M., Ossowoski, R., & Fedelino, A. (Eds) (2003). *Fiscal Policy Formulation and Implementation in Oil Producing Countries.* Washington DC: International Monetary Fund.

Ghana (2005). Economic Governance and Management: Country Self-Assessment, Technical Report prepared for African Peer Review Mechanism, Centre for Policy Analysis, Accra.

Gylfason, T. (2001). Natural Resource and Economic Growth: What is the Connection, CESifo Working Paper No. 530. International Monetary Fund (2008). *Ghana: Enhancing Fiscal Discipline.* IMF Fiscal Affairs Department, Washington D.C.

Moss T., & Young, L. (2009). Saving Ghana from Its Oil: The Case for Direct Cash Distribution. Center for Global Development, Working Paper, 186.

Petroleum Revenue Management ACT, 2011 (ACT 815), Republic of Ghana.

Sachs, J. (2007). How to Handle the Macroeconomics of Oil Wealth. In Humphreys, M., Sachs, J.D., & Stiglitz, J. E. (2007). *Escaping the Resource Curse.* New York: Colombia University Press.

Schwarte, C. (2008). *Public Participation and Oil Exploitation in Uganda.* London: Gatekeeper Series 138 by International Institute for Environment and Development.

Stiglitz, J. (2007). What is the Role of the State? In Humphreys, M., Sachs J.D., & Stiglitz, J. (Eds), *Escaping the Resource Curse.* New York: Columbia University Press, 43-72.

World Bank (2009). Economy-wide Impact of Oil Discovery in Ghana. Report No. 47321- GH.

5

Risks in Gas-Power Project Financing

Francis Mensah Sasraku

Abstract

Bankable project finance is a prerequisite to attracting funding from both local and international sources. In theory or reality, project financing is a positive step if not a panacea to reducing the power supply gap in developing countries like Ghana which continues to experience an energy supply gap. With the discovery of commercial gas reserves offshore, the issue of supply risk, which hitherto had been a big problem because of the undue reliance on the West African gas pipeline, will be mitigated. It appears that the main areas of concern are the country and political risks, force majeure risks, foreign exchange risks, insurance risks, environmental risks and off-take or purchase agreement risks which pertain specifically to the investor country which cannot be easily controlled by international banks. On the other hand, issues of technology risks, site and grounds conditions risks, project planning and preparation risks, construction and project development risks are easily handled by experienced international project finance teams of international banks. This chapter seeks to answer and provide insights into the question: what institutional restructuring should be undertaken to mitigate lender risks to attract project financing into the emerging gas-power generation sector in Ghana? Firstly, expectations of project financiers in power generation plants in developing countries are considered; secondly, risk mitigating measures are developed; and finally, the measures are applied to the environments of developing countries with specific reference to Ghana.

Introduction

The 2007 Ghana Eurobond issue allowed additional infrastructure investments of $600m in 2008 (out of which $500 million was used for electricity), more than the entire publicly funded infrastructural investment reported for the earlier period (World Bank, 2009). The World Bank estimated the cost of providing a standardized infrastructure package in a number of African countries, including Ghana. The package is designed to meet foreseeable economic and social demands for the next decade. In the case of Ghana, the package includes for power, 2,000MW of new generation capacity, and an increase of electrification up to 76 per cent coverage. The doubling of existing capacity to 4,000 MW by 2017 would allow satisfying a domestic demand projected to grow by 7 per cent annually (including a small and constant proportion for exports to neighbouring countries). Additional capacity investment that would make it possible for Ghana to become a large exporter of electricity in the region could be envisaged, with higher gas reserves than currently assessed, among other industrial choices for gas use (World Bank, 2009).

Meeting Ghana's infrastructure needs would cost $1.6 billion per year for the next decade or around 10 per cent of gross domestic product (GDP). Almost half of the total spending requirement is associated with the power sector, with investment needs for that sector as high as $600 million per year (World Bank, 2009). Such power generation gap means that the country's development agenda is being undermined. Studies show that for lenders to finance such projects, they will need to mitigate the risks in the form of construction and project development risks, project planning and preparation risks, implementation risks, shareholder/joint venture risks, site and ground conditions risks, technology risks, supply risk, off-take or purchase agreement risks, market risks, operating and maintenance risks, financing and foreign exchange risks, environmental compliance risks, consents and approval risks, force majeure risks, insurance risks, loan syndication risks, and country and political risks (Smith, 2010). In line with its theme, this material focuses on the risks in the emerging gas-power generation projects in Ghana and their impact on the key areas of energy law and policy as well as the banking sector regulation (National Energy Policy, 2010).

Project Finance and Bankable Projects

Project finance is the creation of commercial structures and financial packages for major development schemes or infrastructure projects by sponsors with their contractors and other project parties, to provide manufacturing or infrastructure facilities which deliver goods and services and generate operational cash flows.

In creating those structures, experienced project sponsors and their advisors will anticipate the needs and requirements of investors and lenders, thereby creating 'bankable' deal structures and commercial packages. A bankable deal is a project transaction which has a sound contractual structure, clear aims and rational, reliable and credit worthy project parties, robust cashflow and a risk profile which is considered to be acceptable by investors and lenders (Smith, 2010).

A 'bankable' power project as shown in Figure 5.1 must therefore satisfy the criteria of bankability by taking into account two important factors. The first is the uniqueness of power projects best described as being asset specific with high capital intensiveness, and having a long gestation period with varying physical or country of location. The second is specific to being located in a developing country where the following issues have to be taken into account: reliability of planned cash flow; scope and operations of the regulatory regime; development risks; environmental, host and political risks.

PROJECT FINANCE, ITS ASSOCIATED RISKS AND ROLE IN DEVELOPMENT FINANCING IN DEVELOPING COUNTRIES

Project finance is useful especially in developing countries to unlock the value of their natural resources and build the infrastructure they need to move forward (Finnerty, 2007). It can provide a cost-effective means of raising funds to support a project that is capable of standing on its own as a separate economic entity as expected by sponsors (Finnerty, 2007).

The theory of corporate finance is relevant to understanding further the role of project finance in development financing and how it should be structured and arranged. In emerging countries such as Ghana characterized by market imperfections, financing constraints have prevented the government from financing a positive Net Present Value (NPV) energy project on its own. Ghana's current rating of BB[1] for example puts it away from an investible grade and is perceived as having a high moral hazard (that is, risk of expropriation).

However, appropriately segregating energy projects based on size, value and time, from the credit rating of the country through project financing that assures the lenders they will be fully repaid with interest can make the difference between projects getting financed or being allowed to languish (Finnerty, 2007).

---

1   Standards and Poors rating 2011.

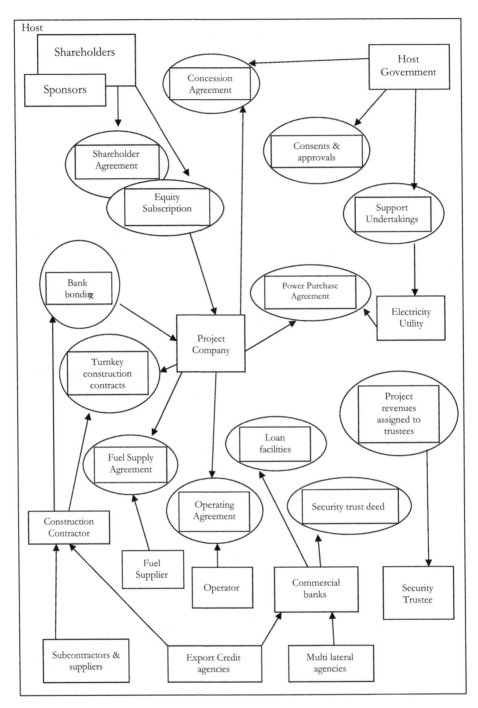

Figure 5.1   **Typical Contractual Matrix for a 'Bankable' Power Generation Project***

* See Smith supra note 4 at 1.5

Earlier studies by Standards and Poors have shown that host country issues and legal or structural deficiencies together account for more than two-thirds of the defaults and just under one-half the rating downgrades (Finnerty, 2007). The pervasiveness of these risks requires a different approach to satisfy the needs of financiers.

PROJECT FINANCE STRUCTURES AND ARRANGEMENTS IN DEVELOPING COUNTRIES

It is reassuring that financiers of power projects in Ghana for example would need country and political risks cover, and the financing package has to maximize the support from export credit agencies (with buyer credit support) and multilateral lending agencies (MLAs) like the World Bank (with co-financing guarantees) through its Multilateral Investment Guarantee Agency (MIGA) or International Development Agency (IDA). These risks can be mitigated through credit guarantee (full or partial) or through political risk insurance as shown in Figure 5.2.

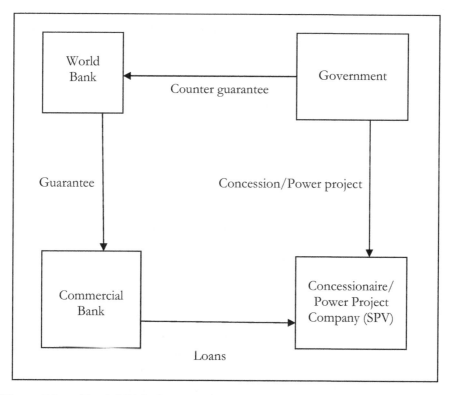

Figure 5.2   Partial Risk Guarantees – Guaranteed Debt Structure for a Typical Power Project

Export credit guarantees or insurance cover losses for exporters or lenders financing projects tied to the export of goods and services. Export credit guarantees or insurance cover some percentages of both political risks and commercial risk (together termed comprehensive risk guarantee or insurance) (Matsukawa & Odo, 2007). Partial Risk Guarantees (PRGs) also termed as Political Risk Guarantees (PRGs) or Political Risk Insurance (PRI) cover losses caused by specified political risk events depending on the provider. In the case of 'enclave projects' which earn foreign exchange revenues such as future potential Ghanaian-controlled cross-border gas and power export projects similar to the West African Gas Project, the International Bank for Reconstruction and Development (IBRD) Enclave PRGs would be required.

The process of structuring power projects in developing countries is first to identify the types of project costs (construction, major plant procurement and services), then determine the offshore and local content (sourcing). Export Credit Agencies (ECA) usually provide cover for up to 85 per cent of the eligible goods and services from the ECA country with European Union (EU) ECAs allowing some other EU countries' content as eligible. The fourth column as illustrated in Figure 5.3 includes the financing plan which is assembled in loan tranches. Often the process will have to go through a number of cycles and the choice of supply may be determined by the availability of country risks cover from individual ECAs (Smith, 2010).

The Figure 5.3 contrasts project financing in a developed country with high credit rating as shown in Figure 5.4 where the banks and other financiers are prepared to absorb the country risk and therefore focuses on counterparty risks as part of credit risks, contractual risk with full or limited recourse depending on the nature of project and the arranging bank.

Local banks in Ghana can participate in major power projects on participating basis. Loan syndication is a key feature of project financing because of the reasons of risk exposure management. Syndicating loans also lead to improvement on return on assets by selling down the loans. However for a developing country like Ghana, an additional government commitment (Stickley, 2006) for both offshore and onshore financial institutions is required against three major risks in the form of regulatory risks, devaluation risk of local currency and sub-sovereign risks (Matsukawa & Odo, 2007). The party taking a loan participation acquires a double credit risk – that of the borrower and of the original lender. If the original lender goes into liquidation, the participant will find that monies subsequently recovered from the borrower will not be

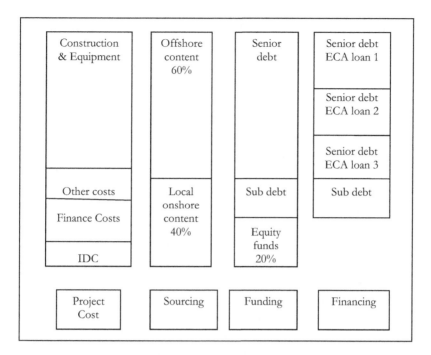

Figure 5.3   Costs, Sourcing, Funding and Financing of Power Projects in Ghana

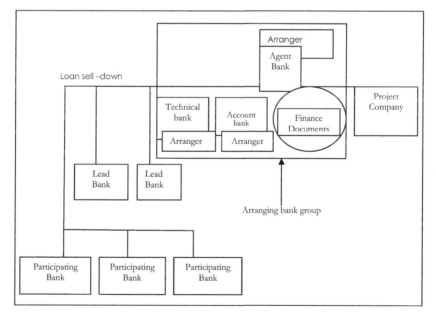

Figure 5.4   Typical Loan Syndication Structure for Projects in Developed Countries with Assumed Political and Legal Risk

applied in satisfying the original lender's liabilities under the participation, but towards the liabilities of the original lender owed to its general body of creditors (Penn, Shea & Arora, 1994). However contractual restrictions in loan documentation may impede the disposal of assets (Penn, Shea & Arora, 1994).

Again a participant will not be able to apply any deposits[2] of the borrower which it holds by way of set-off monies unpaid to the participant. There is no mutuality. The borrower owes the loan to the original lender, most likely the offshore or foreign bank (lead bank) (Penn, Shea & Arora, 1994). The implication is that local and foreign banks will need to protect their loan assets irrespective of their level of participation in the loan syndication and the currencies involved. The risk sharing arrangement if the lead bank is offshore is to seek guarantees from a third party such as the World Bank through its 'multilateral wrap' facility or guaranteed debt structure as illustrated in Figure 5.2. Securing this guarantee, would allow each participant's currency and interest rate risks exposures to be hedged. Hedging instruments may include forward foreign exchange agreements, caps, floors and collars, and interest rate swaps. The documentation should satisfy the standard ISDA documentation for derivatives that helps to mitigate exposures through its netting option (Vinter, 2006).

Institutional Challenges Posed by Power Projects Implementation

Several challenges are posed by the government's drive to attract investors into the power generation sector. There are four specific challenges that explain why investments in the energy sector have not taken advantage of the opportunities offered through international project financing. They are:

1. Inadequate legal and regulatory framework to back and mitigate the risks inherent in gas-power generation value chain investments. For example the current regulator under the Public Utilities Regulation Commission (PURC) and Law (1997), PURC Act 538 has failed to match the cost of generating power to the tariff build up because it is more focused on social and political dynamics than economic viability which underlies bankable projects creating a potential revenue risk.

---

2   Local banks provide utility collection services in their various branches which are finally used to repay VRA or project sponsors.

2.   Failure to fully deregulate leading to the absence of wholesale power markets has prevented and seriously undermined the potential local investments into bulk power purchases to improve cash flows for repayment of any investments in power projects.

3.   The pension sector which has access to contractual savings to support local bond market remains very conservative.

4.   The cultural issues of required state participation or support through the Ministry of Energy and sub sovereign institutions like the Volta River Authority (VRA) which is responsible for power generation specifically has no credit rating as a potential sponsor and both lack project skills at their various institutional levels.

5.   Absence of local well capitalized commercial banks to participate in syndicated loans.

The question still remains as to what specific actions may be needed in areas of policy and law and institutional restructuring to overcome these challenges?

Conclusion

For Ghana to overcome these challenges it needs to strategically reposition the gas-power generation sector and recognize it as the driver of the country's future economic development. That means that some radical changes to the Ghanaian Energy Law and Policy and the regulation of the banking sector.

IMPLICATIONS FOR GHANAIAN ENERGY LAW AND POLICY

1.   There is no law focusing on energy infrastructural development. In addition the existing related laws such as the Ghana Petroleum Revenue Management Law is silent on specific issues of concession, pricing, sale and purchase contracts, taxes and capital allowances and Build, Operate and Transfer (BOT). Regulations for infrastructure are often included in concession or other key contracts between the Government of Ghana and the investor (so-called regulation by contract). Ghana must introduce a law for investments in infrastructure as is the case in Peru (Matsukawa & Odo, 2007). Given Ghana's nascent regulatory framework and its

regulatory agency without a track record the governments have always opted to provide contractual certainty to attract investments bilaterally, multilaterally or privately (Matsukawa & Odo, 2007). More specifically, in designing the law for investments into power infrastructure critical issues regarding concessions are extremely important to remove problems of land tenure and ownership. Provisions on guarantees must be benchmarked against the MLA such as MIGA standards to cover respective contracts of guarantee for loan; for shareholder loans; for non-shareholder loans; and equity investors, and particularly, the place of subordinated loans as a mechanism for early repayment of 'equity funding' to promote assurance and transparency. Given the export revenue potential from power exports, the law must as a matter of strategy strengthen the autonomy[3] of VRA and compel them to seek credit rating.

2. The country has no Gas Law and must develop one as a matter of urgency. This law is important to capture and deal with issues that relate to the type of purchase and sale contracts needed to manage input or supply risks relating to gas-power projects. The infusion of provisions such as 'hell-or-high water' for example would protect the project's lenders against escalation in operating expenses, changes in tax laws, and other factors. Again it protects the project against regulatory lag inherent in the rate-making process (Finnerty, 2007). These stringent terms must be enshrined in the Gas Laws to promote discipline among policy implementers and industry players.

3. Finally potential local sources of financing in the form of pension funds must be integrated into the design of the law. For example the Social Security and National Insurance Trust (SSNIT) must be compelled to allocate a definite percentage of its long-term contractual savings from pensions estimated at $60million US Dollars per month into bankable power projects.

---

3   From its formation the VRA Executive Head was equivalent to a Minister of State and reported to the President until 1998. This privilege needs to be reinstated by future Infrastructure Law to minimize political interference in power projects implementation.

IMPLICATIONS FOR BANKING REGULATION

1.   The banking regulator must encourage local universal banks to increase their equity, institutionalize the Equator Principles and seek ISDA membership for them to potentially participate in project financing.

2.   The existing Foreign Exchange Act, Act 567 must be amended to accommodate expectations of project financiers in the form of availability, convertibility, and full transferability of foreign exchange.

3.   The regulator must promote energy banking and bancassurance and regulate the funds from bancassurance to be invested largely in power projects. This will guarantee liquidity and deepening of the Ghanaian power markets and mitigate project revenue risks and risks faced by local syndicated loans participants as mismatches in their maturity ladder are minimized with the practice that they take short-term deposits with limited long-term savings vehicles against long-term financing needs of power projects.

In conclusion, using experiences in Peru, and project successes and failures in the UK, the impact of specific Laws on Infrastructural Development and Gas Laws in terms of promoting transparency, accountability and project bankability cannot be underestimated. Further deregulation in the energy sector coupled with the incorporation of project finance legal framework into the banking and financial services laws and practices is necessary to deepen and improve the liquidity of the Ghanaian power markets. Should Ghana implement these changes, Ghana should through project financing be able to realize the benefits of its gas reserves, speed up its economic transformation and possibly become a major exporter of power in the next decade.

References

Finnerty, J. D. (2007). *Project Financing Asset – based Financial Engineering* (2nd ed.). New York: Wiley Finance.

Matsukawa, T., & Odo, H. (2007). *Review of Risk Mitigation Instruments for Infrastructure: Financing and Recent Trends and Development*: Herndon, VA: World Bank Publication.

Multilateral Investment Guarantee Agency (2011). *Operational Regulation.* Washington, USA.

National Energy Policy (2010). Ministry of Energy, Republic of Ghana.

Penn, G. A., Shea, M.A., & Arora, A. (1994). *The Law and Practice of International Banking, Volume 2.* London: Sweet and Maxwell.

Smith, V. (2010). *International Project Finance Manual.* Dundee: CEPMLP.

Stickley, D.C. (2006). *A framework for Negotiating and Managing Gas Industry Contracts.* Dundee: CEPMLP.

The World Bank Guarantees: Leveraging Private Finance for Emerging Markets retrieved 5 December, 2011 from http://web.worldbank.org/external.

Vinter, D. G. (2006) *Project Finance* (3rd ed.). Suffolk: Thompson Sweet and Maxwell.

PART II

Entrenching Transparency and Stakeholder Engagement

6

Towards Good Governance in Ghana's Petroleum Sector

Kwaku Appiah-Adu and Nana Kegya Appiah-Adu

Abstract

For Ghana's petroleum resource to yield high dividends for its people, good governance in the sector is absolutely critical. This chapter commences with a definition of good governance in the oil and gas (O&G) sector. Next is a discussion of the building blocks for good governance in the sector. Moreover, the roles of the principal actors in good governance – government, society and operators, are addressed. This is followed by a presentation of good governance functions and three key factors that are inextricably linked to good governance in the O&G sector, namely, transparency, accountability and participation. Additionally, a country example of good governance principles and practices is examined. Finally, efforts made by Ghana to establish a good governance framework, progress made so far and suggestions on the way forward are highlighted.

Introduction

Petroleum is the major source of government revenue in many developing nations. If there is a breakdown in governance of the sector, the consequences can be disastrous for the nation's economy. Conversely, if a country manages to govern this sector appropriately, the results are likely to be growth in the country's wealth, continuous development, and social improvement. A concept of good governance that is comprehensive and practice-oriented enables all stakeholders to understand the subject from a broader perspective so the key issues can be addressed with the objective of finding solutions to them.

Governance in the petroleum sector represents the system for making and putting into practice decisions regarding the development of a country's O&G resources. This involves the configuration and organization of the sector, the decision-making and communication processes, the policies and objectives that govern the sector activities and the regulation of those activities (Lahn et al., 2007).

In discussing governance in the petroleum sector, the significance of issues specific to a country's environment and how these should guide its response to evolving changes over time cannot be ignored. It must be noted that each nation has cultural influences on the sharing and implementation of political authority and legal mandate. Delineating issues involves the following: the political structure, the expected natural life of the resource, the stage of economic and technological advancement, the knowhow and skills set of government institutions, the level of sophistication of civil society, the regulatory structure of the sector, international considerations, the extent of the nation's reliance on petroleum. From the foregoing, it is clear that there cannot be a single complete and prescribed prototype for good governance that suits every petroleum-producing country in this world.

Key players and interested parties in a nation's O&G governance can be classified into three clusters: government (executive, judiciary, regulators); society (legislature, civil society, media, trades unions) and operators (oil companies, private sector institutions, financial institutions). Generally, there are a number of governance functions. These include policy formulation, strategy development, operational level decision making and control. Interestingly, the various stakeholders in petroleum governance play different but sometimes overlapping roles. Policy formulation is usually the task of government. Government tasks operators to undertake O&G operations. Society holds government accountable for policies. While many actors may play overlapping roles in petroleum governance, each has a particular function in the process. The operators make available the information and views/opinions to facilitate suitable regulatory principles and guidelines. Society stimulates and enriches the policy dialogue, and in the final analysis, is a key player in the approval of the selected policy. Society can also support in the control process as they evaluate sector activities via media analysis, sector studies as well as direct interaction and consultation with the industry.

It is generally accepted that good governance in the petroleum sector is built on a number of fundamental tenets. These include the identification of an explicit purpose, with roles and responsibilities clearly outlined. Regarding this point, issues that need to be addressed include the following: who establishes the objectives, targets and regulations; how roles are delineated and functions apportioned; how responsibilities are outlined and authority assigned. Next is facilitating the process of getting each participant to accomplish the functions, roles and responsibilities assigned. Issues that need to be addressed include what each participant requires to fully carry out the tasks assigned; what each participant can do to facilitate the work of other participants; and, creating as well as supporting an enabling environment.

Transparency, including the provision of accurate information, is another pillar of good governance in the petroleum sector. Issues here involve the nature of information required by key actors in the decision-making system to make sound decisions and how the government can recognize that objectives and targets are being realized. When transparency is encouraged, and it is evident that the people's interests are being protected and promoted, there is an enhancement of society's confidence in the political system and public service. Transparency can be enhanced by making available to the public information on decisions concerning the utilization and administration of as well as accounting for petroleum proceeds, so that the citizens can subject the process to thorough examination. Documentation on petroleum income and expenditure associated with the income should be widely made available so that all and sundry can have access to them.

Sometimes confidentiality clauses in petroleum agreements and bills are used as a reason why documents have to be kept confidential. While confidentiality may be necessary on certain occasions to safeguard commercially sensitive information, it is vital that such sensitive sections are subjected to examination by an autonomous body, and not left to the discretion of politicians only, because certain critical issues could be overlooked or missed.

There is an obvious link between transparency and accountability in good petroleum sector governance (Agyare, 2010). For accountability to be effective, the process has to be demand-driven. While in the past, many people in African societies might have been characterized as mere passengers in issues of national interest, we are beginning to see that situation change in the past few years. It is expected that accountability would be further improved when the management of the petroleum resource offers a stage for government officials to be held accountable in the administration and utilization of petroleum proceeds.

When transparency and accountability are primary pillars of the sector, public confidence in the petroleum governance system will be enhanced, and it is expected that there would be useful public participation in decision making, regarding the establishment of priorities in the administering and utilization of petroleum proceeds. A conscious effort should be made to get citizens to actively participate in the setting of development priorities, to which petroleum proceeds shall be applied. This process should include dialogues involving the extent to which spending decisions and prospects are consistent with the country's development priorities. A compilation of the society's evaluations and inclinations on the administration and utilization of petroleum income should be made available to government officials, who as emissaries of the populace, are expected to implement their priorities.

One cannot discuss good governance without highlighting the importance of sustainable development for the gain of future generations. Issues of significance in this respect include the setting of sustainable development objectives for the sector and reasons for doing so and how the objectives and regulations support sustainable development.

Good Governance: The Case of Norway

In Norway, the petroleum industry commenced in the 1970s and it is expected to exist for many decades. A fundamental reason for its stellar performance was the setting up of the Petroleum Fund as soon as it was established that petroleum was a significant component of Norway's resources and assets, and as such, neither bureaucrats nor politicians would be allowed to waste petroleum revenues. In 1990, a transparent system for managing O&G revenues was instituted.

Petroleum proceeds are remitted directly into a foreign currency fund. This fund is managed by professionals. For any use of the fund outside asset management, the Norwegian Parliament has to pass a resolution. There are stringent conditions under which the fund can be used. After decades of accruing surpluses via sound management and investment, Norway's petroleum fund is currently amongst the world's leading institutional investors (Hensley, 2011). The fund, whose results are published openly, is managed on behalf of the Ministry of Finance by Norges Bank. Investments of the fund are made both in Norway and globally to provide for diversity and better risk management.

Since the fund has managed to build up surpluses over the years, it is possible to use it as a hedge for fiscal management in case oil prices take a nosedive. In effect, it is a long-term savings instrument for all the people of Norway. Currently, if required, the fund focuses on covering financing gaps in the pension system. The success of the fund makes it possible for Norway to cater for increases in pension benefits and concurrently sustain investments in long-term assets, in spite of a decrease in petroleum supplies over the long term.

Ghana: Efforts Made in Ghana to Promote Good Governance

Ghana has made significant strides since the Ghana National Petroleum Corporation (GNPC) and its partners Tullow Ghana Ltd and Kosmos Energy announced the discovery of oil in significant quantities off the shore of Ghana's Western Region in 2007. This find, which is approximately 65km from the nearest coastal town, has generated a lot of attention within Ghana and abroad. Not surprisingly, there has been increased interest in exploration in Ghana's waters following the find, which was hitherto not the case. The euphoria that greeted the oil discovery was accompanied by a sincere hope that the discovery would become a much needed blessing to the country and not a curse.

The government of the day immediately established a Ministerial Committee on Oil & Gas to spearhead the development of the necessary preparatory works leading to dialogue with the general populace as well as development partners who had shown an interest in supporting the country. The Ministerial Committee then established a Technical Committee on Oil and Gas and tasked it with the following: the holding of a Forum on Oil and Gas to solicit views from the general populace and to allow interaction with various development partners to map out a strategy O&G development; discussion with the various regions of Ghana through a road show and to further solicit views; formulation of an Oil and Gas Policy for Ghana to be passed by Parliament; crafting of a Petroleum Regulatory Authority Bill; development of an Oil and Gas Master Plan for the country.

The Technical Committee had representation from the following offices: Office of the President; Ministry of Energy; Ministry of Finance & Economic Planning; Ministry of Justice & Attorney General's Department; Ministry of Defence; Environmental Protection Agency (EPA); Internal Revenue Service; and GNPC.

Following the setting up of the committee on O & G, the group set to work on their first task which was the organization of the forum. The National Forum was set for February 2008. The Committee had commitments from the Norwegian Government, World Bank, Department for International Development (DfID), Deutsche Gessellschaft fur Internationale Zusammenarbeit (German Agency for International Cooperation) or GIZ, formerly known as GTZ, International Monetary Fund (IMF), United States Agency for International Development (USAID) and other development partners.

Various meetings were held with the development partners and other interest groups to produce a list of participants. Due to the challenge of numbers, a maximum number of 200 was arrived at. All regions were given a guideline for inviting personalities to the forum. This guide included the following: persons with knowledge of the subject of O&G with ability to make positive contribution to discussions; respected traditional leaders with knowledge of royalties and natural resource management sharing agreements and so on; opinion leaders, and persons within communities who command respect and whose views are held in high esteem within the region or large areas of the region; development-oriented personalities; selected non-government organizations (NGOs) within the region who can contribute to the discussions.

This list was then supplemented with other personalities from the various ministries, departments and agencies, representation from the political parties, religious bodies and other identifiable groups.

The workshop was then organized along the following four main themes. Theme one – turning O&G wealth into sustainable and equitable development – was selected for participants to consider the contribution of O&G to economic growth and development in terms of Ghana's development based on strategies and experiences both positive and negative from around the world. Experts shared views on approaches necessary to achieve sound management of public finances (revenue and expenditure) and particular instruments that have been developed to support this, including petroleum revenue funds.

The second theme – entrenching transparency and stakeholder engagement – sought to examine the role of transparency, accountability and stakeholder engagement in making and implementing good extractive industry policy, using examples from Ghana and elsewhere.

Theme three – effective management of the O&G sector – sought to examine how laws, contracts and regulatory institutions can be used to provide effective management of O&G exploration and production and maximize benefits for Ghana. This will include discussion of licensing and negotiations, fiscal terms and the roles of the regulator and national oil company, using examples from Ghana's own recent experiences with regulatory reform and examples from around the world.

The fourth theme – safeguarding security and the environment – sought to gain best practice experience in ensuring security through examination of security and environmental issues relating to the O&G industry and appropriate safeguard measures suited to Ghana and the best means for their implementation.

Overall, the forum was a big success which won Ghana praise for the process of consultation. Following the forum, the Technical Committee undertook field visits to all ten regions of Ghana and met with stakeholders to solicit further views for incorporation into the draft policy document. The regional visits were again successful and discussions were held with a cross-section of Ghanaians.

These efforts were built on by the new administration after the change in government in 2009. The new government inherited draft bills for: an O&G policy; petroleum revenue management; a petroleum regulatory authority; and a master plan for the O&G industry that covered the legal regime; fiscal regime; local content and private sector participation; downstream and natural gas utilization; security; health, safety, environment and community relations.

Further consultations were conducted involving government officials, civil society, community groups and international agencies and government. Civil society played a major role in organizing a forum where all stakeholders engaged government. This was another giant step taken in the quest for good governance in the O&G sector. Several consultations had taken place with the people of Ghana since oil was discovered and, at the end of the forum, a series of recommendations were presented to Government with copies going to the media.

Many of these proposals were taken into consideration when Government was finalizing the draft petroleum revenue management bill and the draft petroleum regulatory authority bill. Quite clearly, in an environment where civil society is well educated, it would be better placed to make meaningful proposals to government. Moreover, in a situation where government is willing to engage with its citizenry and take into account their suggestions, the result is likely to be win–win situation for all stakeholders and the nation as a whole.

Civil society should serve as watchdogs within the economy and, if the mutual relationship between government and civil society is harnessed to promote good governance in the petroleum sector, such positive developments are expected to be extended to other sectors, and ultimately, it is the citizenry and national economy that will be the overall beneficiaries of the effects of these good governance principles.

Ghana Makes Good Governance Strides in the Petroleum Sector

Several nations that are endowed with rich resources are infamous for secrecy, fraud and the squandering of hundreds of millions in proceeds from petroleum and mining activities. In addition to its natural resources including gold, bauxite and manganese, Ghana became Africa's latest oil producer in December 2010. Ghana has been at pains to ensure that the oil find turns out to be a blessing and not a curse. So far, the evidence points to efforts at incorporating good governance (transparency and accountability) measures in the legal framework for managing its petroleum resources, though it must be said that there is still more work to be done.

In pursuing this goal, the President of Ghana signed the Petroleum Revenue Management Bill soon after it was passed into law. The law requires the Government to publish information on receipts from petroleum companies – online and in national newspapers – on a quarterly basis. The Minister of Finance and Economic Planning will be required to reconcile receipts and expenditures and submit reports to Parliament and to the public every quarter. In addition, audited statements of Ghana's oil accounts will be made public the year immediately following the production of oil.

Further to these transparency and accountability provisions, the law requires the setting up of a Public Interest and Accountability Committee which will include civil society representation. Coupled with new disclosure requirements covering companies registered with the Securities and Exchange Commission (SEC) or receiving World Bank financing, Ghana's new law compels foreign companies playing a role in Ghana's Jubilee Field production to disclose their payments and the country has to disclose the receipts.

Conclusion

Clearly there are still some hurdles to overcome. Ghana has recently put in place an independent regulator for the petroleum sector (the Petroleum Commission) and every effort must be made to make it fully operational within the shortest possible time. In theory, there are respective mandates for the Commission and Ministry of Energy but the relationship between the two bodies has to be delineated so clearly that in practice they will complement each other and not be involved in any turf wars. Clearly, there is a need to build capacity both in new Petroleum Commission and the Ministry of Energy to ensure that they perform their functions in line with international best practices.

Interestingly, this leads to the emergence of a new commercial entity – Ghana's oil company – a role that is expected to be performed by the GNPC. There is no doubt that the GNPC has an appreciable level of skilled staff but it has to be re-engineered to become a learning organization with a stepping up of research and development if it is to compete with international oil companies (IOCs) in the industry. The functions of the national oil company have to be distinctly delineated and the organization has to be equipped with additional requisite skills to complement the existing expertise in order to thrust it into a dimension of competitiveness that makes it possible for it to pitch against industry giants over time. The company has to be able to work IOCS on joint ventures and be able to prime with IOCs in bidding for and winning exploration contracts both within the sub-region and internationally.

Against this backdrop, the Government of Ghana has to ensure that for potential bids in the country, there is no room for controversy where Ghana's national oil company competes with IOCs. In this regard, to every possible extent, legal instruments crafted to establish and delineate roles and responsibilities of the various institutions govern the petroleum sector must be devoid of any ambiguity and leave no room for legal wrangles and tussles.

Another challenge that needs to be addressed as a matter of urgency is the capacity of the institutions that have oversight responsibility for assessing and monitoring the impact of O&G activities on the environment and communities within the proximity of the petroleum find. It is heartening to note that with the support of some development partners, the Government of Ghana is in the process of building capacity particularly within the EPA to make it effective in assessing and monitoring environmental impacts.

On the issue of accountancy and governance, it goes without saying that society would want to see Ghana disclose its financial agreements with IOCs. This is another area in which Ghana has started making progress through the publishing of petroleum agreements for the Jubilee Field, a move which was necessitated by plans by Kosmos Energy, a US company, to become a publicly traded company. The public both in Ghana and globally can now find the contracts on the SEC's website.

A readiness report card has been launched by the Civil Society Platform on Oil and Gas in Ghana. The report was launched in Ghana, the UK and USA. The launches attracted large audiences and there was media coverage by several outlets including Bloomberg, the British Broadcasting Corporation and Voice of America. The report evaluated the preparedness of Ghana's executive, judiciary, legislature and other appropriate stakeholders to manage the oil find. The Government was assessed on ten measures ranging from transparency to independent regulation.

On the whole, Ghana obtained grade C, which indicated fair progress. Many are watching with keen interest to see if Ghana will get it right, sincerely hoping that this expectation will be met with success. It is believed that the Petroleum Revenue Management Law provides a sound platform to address the challenges of turning oil income into enduring benefits for all classes of Ghana's society, particularly the underprivileged.

References

Agyare, J. (2010). Transparency, accountability and participation: a formula to enhance the governance of Ghana's petroleum sector. *The Ghanaian Chronicle*, 3 August.

Hensley, M. (2011). *Avoiding the Curse of Oil: Strategies to Improve Governance and Finance Social Investment in Sub-Saharan Africa*. Virginia: Institute for Public-Private Partnerships.

Lahn, G., Marcel, V., Mitchell, J., Myers, K., & Stevens, P. (2007). Good Governance of the National Petroleum Sector, The Chatham House Document, London: Chatham House.

7

Civil Society and the Evolution of Accountability in the Petroleum Sector

Patrick R.P. Heller

Abstract

As attention to the opportunities and the risks associated with the petroleum industry has risen, so too has the impact of civil society organizations on governance of the sector. Within oil-producing countries, diverse groups of activists, journalists, academics and community representatives have developed sophisticated tools for influencing public policy and promoting more accountable practices. At an international level, civil society has coalesced to organize successful campaigns to develop strong international reporting standards and collect lessons learnt from global practice. This chapter examines the influence that civil society has had on the evolution of norms and procedures for oil sector management, both at a national and international level, and identifies emerging issues and tactics that civil society groups are beginning to utilize as their approaches continue to grow more nuanced.

Introduction

The world has repeatedly witnessed the sad phenomenon of citizens living in poverty or instability in spite of the massive wealth being generated by the oil and minerals being extracted from under their land or off their shores. In Angola, the billions of dollars generated each year by oil produced by the world's most sophisticated companies have done little to improve human development indicators that rank among the world's worst. In Venezuela and Bolivia, control over the petroleum sector has been alternately the source of paralyzing social controversy and a source for the consolidation of power. In Nigeria, the industry has spurred overwhelming environmental damage and violence, particularly in the Niger Delta. In dozens of other countries throughout the developing world, extraction has delivered disappointing revenues to the state or has exacerbated corruption or economic mismanagement with corrosive long-term effects on development.

Weak technical capacity and policy errors within oil-producing governments have unquestionably contributed to these disappointing results. But as Ghana and other new oil producers reflect on the often sad history of petroleum and development, it is increasingly clear that a lack of accountability to the public represents a more fundamental problem. Where citizens lack information on how their governments are managing resources and what is being done with the money generated by extraction, corruption is left to fester in darkness. Where policy makers do not feel the need to answer to their public, decisions are too easily guided by narrow or short-term considerations. Where there is no effective mechanism for communities directly impacted by extraction to express their concerns, the risks of violence skyrocket. When governments have no access to independent analysis, they can be forced to make complex technical decisions without benefitting from comparative perspectives or an effective system for weighing costs and benefits on different stakeholder groups.

This chapter focuses on the role of civil society groups – both within resource-rich countries and internationally – in bridging the accountability gap. In particular, it emphasizes the evolution of civil society organizations, from their roots as watchdogs seeking to expose corruption and generate pressure for transparency, to sophisticated bodies able to influence global policy, provide nuanced technical analysis, and engage in constructive dialogue with governments and oil companies, without sacrificing their commitment to provide a voice for otherwise disaffected stakeholders. As global advocacy for more accountable management of petroleum and minerals advances, civil society is simultaneously building on its core commitment to promoting transparency of extractive industry payments and pushing a number of new frontiers with the potential to dramatically enhance public oversight.

Today, at the outset of oil production, Ghana benefits from a sophisticated network of civil society groups that have developed expertise and effective techniques over years of advocating for more transparency in the mineral sector and are putting it to use to promote responsible management of Ghana's new oil bounty. Ghanaian civil society organizations have conducted sophisticated analyses that have contributed to the promulgation of a forward-thinking system for the management of petroleum revenues, and are now participating in the institutions set up to implement that system. They are working with parliamentarians and journalists to improve capacity for oversight and ensure that the government cannot execute oil policy in a vacuum. They are conducting sophisticated financial analysis and developing nuanced critiques of everything from the contracts signed with international oil companies (IOCs) to the administrative system by which the government will supervise exploration and production.

None of these steps ensures that Ghana will avoid the pitfalls that have impacted so many other oil-producing developing countries. And Ghanaian civil society continues to face serious challenges, from continued limitations on available information to a need to continue to build expertise on complex aspects of oil sector management. But the relative level of sophistication existing within the Ghanaian Civil Society Organization (CSO) world puts Ghana in an advantageous position vis-à-vis many other African oil producers, where there was little expertise or awareness of international expertise, and limited public space for advocacy, at the time that production began. Going forward, the ability of the Ghanaian civil society community to adapt to evolving realities and take advantage of opportunities for policy impact will have a major impact on whether Ghana's oil industry proves a boon to development.

Importance and Origins of Civil Society Engagement

Ghanaians need not look very far to appreciate the importance of a vigilant and engaged citizenry on the governance of natural resources and their contribution to economic development. In Liberia, an unelected transitional government signed dozens of large concession contracts that were out of step with international norms and did little to promote sustainable income for the country (Kaul & Heuty, 2009). In Angola, the Government has developed sophisticated methods for managing relationships with oil companies and generating large public revenues, but a lack of effective citizen oversight of revenue management and expenditure has had pronounced impacts, as evidenced by a 2011 IMF report identifying that $32 billion in public expenditure between 2007 and 2010 (equivalent to a quarter of gross domestic product (GDP)) could not be accounted for (International Monetary Fund, 2011).[1] And

---

1   As of the writing of this chapter, the Angolan Government was said to be conducting an internal review of the discrepancy, looking in particular at expenditures made by the state oil

despite their vast natural resources, these countries remain near the bottom of human development indicators, ranking 182nd and 148th, respectively, out of 187 countries in 2011.

Recognition of the connection between the accountability of resource-rich governments to their citizens and the growth, development and conflict impacts of oil and mineral extraction has represented an important element of major analyses of resource economies since attention to the so-called 'resource curse' phenomenon began to grow in the 1980s and 1990s (Gelb, 1988; Karl, 1997; Sachs & Warner, 1997). Where governments are able to survive on relatively 'easy' extractive rents generated by petroleum or mineral production, the social contract with citizens can break down (or fail to develop), leading governments to make decisions without concern for public perception. This can contribute to weak institutions poorly equipped to assess and promote the long-term interests of citizens (Isham et al., 2003, Brautigam, Fjeldstad & Moore, 2008).

Analysts and citizens have long recognized that civil society groups can play an important role in bridging the divide between citizens and their government.[2] Analysis of civil society influence on extractive industry governments fits within a broader literature on the role of associations on governance both within societies and internationally, which focuses on CSOs' ability to synthesize the views and voices of disparate stakeholders, link everyday citizens with global expertise, and mobilize sophisticated communications techniques to affect policy change (Bratton, 1994; Fiourini, 2000; Scholte, 2004).

Civil society activism around management of oil and mining pre-dates the rise of global organizations explicitly focused on the extractive industries. Activists exemplified by Nigeria's Ken Saro-Wiwa have for decades pushed for greater environmental protection and a more equitable share in financial benefits, particularly for communities directly affected by extractive activities. These organizations have played a crucially important role in calling attention to abuses perpetrated by governments and extractive companies, and to

---

company outside of ordinary budgetary processes, as well as deposits held in escrow accounts outside of the country.

2   It bears noting that there are various definitions of 'civil society'. Rather than wading deeply into a complex debate here, for purposes of this article I use a relatively formalistic approach in line with the World Bank (2010) definition of 'the wide array of non-governmental and not-for-profit organizations that have a presence in public life, expressing the interests and values of their members or others, based on ethical, cultural, political, scientific, religious or philanthropic considerations,' which includes 'community groups, non-governmental organizations (NGOs), labor unions, indigenous groups, charitable organizations, faith-based organizations, professional associations, and foundations.'

mobilizing citizen engagement around issues of justice in the extractive industries. The activities of these national champions around oil and mining were often intricately tied up in broader national movements for democracy, self-determination and environmental justice. The costs they faced were steep; political repression was often harsh, and many paid with their lives.

The global movement for extractive industry transparency began to take something approaching its current form in the late 1990s and early 2000s. Civil society organizations within oil and mineral-producing states collaborated with global organizations like Global Witness, Human Rights Watch, Oxfam America and Save the Children to call attention to the perverse links between natural resource wealth and conflicts that permeated countries such as Angola, Sierra Leone, Liberia and Nigeria. These efforts were undergirded by the library of academic analysis on natural resource economies that had developed during the 1980s and 1990s. The dominant focus of these global efforts was transparency of extractive industry payments by oil and mineral companies to resource-rich governments. In 2002, the Publish What You Pay Coalition was formed as a global campaign to require extractive industry companies to disclose their payments to resource-rich states. Over time, this coalition has developed into one of the most important sources of global information-sharing and collective advocacy, with more than 600 member organizations in 30 countries (van Oranje & Parham, 2009).

International institutions also began to pay close attention to the special challenges facing oil and mineral-producing countries, and to the role that civil society could play in helping alleviate them. The World Bank's 'Extractive Industries Review' represented a systematic attempt to analyse the actual and potential impact for the World Bank Group's policies on natural resource governance. It emphasized the significance of civil society both in its process – the review was developed as a result of extensive multi-stakeholder consultations – and in its conclusions, which emphasized the significance of transparency and consistent engagement with citizens (World Bank, 2004). The IMF's 'Guide on Resource Revenue Transparency', first released in 2005 and updated in 2007, also emphasized the importance in active participation by CSOs in national and international efforts to manage oil and mineral wealth (International Monetary Fund, 2007). The Chad-Cameroon pipeline project represented an early effort to put the growing attention on natural resource governance to the test, as the World Bank backed a controversial effort to help these governments secure financing for the project, backstopped by safeguards to promote transparency and oversight by a multi-stakeholder body including

CSOs. As van Oranje & Parham note: 'The legislation and safeguards for the pipeline project contained several grave weaknesses [which ultimately led to its failure]. However, one positive outcome of the entire effort was that it brought to the fore the fundamental need for civil society oversight in the negotiation of extractive industry projects and the management of resulting revenue flows.'

The 2003 launch of the Extractive Industries Transparency Initiative (EITI) represented another watershed moment in civil society's impact on oil and mineral sector governance. EITI's import has both substantive and process dimensions. By generating more than 50 documents reconciling more than $500 billion in company payment reports against what governments say they receive in 28 countries, EITI has produced a trove of information that national and international civil society organizations can use to hold policy makers to account for their revenue generation and collection methods as well as public expenditure (Revenue Watch Institute, 2011). These reports have served as powerful tools for activists in many countries. In Nigeria, for example, an EITI report identifying more than $800 million in discrepancies between what the Government said it received and what companies said they paid helped spark Ministerial efforts to improve oversight and a national debate about oil sector transparency that includes strong calls to improve reporting practices in new legislation (Extractive Industries Transparency Initiative, 2012).

EITI has provided a mouthpiece for civil society views and a forum for dialogue at a level previously unseen. Civil society occupies seats on the EITI Global Board, and has thus had a major impact on the Initiative itself and the emerging global dialogue around responsible extractive industry management. Within EITI-implementing countries, multi-stakeholder committees bring together civil society, government officials, and companies at a level of frequency and detail previously unseen. This has proven particularly important in countries like Gabon, Niger and the Republic of Congo, where the opportunities for constructive dialogue among these different groups had previously been virtually non-existent. A survey by the Revenue Watch Institute of CSOs active in EITI revealed that this platform for multi-stakeholder dialogue represents the most important tangible impact the Initiative has had on their work (Dykstra, 2011; Heuty, 2012).

Far beyond its direct impacts, EITI has also allowed civil society to influence global standards of resource revenue transparency and to push the growing debate around effective global standards. EITI conferences and board meetings have become some of the most important forums for debates on the state of the art, and CSOs have been right there to push the envelope. Despite these, EITI implementation has several shortcomings including a wide variation in the frequency, level of detail and quality of reports, a failure to cover the most important revenue streams in some countries, a low level of user-friendliness in many country reports and the Initiative's limited scope, which does not cover expenditure transparency or extractive industry contracts (Kolstad & Wiig, 2009; Shaxson, 2010; Gillies & Heuty, 2011; Heuty, 2012). The next section of this chapter details some current movements to deepen EITI and expand its influence on the substance and process of extractive industry reform.

New Skills, Strategies and Directions

Much of the core of the contemporary movement for more accountable governance of extractive industries – the emphasis on transparency, the sharing of international experiences, the interaction between local, national and international advocates – remains in place today. But recent years have seen important evolutions in the influence of civil society groups on global and national processes, and on the tactics they use to wield that emphasis.

ADVOCACY, EXPERTISE AND COLLABORATION

Local and national activists have always possessed the deepest knowledge of the direct impacts and challenges that extraction imposes on citizens. As information dissemination has improved, however, civil society groups have dramatically increased their ability to conduct sophisticated technical analysis and engage with policy makers on key strategic decisions. Extractive industry-oriented civil society groups today are able to carry out activities on a much larger playing field than was possible ten years ago.

This expanded sphere of engagement derives in part from successful advocacy campaigns resulting in greater disclosure of information within resource-rich countries. As CSOs gain a stronger sense of what is going on within their governments, they have moved beyond simply issuing calls for more transparency and have plunged into the weeds of detailed policy analysis. In Mexico, for example, organizations such as Fundar produce regular, detailed briefings on their country's performance on key issues related to oil sector management, including the accountability mechanisms governing the National Oil Company (Lopez, 2011). In Nigeria, the Niger Delta Citizens and Budget Platform conducts rigorous analyses of the expenditure policies and execution of some of the country's most oil-rich states (Niger Delta Citizens and Budget Platform, 2012).

Improved knowledge sharing at an international level has also contributed to this enhanced ability to engage constructively on policy issues. The Publish What You Pay network has proven an invaluable source of shared learning – through regional conferences and workshops, a list served with a constant stream of information and reports, and the development of coalition positions on key issues, the network has provided member organizations with a critical window into the experiences of their peers in other countries. Civil society representatives have taken part in training courses offered by international institutions like Petrad (which brings civil society representatives to Norway to participate in an eight-week training programme on petroleum policy and resource management), the Revenue Watch Institute (which has linked with academic institutions in Africa, Latin America and Eurasia to develop 'regional knowledge hubs' targeting civil society participants), the World Bank Institute and various other global organizations (Petrad, 2012; Revenue Watch Institute, 2012a). Furthermore, a host of efforts to synthesize best practice across the extractive industry value chain – including the 'Natural Resource Charter', the World Bank's 'Extractive Industry SourceBook', the African Union-led 'African Mining Vision' and the International Bar Association's 'Model Mining Development Agreement' – have given CSOs (and governments) a dynamic new set of tools with which to build on international experience in proposing policy solutions for specific challenges.

The conscious effort to build skills has given civil society groups an opportunity to engage more directly with policy makers. International CSOs like Revenue Watch, the African Center for Economic Transformation (ACET) and the International Senior Lawyers Project provide direct technical assistance to reform-minded governments on issues ranging from contract negotiations to transparency processes. National organizations have done likewise, and played a central role working constructively with public officials to base policy decisions on state-of-the-art thinking and a deep appreciation of the needs and desires of citizens. In Mongolia, for example, civil society actors have liaised substantially with government officials and have had a significant impact on the provisions of new mineral legislation and a scenarios-planning exercise designed to promote better decision making about how to spend (and save) large expected new mineral revenue flows (Revenue Watch Institute, 2012b). In Bolivia, the NGO Fundación Jubileo has worked with officials from the Ministry of Hydrocarbons and the National Oil Company to improve transparency practices and support the evolution of petroleum policies that maintain investment while generating fair returns to Bolivia's people (Fundación Jubileo, 2010). In Liberia, civil society groups have begun working with extractive companies and officials from the Public Procurement and Concessions Commission and other government bodies in a multi-stakeholder platform seeking to improve the monitoring and enforcement of key public contracts (Ganteh, 2010).

EITI has unquestionably played an important role in the evolution of these constructive engagements between CSOs and governments. By creating a platform for multi-stakeholder action toward a common goal, the Initiative has given CSOs in many countries an opportunity to demonstrate their expertise and helped develop a common language that public officials, companies and CSOs can use to discuss major challenges of natural resource governance.

New revenue disclosure requirements

The first few years of the 2010s have been characterized by tremendous progress on the flagship goal of the international movement: transparency of payments from extractive companies to national governments. The most significant development was the inclusion in the United States' Dodd-Frank Wall Street Reform Act of Section 1504, which requires all oil and mining companies registered with the Securities and Exchange Commission (SEC) to publish the payments they make to host-country governments on a disaggregated, project-by-project basis. At the time of writing this chapter, the SEC had yet to release regulations implementing the section, and extractive-industry companies were lobbying hard for regulations that would partially neuter the provision.

However, Section 1504 has the potential to have a transformative impact on natural resource governance, by producing regular flows of detailed information in a standard form. The provision will provide citizens in resource-rich countries with unprecedented opportunities to analyse what their governments are earning from their petroleum and minerals, how their country's performance compares to others and whether the state is using these revenues to promote the public good. Section 1504 builds on EITI by rendering the reporting requirements mandatory for all US-listed companies, and by mandating a level of disaggregation that goes far beyond what is reported in many EITI countries.

The US legislation has sparked interest in similar standards in other international financial centres. Notably, the European Commission in late 2011 proposed rules that mirror the core of Dodd-Frank by requiring European Union (EU)-based companies to publish payments they make to governments in natural resource-rich countries on a disaggregated basis. At the time of writing this chapter, these provisions were to be put before the European Council and Parliament for agreement on a final version to be sent to EU member states for consideration. If the provision becomes law in the EU, together with Dodd-Frank these reporting requirements would cover roughly half the global oil and mining sector by market capitalization (Heuty, 2012).

These mandatory standards create new opportunities and new challenges for civil society organizations, commensurate with their role as collectors and interpreters of data, and vehicles for public education. The requirements will produce massive amounts of information, and civil society groups are expected to be at the forefront of pushes to put this information to use to impact policy and performance.

Contract transparency

Transparency promotion efforts have extended beyond the drive for revenue disclosure, with a major focus of civil society groups being on the transparency of extractive industry contracts. Beyond simply knowing how much revenue their states are earning, examining the agreements that their governments have reached with oil and mineral companies is a necessary step to effectively analysing whether rules are being followed and whether the state is generating sufficient value for its resources. Civil society activists have put forward five principal arguments for the disclosure of extractive agreements:

- Contract disclosure gives citizens a well-informed basis for holding their governments to account about the quality of the deals that have been struck and the practices by which they were awarded. Over time, this can have a powerful effect on government behaviour in contracting, generating pressure to refrain from corrupt decision making and signing agreements that provide long-term benefits.

- Transparency gives citizens a basis for monitoring implementation of contracts. Given the weakness of public enforcement agencies and the problems that many governments have been enforcing the terms of their laws and agreements, this can be a powerful tool (Smith, 2011).

- Citizens have a fundamental right to access information on these public resources, particularly given the dominant role petroleum and minerals play in so many economies.

- Public disclosure can promote *constructive* dialogue and criticism between citizens and their governments, as opposed to accusations based on partially-informed rumours. Over time, this improved understanding and climate for dialogue renders contracts more stable and can reduce pressures for renegotiation.

- Public disclosure gives governments a source of independent analysis that can inform decisions. As a global library of contracts develops, this can reduce the information asymmetries that often disfavour governments in negotiations with companies.

In the 1990s and early 2000s, contract transparency was extremely rare, as governments and companies argued that the need to protect commercial secrets and attract large-scale international investment made it a risky strategy (Rosenblum & Maples, 2009). The 2010 *Revenue Watch Index*, which measured the transparency practices of 41 oil- and mineral-rich countries, revealed that only five disclosed their contracts in full by 2009 (Revenue Watch Institute, 2010). But the experience of such pioneer countries as Liberia, Peru and Timor Leste demonstrated that these concerns were ill-founded, and in recent years a wave of new governments have committed to publishing their petroleum and mineral contracts. The wave has been particularly prominent in Africa, where Niger, Guinea and Sierra Leone have included contract disclosure requirements in new laws, and where the Democratic Republic of Congo and Ghana have placed key extractive contracts online (Heller, 2011).

The emerging norm is having an impact at the international level as well; the International Finance Corporation's (IFC) Policy on Environmental and Social Sustainability includes a requirement that, for any extractive-industry project the IFC finances, 'the principal contract with government that sets out the key terms and conditions under which a resource will be exploited, and any significant amendments to that contract, [shall] be public' (International Finance Corporation, 2012). The Policy provides for a loophole that would allow for publication of the key terms of the agreement in lieu of the whole document, which at a minimum would require 'the life of the contract; any material payments due to government made under it; other material fiscal terms and conditions; and a summary of any significant stabilization clauses'. The impact of this limitation remains to be seen, and it could serve to limit disclosure. Nonetheless, the inclusion of a commitment to contract transparency represents a significant step forward for civil society and citizens of resource-rich countries.

Revenue management and expenditure monitoring

Beyond the core promotion of transparency, civil society groups are playing an increasingly dynamic role in monitoring what their governments are doing with the revenues earned from extractive industries. One element of this path focuses on avoiding some of the serious macroeconomic effects that can be generated by dependence on commodities, including excessive budgetary volatility and the crowding out of other productive sectors. Civil society groups in a range of petroleum-rich countries are closely monitoring and reporting on their governments' macroeconomic performance, and in countries like Timor-Leste, civil society groups participate actively in multi-stakeholder bodies specifically tasked with revenue management oversight.

A second element focuses on expenditure monitoring. In order for oil and mineral revenues to contribute effectively to long-term development, they must be invested effectively in key sectors likely to promote sustainable growth. Civil society groups are playing dynamic roles in monitoring both expenditure *policy* and the execution of expenditure. This is happening both at a national level and a local level, particularly in countries like Nigeria, Indonesia and Peru where there is significant sub-national distribution of revenues generated by extractive industries.

Remaining Challenges

The foregoing discussion has focused on the role that civil society plays in promoting effective and accountable management of the extractive industries. It bears noting, however, that civil society groups continue to face serious obstacles in many countries, including the following:

- *Lack of technical capacity.* The efforts of both international and national civil society groups to develop expertise in the extractive industries have generated impressive results, and as noted above the sophistication of civil society groups across the world has increased massively. But given the highly complex, and rapidly evolving, nature of petroleum and mineral economics and technology, civil society groups often still face knowledge gaps when compared to their counterparts in government and within companies. As more information becomes available, and as opportunities to impact policy continue to expand, it is critical that civil society groups redouble their efforts (and that international partners redouble their support) to build expertise. This is particularly severe in the poorest of the poor developing countries.

- *Intimidation and repression.* Democracy and freedom of expression have made major strides throughout the world, but civil society activism remains heavily constrained in many countries, particularly given the close connections between the extractive industries and powerful elites. Petro-states like Equatorial Guinea and Angola have received significant attention for the restrictions placed on civil society behaviour, but recent years have also seen harassment of extractive industry activists in other African countries including Gabon, Niger and the Democratic Republic of Congo.

- *Politicization.* In practice, civil society groups are far from uniform, either in their areas of focus or their political positions. In many developing countries civil society has become inextricably linked to one or more political party or interest group, damaging their reputation for neutrality. In some cases these political allegiances have made essential contributions to the success of civil society groups in mobilizing support for key accountability campaigns. In other situations, however, politicization has damaged CSOs' credibility and impeded their ability to provide an objective perspective focused on the needs of all citizens.

Conclusion

THE CASE OF GHANA: DYNAMIC CIVIL SOCIETY, GROWING INFLUENCE

As Ghana has entered its petroleum industry, a diverse and dynamic set of civil society organizations has made a powerful series of contributions to the national debate around avoiding some of the most serious risks associated with oil economies, and around the best strategies for using oil revenues to promote national development. The sophistication and influence of Ghana's CSOs tracks with the dramatic evolution of civil society groups worldwide, and Ghanaian organizations serve as examples for peer groups elsewhere in Africa.

Among the impacts that Ghana's civil society has had on the evolution of petroleum sector strategy are the following:

- *EITI*: Ghana's civil society has played an active role in an EITI process that is becoming ever more dynamic in the mining sector, and is moving ambitiously as the process expands to oil. In mining, civil society has been a vocal participant in a process that has had meaningful policy impact. The illustration in EITI reports that all companies were paying royalties at the bottom end of the 3 per cent – 12 per cent range that was allowed under applicable laws and contracts generated large-scale public pressure to reform the regime, ultimately prompting the government to increase royalties to 5 per cent. In oil, the EITI multi-stakeholder group is striving to move beyond the Initiative's minimum requirements and track revenue management and public expenditure performance as part of their EITI process.

- *Reporting and analysis on oil sector policy and structure*: Ghanaian CSOs have developed sophisticated policy analyses that have significantly advanced the debates about how the oil sector should be managed. The Civil Society Platform on Oil and Gas produced regular policy briefings and issued a 'Readiness Report Card' in April 2011 that assessed Ghana's performance in the build up to first oil on such issues as licensing, transparency, oversight of Ghana National Petroleum Company (GNPC) and public financial management (Civil Society Platform on Oil and Gas, 2011). The Integrated Social Development Center (ISODEC) collaborated with Oxfam America to produce 'Ghana's Big Test', which included detailed analysis of the reported fiscal terms of the Jubilee field, discussed policy options for utilizing associated gas and analysed the likely impact of tight global credit markets on the development of Ghanaian oil (Oxfam America and ISODEC, 2009).

- *Contract transparency*: Beginning with the release of the first EITI report – which recommended that all mining contracts be made public – contract transparency represented a major push for Ghanaian civil society. President Mills announced an intention to publish major natural resource contracts shortly after taking office, but Government action on this commitment was slow, and civil society groups made contract transparency a core campaign. It was not until 2011, only after Tullow had published contracts on the website of the US SEC as part of its public listing process, that the Government actually put several major oil contracts on the website of the Ministry of Energy. The contract transparency mission is far from fully accomplished; several key documents remain unavailable, transparency remains an ad hoc policy not enshrined in legislation and there have been no major steps to improve the transparency of the licensing process itself (Asafu-Adjaye, 2011).

- *Revenue management*: Civil society played a central role in the development of Ghana's landmark Revenue Management Act, participating extensively in the public consultations that surrounded the development of the Bill, writing analyses that helped advance the Bill's evolution, and engaging with members of Parliament as they brought the Bill into final form. Civil society also has the opportunity to have a major impact on the execution of the Bill, particularly via representation on the Public Interest and Accountability Committee (PIAC), the body established by the Act to monitor compliance with the Act, provide space and a platform for the public to debate revenue management issues and advise Parliament on expenditure decisions. PIAC membership includes one representative nominated to represent 'civil society organizations and community-based organizations,' as well as representatives of think tanks, the Trades Union Congress, the Ghana Journalists Association, the Ghana Bar Association, Ghana's EITI and various religious groups. At the time of writing this chapter the PIAC was preparing its initial assessment of the Government's compliance with the Revenue Management Act for petroleum revenues generated in 2011 vis-à-vis the 2012 budget. The role envisioned for the PIAC represents an important opportunity for civil society groups to serve as an important check to make sure that the government is complying with both the letter and the spirit of the Revenue Management Act, and to promote responsible expenditure that promotes long-term development and guards the country against volatility.

- *New approaches to collaboration between CSOs, governments and academics*: In addition to the more traditional advocacy-oriented organizations, Ghana is home to several non-profit institutions that seek to bridge the gap between research, policy makers and citizens. ACET is one prominent example, housing skilled professionals from all over Africa who provide technical advice to governments and conduct research on key issues related to economic evolution and effective development strategy. ACET has an Extractive Resource Service, which provides high-level advice to governments on oil and mineral policy. At an academic level, the Ghana Institute for Management and Public Administration (GIMPA) has developed a regional knowledge centre that provides training to parliamentarians, local government officials, journalists and civil society representatives from all over Africa, including Ghana itself. These and other organizations have benefitted from Accra's status as a cosmopolitan hub to assemble highly-skilled teams able to develop creative programmes with a direct impact on policy making.

Ghana's civil society faces some of the challenges noted above. There is a continued need for organizations, particularly those based outside of Accra, to develop their capacity to conduct advocacy around complex technical issues. Though Ghana has made some impressive strides vis-à-vis transparency, key pieces of information about how the oil sector is managed remain shrouded in secrecy, limiting the ability of citizen groups to influence policy. And as the thrill of first oil fades, it will be imperative for civil society to maintain a tight focus on oil sector accountability. In many countries once the obvious, concrete tasks such as the passage of legislation have been completed, civil society attention can be distracted by other issues, leaving a void in terms of rigorous monitoring of the conduct of exploration and production and the management by the state of oil revenues. If Ghana is to build on the promise that has developed during the build up to oil production, civil society must remain vigilant, and government must work to ensure that open dialogue is ongoing.

References

African Union (2009). *Africa Mining Vision*, retrieved 6 August, 2011 from http://www.africaminingvision.org/about.html.

Asafu-Adjaye, J. (2011). *The IEA P-TRAC Index 2011 Report: Tracking Transparency and Accountability in Ghana's Oil and Gas Industry*, retrieved 9 August, 2011 from http://www.ieagh.org/index.php/publications/other/300-2011-ptrac-short-final/.

Bratton, M. (1994). *Civil Society and Political Transition in Africa*. Boston: Institute for Development Research.

Brautigam, D., Fjeldstad, O.H., & Moore, M. (Eds) (2008). *Taxation and State-Building in Developing Countries*. Cambridge: Cambridge University Press.

Civil Society Platform on Oil and Gas (2011). *Ghana's Oil Boom: A Readiness Report Card* retrieved 22 January, 2012 from http://www.oxfamamerica.org/files/ghana-oil-readiness-report-card.pdf.

Dykstra, P. (2011). *EITI 2011: Learning from Success and Challenges*. New York: Revenue Watch Institute.

Extractive Industries Transparency Initiative (2012). *Nigeria EITI: Making Transparency Count, Uncovering Billions*, retrieved 22 May, 2012 from http://eiti.org/files/Case%20Study%20-%20EITI%20in%20Nigeria.pdf.

Fiourini, A.M. (Ed.) (2000). *The Third Force: The Rise of Transnational Civil Society*. Washington, DC: Carnegie Endowment for International Peace.

Fundación Jubileo (2010). *Reporte Sobre Transparencia en YPFB y en el Ministerio de Hidrocarburos* (Report on Transparency in YPFB and the Ministry of Hydrocarbons), La Paz, retrieved 30 June 2011 from http://www.jubileobolivia.org.bo/recursos/files/pdfs/Reporte_Transparencia_Hidrocarburos.pdf.

Ganteh, R. (2010). *Liberia: West African Contract Monitoring Meeting Opens in Monrovia Today*, November 30, 2010 retrieved from http://gnnliberia.com/index.php?option=com_content&view=article&id=1125:liberia-west-african-contract-monitoring-meeting-opens-in-monroviatoday&catid=34:politics&Itemid=54/.

Gary, I., & Reisch, N. (2005). *Chad's Oil: Miracle or Mirage – Following the Money in Africa's Newest Petro-State*. Maryland: Catholic Relief Services and Bank Information Center.

Gelb, A. (1988). *Windfall Gains: Blessing or Curse?* New York: Oxford University Press.

Gillies, A., & Heuty, A. (2011). Does transparency work? The challenges of measurement and effectiveness in resource rich Countries, *Yale Journal of International Affairs*, September, Vol 6, Issue 2, pp. 25-42.

Heller, P. (2011). An Emerging Norm of Contract Transparency, New York: Revenue Watch Institute, retrieved January 26, 2012 from http://www.revenuewatch.org/news/blog/emerging-norm-contract-transparency.

Heuty, A. (2012). The Role of Transparency and Civil Society and Civil Society in Managing Commodities for Inclusive Growth and Development. In A. Arezki, C. Pattillo, M. Quintyn & M. Zhu (Eds.) (2012), *Commodity Price Shocks and Inclusive Growth in Low-Income Countries*. Washington, DC: International Monetary Fund. October.

International Bar Association (2010). *Model Mineral Development Agreement*, retrieved January 24, 2012 from http://www.ibanet.org/Article/Detail. aspx?ArticleUid=41f1038e-dcbf-44fd-ad17-898b7aa04a1a.

International Finance Corporation (2012). *Policy on Environmental and Social Sustainability*, Washington, retrieved from http://www1.ifc.org/wps/ wcm/connect/7540778049a792dcb87efaa8c6a8312a/SP_English_2012. pdf?MOD=AJPERES.

International Monetary Fund (2007). *Guide on Resource Revenue Transparency*. Washington.

International Monetary Fund (2011). *Angola – Fifth Review Under the Stand-By Arrangement, Request for Waiver of Applicability of Performance Criteria, and Request for Modification of Performance Criteria – Staff Report, Country Report No. 11/346*, December.

Isham, J., Pritchett, L., Woolcock, M., & Busby, G. (2003). The Varieties of the Resource Experience: How Natural Resource Export Structures Affect the Political Economy of Economic Growth, mimeo, World Bank, Washington D.C.

Karl, T.L. (1997). *The Paradox of Plenty: Oil Booms and Petro-States*. Berkeley, CA: University of California Press.

Kaul, R., & Heuty, A. (2009). *Getting a Better Deal from the Extractive Sector – Concession Negotiation in Liberia, 2006-2008*, Revenue Watch Institute, retrieved December 5 2011 from http://archive-2011.revenuewatch.org/files/ RWI-Getting-a-Better-Deal-final0226.pdf.

Kolstad, I., & Wiig, A. (2009). Is Transparency the Key to Reducing Corruption in Resource-Rich Countries? *World Development* 37(3), pp. 521-532.

López, A. (2011). *Mecanismos de Control y Rendición de Cuentas de Pemex: Retos y Propuestas para su Fortalecimiento (Mechanisms of Control and Accountability of Pemex: Challenges and Proposals for Strengthening)*, Mexico City, retrieved June 18, 2012 from http://www.fundar.org.mx/mexico/pdf/mecanismosdecontrol.pdf.

Natural Resource Charter (2010), retrieved October 6, 2011 from http://www. naturalresourcecharter.org/.

Niger Delta Citizens and Budget Platform (2012). *Analysis of 2011 Budget of Akwa Ibom, Bayelsa, Delta, Edo & Rivers States: 2011*, retrieved June 13, 2012 from http://citizensbudget.org/index.php?option=com_content&view=article&id =140:analysis-of-2011-budget-of-akwa-ibom-bayelsa-delta-edo-a-rivers-stat es&catid=37:publications&Itemid=58.

Oxfam America and ISODEC (2009). *Ghana's Big Test: Oil's Challenge to Democratic Development*, retrieved October 3, 2011 from http://www.oxfamamerica.org/publications/ghanas-big-test.

Petrad (2012). *8-week Programme on Petroleum Policy and Resource Management* retrieved June 13, 2012 from http://www.petrad.no/default.asp?fid=1054.

Revenue Watch Institute (2010). *2010 Revenue Watch Index*, retrieved November 16, 2011 from http://www.revenuewatch.org/rwindex2010/index.html.

Revenue Watch Institute (2011). *EITI Reports: Results and Analysis*, September,, retrieved June 20, 2012 from http://data.revenuewatch.org/eiti/.

Revenue Watch Institute (2012a). *Regional Hubs* retrieved June 30, 2012 from http://www.revenuewatch.org/issues/regional-hubs.

Revenue Watch Institute (2012b). *Support for Mining and Development in Mongolia*, retrieved June 30, 2012 from http://www.revenuewatch.org/grants/support-mining-and-development-mongolia.

Rosenblum, P., & Maples, S. (2009). *Contracts Confidential: Ending Secret Deals in the Extractive Industries*. New York: Revenue Watch Institute, retrieved June 14, 2012 from http://www.revenuewatch.org/publications/contracts-confidential-ending-secret-deals-extractive-industries.

Sachs, J.D., & Warner, A.M. (1997). *Natural Resource Abundance and Economic Growth*. Massachusetts: Center for International Development and Harvard Institute for International Development.

Scholte, J. A. (2004). Civil Society and Democratically Accountable Global Governance, *Government and Opposition*, Vol. 39, Issue 2, pp. 211-233.

Shaxson, Ni. (2009). *Nigeria's Extractive Industries Transparency Initiative: Just a Glorious Audit?* London: Chatham House.

Smith, E. (2011). *Enforcing the Rules: Government and Citizen Oversight of Mining*. New York: Revenue Watch Institute, retrieved June 1, 2012 from http://www.revenuewatch.org/publications/enforcing-rules.

Human Development Report 2011– Sustainability and Equity: A Better Future for All. for the United Nations Development Program, New York.

Van Oranje, M., & Parham, H. (2009). *Publish What We Learned: An Assessment of the Publish What You Pay Coalition*, retrieved May 2, 2012 from www.crin.org/docs/Publishing_What_We_Learned.pdf.

World Bank (2004). *The World Bank Group Management Response to the Extractive Industries Review*.Washington, DC: World Bank.

World Bank (2010). *Defining Civil Society*, retrieved April 4, 2012 from http://web.worldbank.org/WBSITE/EXTERNAL/TOPICS/CSO/0,contentMDK:20101499~menuPK:244752~pagePK:220503~piPK:220476~theSitePK:228717,00.html.

World Bank (2011). *Extractive Industries Source Book*. Washington, DC: World Bank, retrieved April 4, 2012 from http://www.eisourcebook.org.

8

Can Ghana Avoid the Resource Curse?

Inge Amundsen

Abstract

The 'resource curse' refers to the paradox that countries with an abundance of natural resources, specifically petroleum resources, tend to have lower economic growth and less democratic government than countries with fewer natural resources. Democratic institutionalization is important in this respect. It seems that a country will be cursed only when the discovery of petroleum resources is made before democratic institutions are established and consolidated. The question is whether Ghana, as a new petroleum-exporting country, can withstand the pressures that a sudden resource boom will create. Are Ghana's democratic institutions sufficiently strong to withstand the pressures for rent-seeking and political monopolies? Ghana's level of democracy and institutional strengths are analysed using international, comparative governance statistics, like the World Governance Indicators (WGI), the Corruption Perceptions Index (CPI), the Open Budget Index and assessments by international organizations like the Extractive Industries Transparency Initiative and the Revenue Watch Institute. According to these data, which basically picture positively Ghana's level of democratic institutionalization, and the fact that Ghana has held four fully competitive multiparty elections, it is fair to conclude that Ghana can avoid the trappings of the resource curse.

Introduction

The 'resource curse', also called the 'paradox of plenty', refers to the fact that some countries bestowed with high levels of natural resources, in particular oil, gas and diamonds, have little or negative economic growth. It is the paradox that some resource-rich countries are deteriorating in terms of economic expansion and diversification, and have unexpectedly made little progress in terms of redistribution and democratization.

Among the 'resource cursed' countries are Angola, Nigeria, DR Congo, the Sudan, Sierra Leone, Equatorial Guinea, Zambia, Tajikistan, Colombia and Afghanistan. These countries are characterized by poor economic development, low Human Development Index (HDI), and/or poor democratic records, despite substantial incomes from minerals and other resources. On the other hand, a number of countries seem to be protected from – or even blessed – by their resources. Among the 'resource-blessed' countries are Norway, Australia, Canada, Chile, Brazil, Malaysia and Botswana.

Institutionalization and democratization are decisive factors to this curse. It seems that a country will be cursed *only* when the discovery of oil or diamonds, for instance, is made before accountable and democratic state institutions are established and consolidated. It is cursed when its institutions are not strong enough to withstand the pressure from various groups for access to the newly found riches. Countries like Norway and the UK were well-governed *before* they discovered oil and gas (O&G), and their institutions were not influenced negatively by rent-seeking, whereas countries like Nigeria, the Sudan, Sierra Leone and Equatorial Guinea, were authoritarian and institutionally weak.

The discovery and exploitation of resource wealth can create forces that can block the development of 'good quality' political and economic institutions. Rich resources can lead to institutional decay when politicians are obstructing and dismantling state institutions in order to extract the rents for private use. Weak institutions are also incapable of administering the resources in a nationally beneficial way. Institutions of 'poor quality' will fail to protect property rights and contracts, and fail to turn entrepreneurs away from rent-seeking and into production. States with weak institutional capacity cannot hinder group conflict over access to the resource rents; they cannot hinder (economically unproductive) investments in lobbying for protection, subsidies and preferential policies; and they cannot hinder wasteful government investments in luxury goods imports, unsustainable grandiose prestige projects and capital flight.

Particularly harmful is the struggle for the rents controlled by the state, and thus the struggle for control of the state; by for instance political insiders, top-level bureaucrats, military officials, robber barons and warlords. Historically, it is noticeable how the discovery and exploitation of rich resources have led to a *further* weakening when the state institutions are weak or bad in the first place.

The question is therefore if Ghana, as a new petroleum-exporting country, can withstand the pressures that a sudden resource boom will create. Are Ghana's level of democracy and the quality of its institutions sufficient to withstand the pressures created by various forces over access to the riches? Can Ghana withstand the pressure from entrepreneurs and business interests to get preferential government treatment, protection and monopolies? Are Ghana's democratic institutions sufficiently strong to withstand the pressure from political forces that want to extract the rents for private use, to withstand the pressures for rent-seeking and political monopolies?

In order to assess whether Ghana's level of democracy and institutional strengths are sufficient to withstand the political and economic pressures that will be created by a resource boom, we will use available international statistics. We will look at Ghana's institutional quality through the lenses of comparative governance statistics, like the World Bank's WGI, Transparency International's CPI, the Ibrahim Index on African Governance, and the Open Budget Index of the International Budget Partnership (IBP); as well as assessments by international organizations and projects like the Extractive Industries Transparency Initiative and the Revenue Watch Institute. Although these international assessments have some critical limitations, particularly in coverage (do they really cover the institutions essential for stemming the resource curse?) and in time (do they really cover the relevant time period?), we believe they are sufficiently robust, when combined, to assess Ghana's institutional qualities.[1]

The Resource Curse

The 'resource curse' or the 'paradox of plenty' refers to the paradox that countries with an abundance of natural resources, specifically non-renewable resources like minerals and petroleum resources,[2] tend to have lower economic

---

1   A first-hand empirical investigation and evaluation of Ghana's institutions is beyond the scope of this chapter.

2   An *abundance* of natural resources can be measured in many ways, but mostly in terms of *dependency*. Hydrocarbon (oil and gas) export dependency can be measured by the ratio of oil and gas exports to gross domestic product (GDP), or by petroleum sector government revenue to total government revenue. In countries that live from petroleum rents, this figure ranges from a low of 4.9 per cent in Cameroon, a dependent country now running out of oil, to a high

growth, less democratic government,[3] and worse development outcomes than countries with fewer natural resources.

This may happen for many different reasons, and a growing literature is discussing the empirical robustness and modalities of this paradox, and is searching for possible explanations (Sachs & Warner, 2001; Robinson, Torvik & Verdier, 2006; Mehlum, Moene & Torsvik, 2006; Rosser, 2006; Heller, 2006; Humphreys, Sachs & Stiglitz, 2007; Collier, 2010; Cabrales & Hauk, 2011; van der Ploeg, 2011. Among the stronger economic explanations is that an increase in revenues from natural resources appreciates the exchange rate and makes other sectors less competitive, and that the volatility of commodity prices are disruptive. In particular, the negative price effect and a decline in investments 'crowds out' manufacturing and agriculture (Humphreys, Sachs & Stiglitz, 2007:5; du Plessis & du Plessis, 2006:353).

The literature on the resource curse emphasizes three different but interrelated aspects of the phenomenon. As mentioned, economists emphasize the economic factors, and usually call it the 'Dutch Disease'. Then, in political–economy analyses, researchers emphasize corruption, and particularly political corruption, as an explanation to the paradox. Thirdly, political science emphasizes the institutional factors of the curse and argues that the analysis must shift to political institutions to explain the resource curse, and that the main difference between success and failure is in the quality of institutions.

The Dutch Disease

In the 1970s, the Netherlands discovered some of these problems. Following the discovery of a large natural gas field in the North Sea in 1959, the Netherlands experienced a decline of its manufacturing sector. What happened was that the revenues from the petroleum sector made the country's currency stronger, and this made Dutch exports more expensive at the same time as imports became cheaper. Thus, the Dutch manufacturing sector had become remarkably less competitive and the country experienced deindustrialization.

---

of 86 per cent in Equatorial Guinea, one of the newest oil producers. Dependency can also be measured in terms of export profiles, where oil generally makes up from 60 to 95 per cent of an oil dependent country's total exports.

3   One strand of the resource curse theory holds that *no* country has *ever* fully democratised after oil was found. This is true unless you consider Venezuela and Nigeria to be democratic, or you believe foreign military intervention can create democracy in Libya and Iraq.

The same has been the experience of a number of other countries. When discoveries and exports of natural resources increase (or there is a sharp surge in natural resource prices or other inflows of foreign currency like for instance through foreign aid), there is usually an increase of the real exchange rate. Besides, although commodity prices can be very volatile, the main investments, and government concerns and efforts, labour, and personal ambition will still be geared towards the newly profitable extractive industry. Together this makes other economic sectors less competitive, and 'crowds out' manufacturing and agriculture (Sachs & Warner 2001; Humphreys, Sachs & Stiglitz, 2007:5; du Plessis & du Plessis, 2006:353).

Furthermore, extractive industries can bring in additional problems. One is when natural resources begin to dry out or prices are falling, manufacturing industries and agriculture cannot easily catch up, as investments and technology are needed (and this may have been neglected for a long time). Besides, extractive industries are not very technologically advanced and they have few (positive) trickle-down effects in terms of innovation and employment. In particular, offshore oil production will require only a few thousand staff.

The Netherlands later managed to escape the curse owing to its ability to slow down the appreciation of the exchange rate and to boost the competitiveness of the manufacturing sector, mainly by investments in education and infrastructure. Countries with weaker government institutions and a less legitimate government have not been able to do this.

Political Corruption

Political corruption is a second aspect of the resource curse. In particular in political–economy studies, researchers have emphasized how corruption, and in particular political corruption, plays into the resource curse. Some see it as a major explanation to the paradox of plenty, whereas others rather see it as a consequence thereof.

This disagreement notwithstanding, political corruption is defined both with reference to the main actors involved, that is, individuals at the highest levels of the political system, and the purpose of the corrupt behaviour, that is, personal enrichment and the maintenance of positions of power.[4] In other

---

4   Political corruption occurs at the highest levels of the political system and can thus be
     distinguished from administrative or bureaucratic corruption. Bureaucratic corruption takes

words, political corruption may be for private and group enrichment, and political corruption may be for power preservation purposes. These two forms of political corruption are often connected. The latter process, however, is under-researched and underestimated, since much of the focus in the literature has been on accumulation.

Political corruption adds to the problem of the resource curse in several ways. First of all, high levels of corruption will reduce the 'government take' of the resources. Short-term and individual interests will lead to the sale of a country's mineral resources for less than their real value, as the 'commissions' and 'fees' paid out to a few government officials dwarf the value of the under-taxed profits accruing to companies. Political corruption reduces the 'cake' as the resources are plundered and 'privatized' through political corruption.

This is the extractive form of corruption, which occurs when government officials use and abuse their hold on power to extract from the private sector, from government revenues and from the economy at large. These processes of accumulation are referred to as extraction, embezzlement, rent-seeking, plunder and even 'kleptocracy' ('rule by thieves'), depending on the extent and context. Extraction mainly takes place in the form of soliciting bribes in procurement and government projects, in privatization processes and in taxation. Two of the most affected sectors worldwide are military procurement and minerals extraction, because of the involvement of top-level politicians, national interests, and secrecy. Also, political corruption hampers competition because it reinforces economic as well as political monopolistic tendencies. Political corruption creates monopolies because one of the basic favours the corrupters are in the hunt for is favouritist government treatment, preferential contracts and protection from contenders, which can create super profits.

Secondly, political corruption will hamper the redistribution of the revenues. The government's revenues will to a lesser degree be spent on the development of the country; more is siphoned off and spent on consumption and power preservation. Political corruption will lead to more money being

---

place at the implementation end of politics, for instance, in government services like education and health. Political corruption takes place at the formulation end of politics, where decisions on the distribution of the nation's wealth and the rules of the game are made. Political corruption is usually also distinguished from business and private sector corruption. This is only a matter of academic classification; however, since it 'takes two to tango' and because the bribes offered by private companies, both domestic and international, are significant corruption drivers. Sometimes, corruption is indeed 'supply driven' and benefits the briber more than the bribed (this section draws on Amundsen, 2006 and Amundsen, 1999).

spent on government squander, grandiose infrastructure projects, 'white elephants', and capital flight. Individual and group interests will ensure that the resources are 'privatized' (read: pocketed) and exported; illicit money flows out of petroleum-producing countries, sometimes in astronomic proportions.[5] In consequence, the social and economic differences in society will increase. The rich will get richer, and the number of poor people will increase, in absolute and relative terms.

Thirdly, political corruption will undermine the institutions of power sharing, and checks and balances, as the extracted resources are spent for power preservation purposes. Power-preserving political corruption is when the extracted resources (and other public money) are used for power preservation and expansion purposes. It usually takes the form of favouritism and patronage politics, that is, favouritist and politically motivated distribution of financial and material inducements, benefits and spoils, in order to build political loyalty and support.

In line with this is the notion that natural resources, combined with political corruption, increase the autonomy and the powers of the state (and thus, the ruling elite in control of the state). Incomes from natural resource exploitation make the government no longer dependent on taxing the general economy. It suffices to control the extractive sector and the revenues from it. This is the 'unearned' rents and the 'rentier state' that economists talk about.

By controlling the state and the petroleum revenues, there is not much need for additional taxation of domestic economic activity, and consequently no need for a 'social contract' with tax-paying citizens. Those who control the state can fend off the influence of business interests, other economic interests (manufacturing, agriculture), and the middle class, civil society and interest organizations. Thus, in most resource-cursed countries, there are no discussions and agreements between the tax-collecting government and a general population of tax-payers, which will normally reinforce government legitimacy and good public financial management.

---

5   Money is haemorrhaging out of poor countries: in 2006, between $850 billion and 1.06 trillion left developing countries through illicit channels. This includes bribery and theft by government officials, drug trafficking, racketeering, counterfeiting and commercial tax evasion. The figure dwarfs official aid flows; the 22 OECD member countries provided $103.9 billion in aid in 2006 (Fontana, 2010:1). This massive flow of money drains countries of hard currency reserves, heightens inflation, reduces tax collection, hampers investment and undermines free trade. It has its greatest impact on those at the bottom of the income scales, removing resources that could otherwise be used for poverty alleviation and economic growth (Kar & Cartwright-Smith, 2010:1).

The rents also increase the powers of the state, as they provide the means to buy loyalty and allies, and to pay off rivals and perceived and potential opponents. The rents can be used for building clientelist networks, vote buying and to pay off the state institutions of checks and balances and of oversight and control. Parliamentarians can be bought, as can commissioners of election, anti-corruption, auditors and the like. Rivals and opponents can be bought, voters can be bought, and if necessary, loyal decisions from electoral commissions can be bought to secure re-election. Investigations and audits can be halted, and judicial impunity gained. In the final instance, those in control of the state can purchase the necessary military and security hardware. The elite controlling the state have access to the means and necessary instruments of coercion.

The consequences of the 'power-preservation' form of political corruption are grave, and perhaps even worse than the consequences of extractive political corruption. Political corruption for power preservation purposes leads to bad governance in the form of unaccountable and favouritist political decisions; manipulated, weak and distorted institutions; lack of transparency and accountability; immunity and impunity; and elections that are not free and fair. The two processes of political corruption – extraction and power preservation – are often connected. Many of the larger political corruption scandals include both aspects: large-scale bribery schemes are concluded when the extracted money is used to buy political support, and the full circle is made when the purpose of power is wealth and the purpose of wealth is power.

Corruption in Oil

Corruption and economic mismanagement can take place all along the petroleum value chain. What follows is an outline of possible corruption problems in the petroleum sector. The list is not exhaustive, but it includes some of the better-known and well-described problem areas, in addition to some lesser-known ones.

One of the first and fundamental decisions a government has to make is whether to regulate petroleum production by law (a petroleum law, also called concessionary system, which is common in countries like Norway and the UK) or by a licence system (usually referred to as a production-sharing agreement or contract, common in most developing countries).[6] Issues like the concession

---

6   A production sharing contract (PSC) is typically between the President of the Republic, the Minister of Energy (or Petroleum), and/or the state-owned national petroleum company (NOC),

period, taxation levels and procedures, technology transfers, environmental protection, local content, security issues, inspection and control regimes can either be determined by law in a concessionary system, with each individual contract referring to the respective law, or it can be regulated by individual contracts in a licence system, where the individual contracts will stipulate the conditions.

The latter involves a considerably higher corruption risk (Al-Kasim, Søriede & Williams, 2008; Rosenblum & Mapels, 2009). Where government officials and companies have to deal with conditions embedded within individual contracts, it opens up for negotiations, re-negotiations and the influence peddling that comes with it. The regulatory capacity of the state is diluted, as conflicts become subject to international arbitration rather than domestic courts, and the many different contracts (made at different points in time and with different companies) will make government monitoring cumbersome. Furthermore, production sharing agreement (PSA) contracts usually contain confidentiality clauses.

Contract transparency is critical for better addressing the resource management of the petroleum industry. With contract transparency, governments will be able (in the long term) to negotiate better deals, as the information asymmetry between the government and companies closes. Contract transparency will also (in the shorter term) help government agencies responsible for managing and enforcing contracts to collaborate. 'With contracts publicly available, government officials will have an incentive to stop negotiating bad deals, owing to corruption, incompetence, or otherwise' (Rosenblum & Mapels, 2009:11).

Besides, citizens will better understand the complex nature of extractive agreements if they are out in the open. Contract transparency will result in more stable and durable contracts, both because they are less subject to the population's suspicions and because the incentives for governments and companies to negotiate better contracts will be increased (Rosenblum & Mapels, 2009).

---

and private companies chosen as onshore contractors in the petroleum industry. The contract details the specific rights and provisions these contracting partners have when taking part in a particular petroleum production field. A typical oil project can have around 100 subcontracts uniting a large number of parties in a vertical chain from input supplier to output purchaser. Among these is one 'primary' contract between the state (or the NOC) and the (private, foreign) company (or consortium of companies) that is superior to the other contracts.

Therefore, host states should create robust legal regimes to govern relationships with investors instead of individual contracts. Model contracts with as few variables as possible should be adopted and permissible modifications specified. This reduces transaction costs and corruption pressures by reducing the number of costly negotiations. It further reduces the technically difficult and costly regulatory oversight (Rosenblum & Mapels, 2009).

Let us take Nigeria as an example. From 1985 to 1993, the military ruler General Ibrahim Babangida (IBB for short) governed Nigeria, a period that proved disastrous as IBB institutionalized corruption as a tool of political control. A recent report estimates that Nigerian leaders stole more than $89.5 billion from the national treasury from 1970 to 2008, and that Nigeria lost more money through illegal outflows than any country in the world during that period (Kar & Cartwright-Smith, 2010).

In Nigeria, extractive political corruption takes place above all in awarding upstream licences. During military rule, most licences were awarded on a discretionary basis by the head of state. At the height of personal power concentration under General Abacha (1993–1998), the President took control of the entire oil sector by giving the presidency full control of the national oil company and all oil trading. The president and minister of oil awarded oil blocks on a discretionary basis. Fees for the blocks were negotiated behind closed doors, upfront, and were completely open to usurpation and corruption.

Although Obasanjo set out to make Nigeria's oil block bid rounds more competitive (and held bid rounds in 2000, 2005, 2006 and 2007), these bid rounds also had serious shortcomings. Nigeria's Petroleum Act still gives the Minister of Petroleum full authority over the allocation of licences for the exploration, prospecting and mining of oil. There are consequently no legally mandated processes or oversight mechanisms for the allocation of blocks. Besides, in his second term as elected president, Obasanjo also remained Minister of Petroleum for six years, micromanaging the petroleum sector from the presidency (Amundsen, 2010; Soares de Oliveira 2007b).[7]

In Nigeria, the awarding of large-scale contracts to oil service companies is also riddled with corruption. Aspiring contractors have used fake consultancy

---

7   In Nigeria, a new *Petroleum Industry Bill* is currently under consideration in the National Assembly. It aims to replace all existing legislation relating to the oil and gas sector and to fundamentally revamp the institutional set-up of the industry by breaking up the powerful NNPC. It can, however, also be seen as a step in the direction of executive control of the industry itself.

firms to channel payments to the government, manipulated their own company's financial systems to acquire extra cash and distributed payments to representatives designated by those at the highest levels of government (Amundsen, 2010).

Furthermore, most Nigerian presidents have been using Nigeria's national oil company (the Nigerian National Petroleum Corporation, NNPC) as a private purse. Former President Yar'Adua admitted that the NNPC 'has not been transparent, and it is one of the most difficult agencies of government to tackle because of vested interests of very powerful people in the country'.[8] The NNPC allocates contracts which 'do not always follow advertised criteria or guarantee competitive pricing', and handles the crude sales and remittances of proceeds without, however, always remitting all revenues (Amundsen, 2010:26).

Whenever direct bribery and the embezzlement of funds from the national treasury has to some degree been restricted (like in an increasing number of oil-producing countries through the introduction of an improved revenue management system), another mechanism for the misappropriation of funds emerges. Increasingly, national private oil companies are set up to collaborate with international oil companies (IOCs) in consortia to win petroleum production contracts. These are not always genuine oil companies, however, but 'front' companies owned by former and current government ministers, ruling party officials, state oil company directors and members of the ruling families. Sometimes, they even default on their initial payments until they get their share of the profits.[9]

According to 'local content' policies, multinational companies are sometimes requested to 'invite' local national oil companies into their consortia to bid for the exploration and production of oil. These local companies can contribute very little in terms of financing, technology or other inputs, and the real ownership of some of these is in fact unknown to the operators.

This is an increasing practice in Nigeria, where government officials have benefited from procedures that favour companies in which they have a financial stake. For instance, senior political leaders have reportedly manipulated tenders to benefit large logistics companies for their own private gain and officials have given preference to companies owned by their political and economic allies

8   *This Day*, Lagos, 15 December 2007.
9   What a representative of *ChevronTexaco* in Angola referred to as 'dead meat companies'.

(Amundsen, 2010). According to a report on the Norwegian company Hydro in Angola, it was 'in partnership with a local private oil company despite suspicions that the company's undisclosed owners may include government officials, in a country perceived to be one of the most corrupt in the world' (Global Witness, 2008:1).

Ironically, activities and funding schemes labelled 'corporate social responsibility' (CSR) can sometimes add to the corruption problems in the petroleum industry. Donations by multinational petroleum companies have an underlying profit-maximization motive and rationale. Through 'branding' and reputation management, involvement in social projects can improve their reputation and thus increase their odds of winning contracts (Amundsen & Wiig, 2008:6).

These corporate objectives do not necessarily correspond with the interests of society and we have seen the duplication of work and projects that are unsustainable because they have no public follow-up mechanisms (schools without teachers, for instance). More importantly, it is relatively easy to manoeuvre social projects into serving the political and clientelist interests of the ruling party and of the government.

In Angola, for instance, there are two basic streams of foreign private contributions from petroleum companies. The first stream (and the most important in terms of amounts) is the money paid by the commercial companies in the petroleum sector based on the signature bonus system. Signature bonuses may include a 'social bonus' component, which is either a percentage or a round sum donated for unspecified 'social projects' or broad social areas like education and health.

The amounts for signature bonuses and social bonuses have increased considerably over the last few years, and the money arrives in tsunami-like waves following the bidding rounds. A fair estimate is that the social bonuses on oil contracts in Angola are worth at least $100 million per year, and steadily increasing.[10]

---

10 In 2004, Chevron paid a social bonus of $80 million on the extension of its licence for Block 0, in addition to a signature bonus of $210 million. The accounting firm KPMG, which carried out a diagnostic study of the Angolan oil sector in the early 2000s, noted before the payment of this bonus in 2004 that the management of social bonuses was opaque. The consultants were unable to find any record of which social projects benefited from such bonus payments (Global Witness, 2010).

Although the signature bonuses now figure in the Angolan state budget, the social bonuses do not. Sonangol manages social and signature bonuses (Amundsen & Wiig, 2008). This opens up opportunities for all kinds of misuse of the funds; the companies themselves serve as the only accountability mechanism; yet they are eager to be on good terms with the government. This enables the presidency and the ruling party to determine the physical location of projects in accordance with their political needs.

The second stream is the post-tax voluntary contributions of companies for social projects that are managed directly by the companies either through their own charity organizations (such as the Shell Foundation) or through various charity organizations, churches, foundations and NGOs. The post-tax voluntary contributions are modest in size, but they are much more visible and actively promoted by the companies. For the operator Esso, the contribution is around $ 5 million a year through the ExxonMobil Foundation. ChevronTexaco donates around $10 million (Amundsen & Wiig, 2008).

The problem with this is that the motivation of oil companies to provide social funds is guided by corporate objectives rather than altruism, and that these corporate objectives do not necessarily correspond with the interests of society. Besides, information about oil companies' social activities is quite opaque, and it is difficult to monitor what the oil companies are actually doing. It might be that petroleum companies have certain strategic advantages in project implementation (as large and sometimes powerful negotiators with strong technological and political capability), but their social activities may increase the lack of political will by the government to provide services, and add to the problems of corruption and clientelism.

THE INSTITUTIONS THAT MATTER

Political and institutional factors are increasingly highlighted in the literature on the resource curse. According to Heller (2006:24), the analysis must shift to political institutions to explain the resource curse, and according to Mehlum et al. the main difference between success and failure is in the quality of institutions (2006:1119).

Basically, rents generated from mineral and other easily accessible resources can either be channelled into the productive economy, or be captured by the ruling elite for personal enrichment, status gain and power purposes. Whether the resource rents are spent to stimulate production and national economic development, or spent on consumption, capital flight and non-productive investments, is largely a question of institutional quality. Government mismanagement of resources, as well as weak, ineffectual, unstable and corrupt institutions is largely due to the easily diverted actual or anticipated revenue stream from extractive activities.

There seems to be a convergence in economic theory that the availability of rich resources, the quality of state institutions and development outcomes are connected. Economists are mainly preoccupied with institutions with a direct effect on economic performance and the profitability of private enterprises, like the institutions governing tax regimes, the protection of property rights and contract enforcement, bureaucratic efficiency and the 'business climate'. There is, however, an entire political economy tradition of institutional analysis, called 'new institutionalism', which emphasizes the role of a broader set of political institutions in economic development (See for instance Hall & Taylor, 1996:936–957; Powell & DiMaggio, 1991). There is a need to outline in some detail the institutions that matter the most in the face of the resource curse.

Firstly, there is an analytically important distinction between the institutions of extraction and the institutions of redistribution. The institutions of extraction are necessary for the production and extraction of economic resources and for extracting the rents from the minerals sector, in particular. The institutions of redistribution are the institutions of power sharing (elections, checks and balances) and of revenue redistribution (infrastructure, health and education, social security and other state services).

Secondly, there is a need to specify the institutions that can stem the resource curse. These are the institutions of power redistribution and the institutions of wealth redistribution such as electoral commissions, parliaments (legislatures), judiciaries, civil society and the media. These are all intertwined; power sharing and the sharing of economic resources tend to go hand-in-hand (in the same way as political monopolies and economic monopolies do). Thus, we can regard these as two parts of the same mechanism, and we will be looking at them together under the assumption that power redistribution will lead to economic redistribution.

The Institutions of Extraction and Redistribution

The institutions of extraction usually work relatively efficiently, even in resource-cursed countries, because they are needed. Ruling elites use these institutions for the extraction (or looting) of resource rents. Therefore, they are politically protected, sometimes above the law, and at times kept outside of the bloated and inefficient modus operandi of the ordinary state bureaucracy.[11]

At the same time, the institutions of redistribution, which serve the purpose of sharing economic and political resources, function poorly because they are unwanted and only necessary to limit social unrest and power rivalry (from the ruling elite's point of view), and are consequently manipulated politically and side-lined.

The institutions of extraction, which enable the ruling elite to extract and enrich itself, typically include institutions like the presidency (presidential powers and the executive branch), the national petroleum companies (NOC), ministries of finance and petroleum, tax authorities, the central bank and the ruling party.[12] These institutions are necessary for revenue generation and government extraction in any country, but they may also facilitate rent-seeking, patronage and looting in some countries. In the absence of democratic controls, these institutions can facilitate 'primitive accumulation', unproductive investments and 'suspicious consumption'.

The institutions of extraction also include the institutions necessary for protecting resource and rents extraction, like the army, security companies and the police. When access to the rents is politically disputed, when there are rivalries over the control of the state apparatus and its extraction capacities, controlling the security apparatus becomes pivotal. In short, the resource rents increase the prize of controlling the state (the incentives for rent-seeking) and

---

11 In Angola, for instance, the state oil company Sonangol as an essential tool for the empowerment and enrichment of the Angolan ruling elite 'was from the very start protected from the dominant (both predatory and centrally planned) logic of Angola's political economy. Throughout its first years, the pragmatic senior management of Sonangol accumulated technical and managerial experience, often in partnership with Western oil and consulting firms. By ... the early 1990s, Sonangol was the key domestic actor in the economy, an island of competence thriving in tandem with the implosion of most other Angolan state institutions. However, the growing sophistication of Sonangol ...has not led to the benign developmental outcomes one would expect ... Instead, Sonangol has primarily been at the service of the presidency and its rentier ambitions ... This highlights the extent to which a nominal 'failed state' can be successful amidst widespread human destitution, provided that (in this case, Sonangol and the means of coercion) exist to ensure the viability of incumbents' (Soares de Oliveira, 2007a:1).

12 In the 1970s and 1980s, the list would also include 'stabilization funds' and 'marketing boards', which enabled the government to appropriate the export rents by acting as a middle-man 'guaranteeing' the local producers a fixed price well below the international market price. One example is the now defunct 'Caisse de Stabilisation' which enabled former President Houphouët-Boigny to appropriate the rents of the coffee and cocoa production of the Côte d'Ivoire.

the resource rents increase the autonomy of the state (the means to protect a rent-seeking position).

The institutions of redistribution are primarily the institutions of power sharing; that is, the institutions of checks and balances, but also the institutions of wealth sharing, that is, the institutions of economic redistribution, which are rooted in and sometimes supplement the institutions of power sharing. The main institutions of political power sharing are the parliament (legislature, national assembly) and the judiciary (high or supreme court), which curb the 'government's' and presidential and ruling elite's domination.

Institutions to Stem the Resource Curse

Parliament is the primary institution of checks on executive powers. One of the most basic functions of any parliament is to make the laws, including the Constitution and amendments to it, and the state budget (which is usually formulated as a bill). The power of legislation thus includes the power to establish the political and institutional 'rules of the game', and the distribution of material benefits. The parliament is responsible for raising and using public funds, and for checking on the government's spending of public money.

Parliament is important for stemming the 'resource curse' because it can (potentially) balance the powers of the president and ruling elite, reduce government rent-seeking and patronage, and redistribute income. A vibrant parliament and a genuine opposition can reduce the predatory tendencies of the ruling elite. A responsible parliament can control and restrict lobbying for protection, subsidies and preferential policies; it can reduce wasteful budgetary expenditures that favour the reproduction of politically and economically dominant elites; and it can ensure 'development friendly' policies through its taxation and investment policies.

The *judiciary* (and especially the high courts) is the second most important institution for stemming the 'resource curse', in particular in safeguarding the rule of law, in performing judicial reviews and in adjudicating economic cases. The judiciary is important for stemming the 'resource curse' through its protection of property rights and through its protection of fair competition. The judiciary can stem the tendencies of monopolies, economic crime and mafia methods.

As a subset of parliamentary or judiciary institutions, we also find a number of *special agencies* of oversight and control, like ombudsmen, auditors and commissions. Together with the parliament and judiciary, they make up the institutions of 'horizontal' accountability.

The institutions of redistribution also include the institutions of 'vertical' accountability, of popular participation, voice and control. The most important of these institutions are free and fair *elections* (without elections, there is no democratic accountability), which includes functioning and credible opposition and political parties, followed by civil society organizations and the media.

Through elections, citizens can possibly elect another ruling elite and another economic policy. Free and fair elections and genuine political parties are prerequisites, however. There should be a viable, sustainable, realistic policy alternative to the government in place, that is, parties with alternative programmes and different candidates that people can vote for at elections, and there should be an independent electoral commission to administer elections.

Besides, power sharing and revenue sharing can be accomplished through open political debate on economic policies and direct citizen participation in policy making (through for instance manifestations and direct action). Both *civil society organizations* and the *media* have important control functions. Civil society organizations can for instance demand information and justification of – and monitor – public spending; and the media can keep up transparency and information levels, if there is freedom of organization, information and speech.

GHANA'S DEMOCRATIC INSTITUTIONALIZATION

Ghana is today an oil-producing and exporting country. The first offshore oil discovery of commercial quantities was announced in June 2007 (now known as the Jubilee Field), and production began in December 2010. The Ghanaian oil reserves are estimated at between 800 million and 1.8 billion barrels (bbl.), and with an estimated production of about 40,000–150,000 bbl. per day, oil is expected to generate over US$1 billion per year in export revenues over the next 20 years.[13]

Although still not an oil-dependent country, can Ghana withstand the pressures that will be created by the oil income, and avoid the resource

---

13 Source: Revenue Watch: http://www.revenuewatch.org/countries/africa/ghana/extractive-industries.

curse? Will Ghana's institutions be able to promote accountability and state competence to ameliorate the perverse political incentives that an oil boom can create? According to some of the more general and broad-spectrum comparative governance statistics available, Ghana seems to have undergone a slow but steady progress over the last ten to 15 years, and to have reached a current level of democracy and good governance that is possibly sufficient to keep the resource curse at bay.

Governance Statistics

According to the World Bank's WGI,[14] the overall picture is positive, with significant improvements achieved on most indicators since 1996. Ghana is now in the 50–75 percentile range for all indicators (100 represents the highest level), which ranks Ghana much higher than most of Africa, and puts it on par with African countries like Botswana, South Africa, Namibia and the Seychelles.

Compared to the resource-rich and resource-blessed developing countries – Chile, Brazil, Malaysia and Botswana, Ghana is on par with all of these on all (but one) of the indicators. That is, Ghana scores in the 50–75 percentile range on all indicators, and so do the resource-blessed countries (although Chile, Malaysia and Botswana score even higher, in the 75–100 percentile range, on some indicators). The only exception is that Ghana scores relatively low, like Brazil, on 'political stability'; and that Malaysia scores significantly below the others on 'voice and accountability'.

Compared to resource-cursed countries like Angola, Nigeria, DR Congo, the Sudan, Zambia, Tajikistan and Colombia, Ghana scores much higher than all of these on all indicators, with one exception: Ghana scores in the 50–75 percentile range on all indicators (except for one), and all the resource-cursed countries score in the 0–25 percentile range on most indicators and in the 25–50 on some indicators. Only on two indicators does Colombia also score in the 50–75 range. The only exception to this trend is that Ghana scores relatively low, on par with Angola and significantly below Zambia, on 'political stability'.

---

14 WGI: http://info.worldbank.org/governance/wgi/index.asp and http://info.worldbank.org/governance/wgi/pdf/c82.pdf. The WGI indicators are: Voice and Accountability, Political Stability and Absence of Violence, Government Effectiveness, Regulatory Quality, Rule of Law and Control of Corruption.

According to the Mo Ibrahim Foundation's Ibrahim Index of African Governance[15] (which is quite similar to the WGI, as it draws upon many of the same sources, but is limited to Africa), Ghana scores 66.0 overall (in a range from 0 to 100), and ranks seventh in Africa (after Mauritius, Cape Verde, Botswana, Seychelles, South Africa and Namibia). Ghana has been stable over the last five years, and it is well above the African average. Rule of law, national security, participation, rights, and health are Ghana's best-governed areas (above 70 in score). The country is only comparatively and absolutely weak in infrastructures.

Compared to two of Africa's resource-cursed countries, Ghana scores very much better, according to the Ibrahim Index. Angola and Nigeria score well below the 50 mark on all of the governance indicators ('rule of law', 'accountability', 'participation' and 'rights'), whereas Ghana scores 85, 61, 72 and 75 on these indicators, respectively.

Another global composite statistical source is the UNDP's HDI.[16] According to this Index, Ghana is a 'medium human development' country, whereas all the resource-cursed countries in Africa (Angola, Nigeria, DR Congo, the Sudan and Zambia) score low on human development. Outside of Africa, Tajikistan scores medium and Colombia scores even higher. The relevance of this Index is negligible, however, as the HDI is not a governance index but a composite index on living conditions like health, education, income, inequality, poverty, gender and environment.

More relevant as general, global indicators are the Freedom House Freedom in the World 2012 Index and the Economist Intelligence Unit's (EIU) Democracy Index 2011.[17] According to the former, Ghana is an electoral democracy (among the 117 electoral democracies in the world) and it is free (among the 87 free countries). Then there are 48 not free and 60 partly free countries in the Index. Ghana's scores on political rights and civil liberties are 1 and 2, respectively,

---

15 The Ibrahim Index: http://www.moibrahimfoundation.org/en/section/the-ibrahim-index and http://www.moibrahimfoundation.org/en/media/get/20111003_ENG2011-IIAG-ScoresTable. pdf.

16 The HDI: http://hdr.undp.org/en/data/map/; http://hdr.undp.org/en/media/HDR_2011_EN_ Complete.pdf and http://hdrstats.undp.org/en/countries/profiles/GHA.html. The Human Development Index (HDI) is a comparative measure of life expectancy, literacy, education and standards of living for countries worldwide. It is used to distinguish whether the country is a developed, a developing or an under-developed country, and also to measure the impact of economic policies on quality of life.

17 The Freedom in the World 2012 Index: http://www.freedomhouse.org/report/freedom-world/ freedom-world-2012. The Democracy index 2011: http://www.eiu.com//public/topical_report. aspx?campaignid=DemocracyIndex2011.

on a scale from 1 (most free) to 7 (least free). Compared to other mineral-rich countries, the resource-blessed Brazil, Botswana and Chile are free like Ghana, whereas Malaysia is partly free. The resource-cursed Angola, DR Congo, Sudan and Tajikistan are not free, and Nigeria, Zambia and Colombia are partly free.

According to the latter, Ghana is a 'flawed democracy', ranking 78 in the world. Ghana ranks the last of 52 'flawed democracies', which is below the 25 'full democracies' but above the 26 'hybrid regimes' and 51 'authoritarian regimes'. Ghana scores an overall of 6.02 on this Index, which ranges from North Korea's 1.08 to Norway's 9.80. Here, Ghana's score is particularly high on 'electoral process and pluralism' with 8.33. Among the resource cursed countries, Angola, Nigeria, DR Congo, Sudan and Tajikistan are 'authoritarian', whereas Zambia and Colombia are also 'flawed democracies'.

Elections

There is a political science thumb rule, which holds that democracy is consolidated in a country when the executive (president and government) has stepped down at least twice, peacefully, as a consequence of electoral defeat to another political party/candidate. If this is the case, electoral democracy has become legitimate and the 'only game in town'.

Ghana has held regular elections every four years since 1992, and four fully competitive multiparty elections since 1996. Furthermore, the incumbent president has stepped down twice because of the election results. The first time was with the presidential elections in December 2000 when John Kufuor won and John Rawlings stepped down, and the second time was in December 2008 when John Atta Mills won the presidential elections and John Kufuor stepped down.

This suggests that Ghana is a consolidated electoral democracy. In 2000, international as well as domestic observers concluded the elections were free and fair (CODEO, 2001). In 2009, the European Union Election Observation Mission (EU EOM) concluded that 'these presidential and parliamentary elections were conducted in an open, transparent and competitive environment. Fundamental freedoms such as the right to stand for election, the right to vote and the freedoms of assembly, expression and movement were respected across Ghana' (European Union Election Observation Mission, 2009:4).

The two largest political parties that dominate contemporary politics in Ghana, the NPP and the NDC, have both enjoyed two consecutive terms with a parliamentary majority and in presidential office. However, whilst the two larger parties claim to have divergent political views, their manifestos for these elections were fundamentally similar with little to differentiate the political parties in terms of policy directions (European Union Election Observation Mission 2009:8).

The Parliament

As mentioned, the parliament is important for stemming the 'resource curse' because it can balance the powers of the president and ruling elite, reduce government rent-seeking and patronage, and redistribute income. Good, reliable and publicly available statistics on parliament's performance and levels of parliamentary accountability do not exist. There is no general agreement on the role of parliaments in liberal democracies, and little systematic data on parliamentary performance that is comparable in time and space (Tostensen & Amundsen, 2010:9).

One exception is the Parliamentary Powers Index (PPI).[18] In this, the Parliament of Ghana scores 0.47 (on a scale from 1 to 0, where one suggests a total parliamentary power over the executive and zero suggests a total parliamentary subservience to the executive). Comparatively, Ghana is here on par with Nigeria, weaker than Colombia, and significantly better than the other resource-cursed countries mentioned earlier. Compared to the resource-blessed developing countries, Ghana scores better than Malaysia and Botswana, but not as good as Brazil and Chile (both with a 0.56 score). This indicator is rather inconclusive, and this snapshot at one particular point in time is unsuitable for tracking changes over time.

However, some proxy indicators are more revealing. One is on transparency in the budget process. Since the parliament is the main institution responsible for raising and using public funds, and for checking on the government's spending of public money, this is a good indicator of parliamentary performance. On the IBP's Open Budget Index 2010 (OBI), Ghana has a score of 54, which means the

---

18 The PPI by Fish & Kroenig (2009) provides a snapshot of the state of legislative power in the world as of 2007, and it uses a panel of experts to gauge the legislature's sway over the executive, its institutional autonomy, its authority in specific areas, and its institutional capacity. The background data are not available.

government provides *some* information to the public in its budget documents (the scale ranges from scant or no information: 0–20, minimal: 21–40, some: 41–60, significant: 61–80 and extensive information: 81–100.[19] This means that the information level in Ghana is 'far less than what is required for the public to obtain a clear understanding of the budget and to provide a check on the executive'.

Ghana is in the upper medium range of the OBI, but the resource-cursed countries' scores are all much lower, in the 'minimal' and even 'scant/no information' range (with the exception of Colombia with a 'significant' 61 score). Two of the resource-blessed countries, Chile and Brazil, have a 'significant' score of 72 and 71, whereas Botswana is on par with Ghana with 51 and Malaysia has a 'minimal' score of 39. These figures are not particularly conclusive, but the IBP observes that 'Ghana's OBI 2010 score of 54 is higher than the score of any other country surveyed in West Africa and is higher than the worldwide average of 42. Ghana's score increased from 42 to 54 from 2006 to 2010 largely because the government now publishes a Mid-Year Review, a Year-End Report, and an Audit Report. Ghana's score, however, shows that the government still provides the public with only some information on the central government's budget and financial activities during the course of the budget year. This makes it challenging for citizens to hold the government accountable for its management of the public's money'. Besides, the IBP reports that Ghana's Parliament and supreme audit institution (the Auditor General) are 'moderately effective' as budget oversight bodies.[20]

However, Ghana is one of (currently) 11 compliant countries of the Extractive Industries Transparency Initiative (EITI). This means that Ghana is found to be compliant with the EITI Implementation Criteria, which is a global standard for transparency in the oil, gas and mining sectors. Ghana submitted its final validation report to the EITI board in June 2010 and was designated EITI compliant status in October 2010.[21] However, Ghana's mining industry is

---

19   Source: International Budget Partnership's Open Budget Survey: http://internationalbudget. org/what-we-do/open-budget-survey/.
20   Source: International Budget Partnership main report on Ghana: http://internationalbudget. org/wp-content/uploads/2011/04/OBI2010-Ghana.pdf. The recommendations are that Ghana should improve the comprehensiveness of the year-end report and the executive's budget proposal; publish timely and regular in-year reports; publish a *Citizens Budget*; produce and publish a pre-budget statement; provide opportunities for the public to testify at legislative hearings on the budget for individual administrative units; and enable the legislature and Auditor General to provide more effective oversight of the budget.
21   Source: Extractive Industries Transparency Initiative (EITI): http://eiti.org; http://eiti.org/ Ghana, and http://www.geiti.gov.gh/site/. The initiative encourages, government, extractive

dominated by gold, diamond, bauxite, manganese and salt. Gold represented 34 per cent of the country's exports and 12 per cent of GDP in 2000–2003. Ghana's EITI implementation covers first and foremost the revenues from this traditional mining industry, but Ghana will most probably also be a compliant country when it comes to O&G revenues in the future. Publications have already begun, as total O&G output lifted and the reference price is published on a quarterly basis according to law, and the first oil receipts (for first to third quarter, 2011) are now available.[22] While the EITI initiative basically covers the revenue side (government income) of the extractive sector, the Revenue Watch Institute reports that also on the expenditure side, the Government and the Parliament are making progress in improving transparency.

Ghana has introduced targeted legislation in recent years designed to ensure accountability, transparency and efficiency in public resource management, including the Financial Management Act of 2003, which regulates the public sector to ensure transparent and effective management of state revenues and expenditures, the Public Procurement Act of 2003, which aims to foster competition, efficiency, transparency and accountability in procurement, and further efforts in expenditure transparency include the 2007 launch of Public Expenditure Tracking Surveys (PETS) in the education and health sectors. Besides, Ghana has included a requirement in its EITI framework that district, municipal and metropolitan assemblies report royalty receipts and how they are used. Also Ghana's Publish What You Pay (PWYP) coalition is supporting an ongoing community capacity-building exercise to track these disbursements.[23]

Thus, the public financial management system in Ghana 'is based upon a solid legal and regulatory framework'.[24] Nevertheless, some weaknesses remain in budget documentation, in the transparency of inter-governmental fiscal relations, and the internal audit systems. There is also room for improvement with respect to public involvement in monitoring and auditing processes.

companies, international agencies and NGOs to work together to develop a framework to promote transparency of payments in the extractive industries.

22 Published according to Section 8 of the Petroleum Revenue Management Act, Act 815, 2011 (PRMA), at Ghana EITI's webpage: http://www.geiti.gov.gh/site/index.php?option=com_content&view=article&id=140:oil-receipts-for-1st-3rd-quarter-2011&catid=1:latest-news&Itemid=29.

23 Source: Revenue Watch Institute: http://revenuewatch.org.

24 Source: http://www.revenuewatch.org/countries/africa/ghana/transparency-snapshot.

The Judiciary

Data on the effectiveness of the judiciary systems of the world do not exist, and comparable, international data on judiciaries' performance in terms of judicial reviews, adjudication in economic cases are not available. However, data on the rule of law are easily available, and data on the ability of the judiciary to hold the executive to account (judiciaries' checks and balances capability) are possible to find. There are individual country reports of quality, such as the US Department of State Human Rights Country Reports 2010,[25] which claims that Ghana's judiciary is 'inefficient and subject to influence and corruption' (p. 10).

Some comparative and longitudinal data on the rule of law are available, and these data are important indicators on judiciaries' ability to stem the 'resource curse' through safeguarding the rule of law. According to the World Bank's WGI, rule of law in Ghana has been relatively high (in the 50–75 percentile) and quite stable since 2000, as have most of the other (five) indicators.[26] Compared to the resource-cursed countries, Ghana scores in 2010 better than any of the countries mentioned, and compared to the resource-blessed developing countries, Ghana scores on par with Brazil, although not as good as Malaysia, Botswana and Chile.[27]

According to the World Justice Project's Rule of Law Index, Ghana is as good as any of the other resource-blessed countries on average, scoring even better than Malaysia, and almost as good as Brazil and Chile.[28] In particular, Ghana scores high on the indicator 'Limited government powers' and comparatively well on the indicator 'Government powers are effectively limited by the judiciary' (even better than the resource-blessed Brazil, Malaysia and Chile). This indicates that those who govern are subject to law and accountable under the law. The report says further that Ghana is the best performer among low-income countries, enjoying a good system of checks and balances, and that public administration bodies are relatively effective and corruption levels relatively lower.

---

25 Source: US Department of State, *Human Rights Country Reports*: http://www.state.gov/j/drl/rls/hrrpt/2010/index.htm and on Ghana: http://www.state.gov/documents/organization/160124.pdf.

26 WGI: http://info.worldbank.org/governance/wgi/index.asp.

27 Ghana is with all the resource-blessed countries in the two upper categories (50–75 percentile and 75–100 percentile), whereas all resource-cursed countries are in the two lower categories (0–25 and 25–50 percentile rank) and the majority in the lowest category (0–25 percentile rank).

28 Source: World Justice Project's Rule of Law Index: http://worldjusticeproject.org/rule-of-law-index/index-2011 and the report: http://worldjusticeproject.org/sites/default/files/wjproli2011_0.pdf.

Respect for human rights is another aspect of judicial quality and independence. According to one dataset, the Escola de Cultura de Pau Human Rights Index 2010,[29] Ghana has a better human rights record than any of the resource-cursed countries mentioned, and also better than Malaysia and Brazil. Ghana has a record on par with Chile (and other countries like Benin and Japan). The Index is, however, weighted and calculated in a way that is rather contested and not necessarily reflecting the main idea of human rights as a quality of the judiciary.

The Special Agencies

The special agencies can in some respects be part of the regulatory framework for the oil sector. For instance, anti-corruption agencies (ACAs) are important, and contested, players in the fight against corruption in the petroleum sector. They are, however, generally less equipped (and backed politically) to tackle high-level political corruption than they are to handle smaller cases of bureaucratic corruption, and ACAs are not considered to deliver on the high expectations bestowed upon them.

There are no international statistics on the efficiency of the world's many anti-corruption commissions, but there are some (older) evaluations of individual agencies. Ghana's anti-corruption commission, the Serious Fraud Office (SFO) is not covered in the only cross-country portal on ACAs,[30] but it figures in a 2005 report (Doig, Watt & Williams, 2005). This report claims that the SFO has adequate powers and operational independence, and that it is able to deal with serious (high-level) cases, but it is constrained by the delays in prosecutions by the Attorney-General (ibid., p. 58–59). In 2010, the SFO was replaced by the Economic and Organized Crime Office (EOCO), which was granted expanded powers to investigate and prosecute corruption and economic crime.

Two comparative dataset on corruption exist, however, that can serve as a proxy not of the efficiency of ACA as such, but of national anti-corruption measures in general. One is Transparency International's CPI.[31] According to the CPI (2011), Ghana scores 3.9 (on a scale from 0, highly corrupt to 10,

---

29 Souces: Escola de Cultura de Pau Human Rights Index 2010: http://escolapau.uab.cat/index.php?option=com_content&view=article&id=77&Itemid=97&lang=en
30 Source: http://www.acauthorities.org/aca/.
31 Source: TI's Corruption Perceptions Index: http://cpi.transparency.org/cpi2011/.

very clean). This is above the African average, but still not a very good rating. Compared to the oil-cursed countries, this is significantly better than all the ones mentioned, with for instance Angola and Nigeria scoring 2 and 2.4, respectively. Compared to the resource-blessed developing countries, Ghana matches Brazil (with 3.8) and Malaysia (with 4.3), but lags behind Botswana and Chile's 6.1 and 7.2 respectively. The CPI is much criticized for being based only on perceived corruption, however, and for not distinguishing between political and bureaucratic corruption, and using the CPI to find trends over time is not recommended.

The other is the World Bank's WGI mentioned above, in which one of six governance indicators is precisely 'control of corruption'.[32] On this indicator, Ghana scores much higher than all resource-cursed countries mentioned – Tajikistan, Sudan, Angola and DR Congo are extremely low on this indicator. Compared to the resource-blessed countries, Ghana scores the same as Brazil and Malaysia, but Chile scores much better. In other words, Ghana's control of corruption is on par with the resource-blessed developing countries.

There are some other special agencies in Ghana responsible for tracking oil revenues and keeping the government accountable on financial matters. One is the 13-member Public Interest and Accountability Committee (PIAC), put in place by Government in 2011 to monitor Ghana's petroleum revenue and investments, but this still lacks a secretariat and an operational record, and it is too early to evaluate. Other institutional instruments established to manage Ghana's petroleum resources include the national state oil company Ghana National Petroleum Corporation (GNPC), the national savings and stabilization funds of Ghana Petroleum Funds, the Commission on Human Rights and Administrative Justice (CHRAJ), the Auditor General and the Ghana Revenue Authority (GRA). There are no comparable, international data on these institutions.[33]

---

32 WGI: http://info.worldbank.org/governance/wgi/index.asp and http://info.worldbank.org/governance/wgi/pdf/c82.pdf. The WGI indicators are: Voice and Accountability, Political Stability and Absence of Violence, Government Effectiveness, Regulatory Quality, Rule of Law, and Control of Corruption.

33 There are some data available on fiscal regimes and the 'government take' from petroleum exploration and production, but these are hardly comparable. The Angolan Government's tax take from multinationals in the oil sector is high and increasingly sophisticated, for instance, perhaps as much as 85 per cent already in 2006 (which is 'very tough' according to the industry), and Norway's take is also in the range of 80–90 per cent. For developing countries like Ghana, a combination of royalties and profit-sensitive taxes is often appropriate, with close attention to detail and implementation. While royalties can distort extraction and investment decisions, they pass additional risk to investors (who may be better placed to accept them than are the governments of many lower-income countries) and assure an early and visible revenue return

Civil Society and the Media

Civil society organizations and the *media* have important control functions. Both can monitor government incomes and expenditures, check on public service delivery, monitor business ventures, create public awareness and encourage public debate.

There is one interesting data source on civil society from the Rule of Law Index. According to this source, Ghana scores high on the indicator 'Freedom of assembly and association', and even slightly better than the resource-blessed Brazil, Chile and Malaysia.[34] Indeed, in Ghana freedoms of association, movement, assembly and speech as well as citizens' political and civil rights are all guaranteed in the Constitution. The Constitution also protects other fundamental freedoms and political rights including the right to vote, the right to participate in public affairs, and the right to a fair trial (EU EOM[35] 2009:9). And, according to the US Department of State, there were no reports that police denied demonstration permits to anti-government groups (only the ban on campus demonstrations at Takoradi Polytechnic, where 64 students were arrested in 2007, remained in effect) (US Department of State, 2010:14).

According to Freedom House' Freedom of the Press Index 2011, Ghana's press is free, with a relatively constant score over the last ten years.[36] Ghana scores 26 in 2011 (on a scale from free: 0–30, partly free: 31–60 and not free: 61–100), and its press is thus deemed 'free'. This is in contrast to the resource-cursed countries which all are classified as not free or partly free (Nigeria and Colombia). The resource-blessed countries vary, from Chile's free press to Brazil and Botswana's partly free and Malaysia's not free press.

Although this looks good, there is, according to Revenue Watch Institute, a 'strong call for Ghana to enact a Freedom of Information Law and [to] affirm the public's right to information as a critical means to bolster and promote

---

to the government. Profit-sensitive taxes can ensure that the government shares visibly in any rents, not least when prices are high, and this is both fair in itself and potentially conducive to sustainability and credibility of tax regimes. Schemes of broadly this kind are in place in, for instance, Angola, Mozambique and Namibia for petroleum, and in Botswana, Liberia and Malawi under general legislation for mining (See: International Monetary Fund, 2011:66).

34 Source: Rule of Law Index: http://worldjusticeproject.org/rule-of-law-index/index-2011.
35 European Union Election Observation Mission.
36 Freedom House's Freedom of the Press Index: http://www.freedomhouse.org/sites/default/files/inline_images/FOTP%20Detailed%20Data%20and%20Subscores%201980-2011.xls

transparency'.[37] And, more specifically on accountability, transparency and efficiency in public resource management, Revenue Watch Institute claims there are 'critical weaknesses in budget documentation, in the transparency of inter-governmental fiscal relations, and ... in internal audit systems in Ghana. ... Room for improvement with respect to public involvement in monitoring and auditing processes remains'. Furthermore, the secrecy surrounding mining and oil contracts is an issue in Ghana. Before Ghana endorsed the EITI principles, all discussions of contract transparency were branded as anti-business, but much has been achieved since the first EITI report recommended that all of Ghana's mining contracts, including investment agreements, be made public.

Besides, according to Revenue Watch Institute, the GNPC is not committed to contract disclosure. It has issued a model contract and related laws, available in CD-ROM format, but this presents a technological barrier and does not address the fundamental problem that actual contracts remain unavailable for comparison. The model contract, drafted in the 1980s, also faces criticism over whether it adequately addresses contemporary market realities, and minerals contracts still contains a confidentiality clause.[38] Besides, individuals involved in the negotiation of Ghana's recent oil contracts report that the Government was concerned about companies' reaction if it committed to contract transparency, although Ghana has recently announced that its oil contracts will be made public (Rosenblum & Mapels, 2009:44).

Conclusions

As we have seen, there are numerous mechanisms by which power-holders and government insiders can extract from the petroleum sector. They can take bribes directly in the commissioning and contracting phases, especially when negotiating and renegotiating PSA arrangements, and they can take 'signature bonuses' and 'facilitation money' upfront. Then, they can siphon

---

37 Source: Revenue Watch Institute: http://www.revenuewatch.org/countries/africa/ghana/transparency-snapshot.

38 'Information or material supplied by the Company to the Government pursuant to the provisions of this Agreement shall be treated by the Government, its officers and agents as confidential and shall not be revealed to third parties, except with the consent of the Company (which consent shall not be unreasonably withheld), for a period of 12 months, with respect to technical information, or 36 months, with respect to financial information, from the date of submission of such information. The Government and persons authorized by the Government may nevertheless use any such information received from the Company for the purposes of preparing and publishing general reports on minerals in Ghana' (Cited in Rosenblum & Mapels, 2009:75).

money off from the national oil company (NOCs being used as the private purse of government officials) and they can use fake private oil companies and subcontractors to 'free ride'. Furthermore, power-holders and government insiders can use the petroleum sector in different ways to preserve and enhance their positions of political power. Essentially, they can spend the rents on power preservation. More specifically, they can also request donations and 'favours' from companies to acquire campaign and party funds and ensure that oil companies' CSR projects and infrastructures benefit their political allies.

To restrict these practices and to reduce the possible impact of the resource curse, long-term efforts have to be made on all fronts simultaneously and to be implemented in both the economic and political spheres. Some priorities stand out, however. In the economic realm, it is a question of reducing the petroleum industry's 'crowding out' effect on agriculture and manufacturing, by improving the business climate, by generating new economic activities and through economic diversification. This can potentially lead to the development of a middle class in the long term, which historically is the best guarantee for liberal politics.

In the political realm, it is a question of strengthening the institutions of checks and balances, accountability and control. The political response to the resource curse is the reduction of political monopolism and the institutionalization of efficient democratic control mechanisms. The solution is, particularly, in the institutionalization of public control mechanisms and in the 'ring-fencing' of informal practices. It is a question of the ability of Ghana's public as well as private institutions to control and withstand the pressures for extraction ('privatization' and usurpation of oil wealth and public money) and favouritism (clientelism, patronage, elitism). This should take place at a broad front and include the horizontal institutions of accountability (separation of powers, legislature and judiciary and special agencies of restraint and control), as well as the vertical institutions of accountability (elections, civil society and the media).

According to available statistics, like the WGI, the overall picture is positive for Ghana, with significant improvements achieved on most of these indicators since 1996, and a ranking of Ghana on par with the resource-rich and resource-blessed developing countries Chile, Brazil, Malaysia and Botswana. This puts Ghana well above the resource-cursed countries like Angola, Nigeria, DR

Congo, the Sudan, Zambia, Tajikistan and Colombia.[39] This picture is confirmed by the Ibrahim Index of African Governance. Here, Ghana ranks much better than Angola and Nigeria on all governance indicators. Also according to the Freedom in the World 2012 Index, Ghana is an electoral democracy and it is free, as are all the mentioned resource-blessed countries (except Malaysia which is partly free). The resource cursed countries are classified as not free or partly free.

More specific data sets on areas deemed important for curbing resource curse tendencies are harder to come by, but some data are available on elections and the parliament. Ghana's elections since 2000 have generally been considered to be free and fair by most observers, and the PPI ranks Ghana as a medium-range country, on par with Nigeria, weaker than Colombia, and better than the other resource-cursed countries mentioned. Also, Ghana scores not as good as Brazil and Chile on this indicator, which suggests that parliamentary control of the executive is not sufficient in Ghana. This is also indicated by the Open Budget Index on transparency in the budget process. This indicator demonstrates that the government provides only *some* information in its budget documents, which is less than what is required for the public to provide a check on the executive and that the parliament and the Auditor-General are only 'moderately effective' as budget oversight bodies.

Data on the effectiveness of the judiciary systems is harder to come by, but data on the rule of law are easily available, and can serve as a proxy. The WGI rank Ghana's rule of law relatively high, much better than all the before-mentioned resource cursed countries, on par with Brazil, but not as good as Malaysia, Botswana or Chile. When the Rule of Law Index ranks Ghana as good as any of the other resource-blessed countries on average, better than Malaysia and almost as good as Brazil and Chile, we can conclude that Ghana belongs to the resource-blessed group when it comes to the rule of law, even when there are data discrepancies. The conclusion is further supported by some data suggesting that executive powers are effectively limited by the judiciary, and that Ghana has a particularly good human rights record.

The legal regime on accountability, transparency and efficiency in public resource management seems to be well developed in Ghana, and particularly important in this respect is the fact that Ghana is a *compliant* country of the Extractive Industries Transparency Initiative (EITI). Full disclosure of O&G

---

39 The only exception is that Ghana scores relatively low, on par with Angola and significantly below Zambia, on 'political stability'.

revenues has begun, which is a particularly good indication. However, some of the special agencies relevant for petroleum resource management have weaknesses. Ghana's ACAs are only beginning to tackle high-level political corruption, although corruption control in general seems to be strong, and Ghana's PIAC has been only recently established. Comparative data on the other institutional instruments established to manage Ghana's petroleum resources do not exist. Regarding *civil society*, Ghana scores high on freedom of assembly and association, and this is also guaranteed in the Constitution. The same is the case with freedom of the press, where the Freedom of the Press Index 2011 classifies Ghana's press to be free. However, it is notable that Ghana still needs to enact a Freedom of Information Law.

It is a main argument of this chapter that institutionalization and democratization are decisive factors deciding whether abundant resources will be a curse or a blessing for a developing country, and that a country will be cursed *only* when the discovery of petroleum resources, for instance, is made before accountable and democratic state institutions are established and consolidated. Ghana has held four free and fair competitive, multiparty elections since 1996, and the incumbent ruling party and president have stepped down peacefully, twice, as a result of the popular will as expressed in the elections. Furthermore, the country's institutions have *not been* destroyed by civil war and conflict like the institutions of Angola and the DR Congo, and it has not gone into petroleum production shortly after independence, with an authoritarian government, like Nigeria and the Sudan. Combining the above points with data on institutionalization in Ghana, it seems fair to conclude that Ghana has reached a sufficiently high level of democratization and institutionalization to avoid the trappings of a resource curse, and perhaps even be blessed by its newly found petroleum resources.

References

Al-Kasim, F., Søreide, T., & Williams, A. (2008). Grand Corruption in the Regulation of Oil. Bergen: Chr. Michelsen Institute (U4 Issue 2).

Amundsen, I. (1999). Political Corruption: An Introduction to the Issues. Bergen: Chr. Michelsen Institute (CMI WP 7).

Amundsen, I. (2006). Political Corruption. Bergen: Chr. Michelsen Institute (U4 Issue 6).

Amundsen, I. (2010). Good Governance in Nigeria: A Study in Political Economy and Donor Support. Oslo: Norad (Norad Discussion Report No. 17).

Amundsen, I., & Wiig, A. (2008). Social Funds in Angola – Channels, Amounts and Impact. Bergen: Chr. Michelsen Institute (CMI WP 8).

Cabrales, A., & Hauk, E. (2011). The quality of political institutions and the curse of natural resources. *Economic Journal*, 121(March), 58–88.

Coalition of Domestic Election Observers (CODEO) (2001). Final Report on the December 2000 Elections in Ghana. Accra, Ghana (Ghana Centre for Democratic Development (CDD-Ghana) and Coalition of Domestic Election Observers (CODEO).

Collier, P. (2010). *The Plundered Planet. How to Reconcile Prosperity with Nature*. London: Allen Lane.

Cramer, C. (2003). Does inequality cause conflict? *Journal of International Development*, 15(May), 397–412.

Doig, A., Watt, D., & Williams, R. (2005). Measuring 'Success' in Five African Anti-Corruption Commissions – the Cases of Ghana, Malawi, Tanzania, Uganda & Zambia. Bergen: Chr. Michelsen Institute (U4 Report May).

du Plessis, S., & du Plessis, S. (2006). Explanations for Zambia's economic decline. *Development Southern Africa*, 23(September), 351–369.

European Union Election Observation Mission (EU EOM) (2009). Ghana Final Report Presidential and Parliamentary Elections 2008. Brussels, February 2009, European Union Election Observation Mission.

Fish, M.S., & Kroenig, M. (2009). *The Handbook of National Legislatures: A Global Survey*. New York: Cambridge University Press.

Fontana, A. (2010). What Does Not Get Measured, Does Not Get Done. The Methods and Limitations of Measuring Illicit Financial Flows. Bergen: Chr. Michelsen Institute (U4 Brief 2).

Global Witness (2008). *StatoilHydro's Libyan 'Corruption' Scandal Shows Need for Oil Industry Disclosure Laws*. London: Global Witness.

Global Witness (2010). *Oil Revenues in Angola: Much More Information but Not Enough Transparency*. London: Global Witness and Open Society Initiative for Southern Africa-Angola (OSISA-Angola).

Hall, P.A., & Taylor, R.C.R. (2996). Political science and the three new institutionalisms. *Political Studies* 44(5), 936–957.

Heller, T.C. (2006). African transitions and the resource curse: an alternative perspective. *Economic Affairs* 26(4), 24–33.

Hodges, T. (2004). *Angola: Anatomy of an Oil State*. Lysaker: Fridtjof Nansen Institute.

Humphreys, M., Sachs, J.D., & Stiglitz, J. E. (2007). *Escaping the Resource Curse*. New York: Colombia University Press.

International Monetary Fund (IMF) (2011). *Revenue Mobilization in Developing Countries*. Washington, DC: International Monetary Fund.

Kar, D., & Cartwright-Smith, D. (2010). *Illicit Financial Flows from Africa: Hidden Resource for Development*. Washington DC: Global Financial Integrity/Center for International Policy.

Mehlum, H., Moene, K., & Torsvik, R. (2006). Cursed by Resources or Institutions? *The World Economy* 29(August), 1117–1131.

North, D.C. (1990). *Institutions, Institutional Change, and Economic Performance*. Cambridge: Harvard University Press.

Powell, W.W., & DiMaggio, P.J. (Eds) (1991). *The New Institutionalism in Organizational Analysis*. Chicago, IL: University of Chicago Press.

Robinson, J.A., Torvik, R., & Verdier, T. (2006). Political foundations of the resource curse. *Journal of Development Economics* 79(February), 447–468.

Rosenblum, P., & Maples, S. (2009). *Contracts Confidential: Ending Secret Deals in the Extractive Industries*. New York: Revenue Watch Institute.

Ross, M.L. (2001). Does oil hinder democracy? *World Politics* 53(April), 325–361.

Ross, M.L. (2004). What do we know about natural resources and civil war?' *Journal of Peace Research* 41(May), 337–356.

Rosser, A. (2006). Escaping the resource curse. *New Political Economy* 11(December), 557–570.

Tostensen, A., & Amundsen, I. (2010) Support to Legislatures. Synthesis study. Oslo, Norad (Evaluation Report no. 2, January).

Sachs, J.D., & Warner, A.M. (2001). The curse of natural resources. *European Economic Review* 45(May), 827–838.

Soares de Oliveira, R. (2007a). Business success, Angola-style: postcolonial politics and the rise of Sonangol. *Journal of Modern African Studies* 45(4), 595–619.

Soares de Oliveira, R. (2007b). *Oil and Politics in the Gulf of Guinea*. London: Hurst and Company.

US Department of State (2010). 2010 Country Reports on Human Rights Practices: Ghana. Washington, August 2011, US Department of State, Bureau of Democracy, Human Rights, and Labor.

Van der Ploeg, F. (2011). Natural resources: curse or blessing? *Journal of Economic Literature* 49(June), 366–420.

PART III
Effective Management of the Oil and Gas Sector

9

Ghana's Present Legal Framework for Upstream Petroleum Production

Ama Jantuah Banful

Abstract

In discussing this chapter on Ghana's current legal framework, a brief history of the country's exploration exploits and a chronological analysis of the laws governing the upstream sector are presented. Also explored is the law governing petroleum discovery, the tenets of petroleum agreement and issues regarding associated and non-associated gas. Next is a discussion of the development of a work programme in which parties agree to the minimum work and expenditure obligations of the contractor during the initial exploration period and negotiation of these terms in each subsequent extension period. Moreover, the rights and obligations of contractors and subcontractors are spelt out. Other subjects highlighted include efforts at promoting local content, dealing with offences and penalties, and the significance of regulations. Thereafter, issues involving environmental protection, crude and natural gas production as well as decommissioning are addressed. Furthermore, petroleum income tax and the Petroleum Revenue Management Act (PRMA) are highlighted. The penultimate section sheds light on the legal mandate of the Ghana National Petroleum Corporation (GNPC), being mindful of the possible changes that would take place in the regulatory landscape when Ghana's petroleum regulatory body is established. Finally, suggestions are made on how Government would gain optimal benefits in the petroleum sector through an effective legal regime.

Introduction

Ghana announced the discovery of oil in commercial quantities in June 2007.[1] Prior to this Ghana had in place a legal framework for the regulation of the industry in the country. This framework has been in place since 1984.

Oil exploration dates back to the nineteenth century in the Onshore Tano Basin,[2] but it was not until the 1980s that Government realized the potential for oil in the country and began to put in place laws, in an attempt to manage exploration and production activities. The legal framework was established and came into force in 1983 through two main statutes: (1) the Exploration and Production Law (PNDCL 84), which currently provides the framework for the management of upstream oil and gas (O&G) exploration, development and production in Ghana; and (2) the GNPC which was then set up by PNDCL 64 of 1983 to manage and regulate the industry, and also participate in exploration and production. The Petroleum Income Tax Law, PNDCL 188 of 1987 was later put in place to deal with fiscal and taxation issues relevant to the industry. The three laws are synthesized into the Model Petroleum Agreement (MPA) that forms the basis for negotiation between Government and prospective oil companies. Recently the Petroleum Resource Management Act has been passed to deal with petroleum resource management and amendments to the existing PNDCL 84 are also being considered. These laws have constituted the existing legal framework to date. This chapter will attempt to look at the legal framework and give a synopsis of the contents of these laws and consider briefly their adequacy and relevance to the industry in Ghana. The chapter will also make some suggestions as to the way forward.

In 1982 the Geophysical Services Incorporated (GSI) acquired for the Government of Ghana a non-exclusive seismic survey offshore, the data covered the area from the Eastern Border of Ghana to the Cape Three Points. It was then that the government of the day decided to establish the institutional capacity, statutory legal framework for the petroleum industry and that effort on the part of the Provisional National Defence Council (PNDC) Government accelerated Ghana's Exploration and Production efforts and subsequently the above mentioned laws were enacted.

---

1   The discovery of oil by Tullow Oil PLC Ghana in commercial quantities in its Mahogany 1 Hyedua in the Jubilee field.

2   Ghana Geological Survey Bulletin No. 40 authored by Dr Moshin H. Kan.

The Laws

PNDCL 84

The legal framework for upstream petroleum production is provided for by PNDCL 84. This law gives the GNPC the right to extract petroleum resources as well as regulate the industry. The regulation is undertaken by GNPC because currently the Ministry responsible does not have the requisite expertise to fulfil that function, however, Parliament has enacted a law establishing the Petroleum Commission that will take over the regulatory function of GNPC when it is fully set up. The Commission is yet to be set up.

The Act vests the ownership of all petroleum existing in its natural state and found within the jurisdiction of Ghana in the President for the people of Ghana and so all petroleum found in Ghana is the property of the Republic of Ghana.[3]

The Republic is represented by the Minister in Petroleum negotiations; a contract is negotiated after an application by the Contractor has been made to the Minister for the acquisition of a petroleum block and the request has been granted. The negotiated petroleum agreement goes to the Minister and then to Cabinet for approval, and it is then taken to Parliament for ratification (a requirement of Article 268(1) of the 1992 Constitution). The execution of the petroleum agreement by a Contractor is deemed requisite and sufficient authority over the land in relation to which the terms of the agreement are carried out.[4] Development of petroleum can only be done by a Contractor in accordance with a petroleum agreement entered into between the Republic and the GNPC. The negotiated agreement specifies how petroleum operations are to be carried out.

The Act gives the right to a licensed Contractor to enter the land to carry out petroleum operations. The law specifies that any person who has title or an interest in land in which a Contractor or Subcontractor proposes to carry out petroleum operations shall permit the carrying out of such operations after consultation with GNPC.[5] Compensation is to be paid to any title holder of the land taken for petroleum operations after consultations have taken place with GNPC.

---

3   PNDCL 84 Section 1(1).
4   Sections (1)(4) of the Act.
5   Section 6 (2).

Compensation is to be paid to the title holder; this compensation for the land is calculated based on the value of trees and crops on the land, disturbance of subdue rights and damage to the building and livestock as a result of the petroleum activities.[6]

When a Contractor enters into a petroleum agreement, the Contractor cannot directly or indirectly assign any part of that agreement to any other person without the prior consent in writing of the Minister.[7] The law makes it clear that a petroleum agreement when executed cannot change parties without Government consent. The consent required to assign is also reiterated in the section that spells out the rights and obligations of Contractors and Subcontractors. There the law goes further to state that the 'Contractor or Subcontractor shall not assign his rights and obligations under a petroleum contract or subcontract either in whole or in part to a third party without the prior written consent to the Minister'. The issue of written approval to reassign a petroleum contract or rights and obligations under a petroleum contract, is imperative and failure to adhere to it may end in the loss of the licence to the Contractor. The same condition is spelt out in the model agreement. The reason for written approval is based on the fact that all minerals are owned by the country and its people. It is the Government's duty to know whom it is dealing with especially in respect to the contract, Government must be comfortable with the contract or since Government is a trustee of the petroleum being explored and produced for the people of Ghana, and is accountable to them.

The law requires that the Contractor is obliged to submit to the Minister a development plan and a long-term production programme in respect of the field to be developed. Currently these plans need to go directly to the Minister,[8] but this may change if there is put in place an Upstream Petroleum Regulatory body which would take over the role of the Minister in these circumstances.

Petroleum Discovery

Where a petroleum discovery is made, by the Contractor or if GNPC has made the discovery, the Contractor should notify the Minister and furnish him with the full particulars in writing of the discovery indicating which merits

---

6   Section 6(2) (a) & (b) and Section 7.
7   Section 8.
8   See Section 10(2).

appraisal.[9] After indicating that the discovery merits appraisal the Contractor shall submit a timetable by which it intends to carry out an effective and adequate appraisal to enable a determination to be made, as quickly as possible, as to whether the discovery constitutes a commercial field. Where the Contractor declares a discovery to be non-commercial the area that comprises the geological structure in which the discovery was located shall be relinquished by the Contractor.[10]

It must be noted that the Minister may direct a Contractor to increase or reduce the rate at which petroleum is being recovered from the field.

The Petroleum Agreement

Every Contractor who is licensed has to develop the area given in accordance with the terms of a petroleum agreement. This agreement is executed between the Contractor, the Republic, represented by the Minister responsible for Energy and the GNPC.[11] The Petroleum Agreement is valid for a period of 25 years, but if the Contractor does not make a commercial discovery within seven years from the effective date of the agreement, the licence shall terminate.[12] If however a discovery is made in the last year before termination of the Petroleum Agreement the Minister may grant an extension on such terms and conditions as the Minister deems fit to enable a determination to be made as to the commerciality of the discovery.

The agreement provides for a review of its terms any time any significant change occurs in the prevailing circumstances that existed at the time of the execution of the contract, the agreement also provides for relinquishment in a phased manner of portions of an area which the agreement relates to after the expiration of the initial exploration period, and any area relinquished at any guideline shall be, as much as possible, contiguous and compact and of a size that will enable petroleum activities by another Contractor to be carried out in the relinquished area.[13] These terms are negotiated during contract negotiation between the parties and the conditions and times for relinquishment are a standard and are negotiated when parties are negotiating the Contractor's work plan. The work plan is binding on the Contractor and he is expected to

---

9   See Section 9(2) PNDCL 84.
10 See Section 9(5) of PNDCL 84.
11 See Section 2(1) of PNDCL 84.
12 Section 12(1) of PNDCL 84.
13 PNDCL 84, Section 14(2).

abide by the terms of this negotiated work plan. The area retained at the end of the exploration period shall in so far as it is possible include all the petroleum reservoirs for all discoveries of petroleum which were made in the agreement area approved by the Minister.[14]

The terms for the production of natural gas are provided for separately in the Petroleum Agreement, the law stipulates that any natural gas produced in association with crude oil may be used in petroleum operations, but where such gas is not issued in petroleum operations it shall be the property of GNPC and the state.[15] It must be mentioned here that the exact terms are spelt out in the Petroleum Agreement in Article 14. This provision spells out the special terms for the exploration and production of natural gas.

The article stipulates generally how natural gas produced from a development and production area can be used for reinjection for pressure maintenance and or power generation. It can also be flared under specific circumstances. This is spelt out in the Act.[16] However associated gas has its own special provisions in Part II of Article 14 of the Petroleum Agreement.

Associated Gas

The Petroleum Agreement states the principle that there must be full utilization of associated gas with no impact to the production of the crude and it is a requisite that a Contractor's development plan for each production area shall include a plan for the utilization of associated gas and if the Contractor considers the production and utilization of this gas as uneconomic, GNPC has the option to off-take such associated gas. Where GNPC does so, it has to pay for any additional facilities and production costs required to have the gas delivered to GNPC. There are other provisions that spell out the Contractor's liabilities if the Contractor later decides to participate in GNPC's gas utilization programme.

Non-Associated Gas

The Petroleum Agreement in Part III spells out the provision for non-associated gas. It stipulates that the Contractor should notify the Minister as soon as there

---

14   See Section 14(3).
15   Section 16, PNDCL 84.
16   See Section 14.2 of the Model Petroleum Agreement.

is a discovery of non-associated gas. The agreement has terms that require the Contractor to facilitate a technical evaluation of the find and if in the Contractor's opinion the discovery merits appraisal the Contractors shall communicate this opinion in writing in a further notice to the Minister. If in the notice the Contractor indicates that the discovery merits the drilling of one or more appraisal wells at a time, the Contractor shall submit to the Joint Management Committee (JMC) an appraisal programme which shall be completed in two years. Sections 14(12) to 14(14) spell out the other terms on non-associated gas in the Petroleum Agreement. It is obvious that the production of non-associated gas could result in the Contractor requesting changes in the fiscal and other related terms in the existing arrangements which may, in the opinion of the Contractor, affect the already agreed terms for the production of crude oil from the contract area. Part IV of Article 14 in the Petroleum Agreement deals with gas projects, and here the Petroleum Agreement stipulates that while assessing the commerciality of the gas discovered, the Contractor can inform the Minister of commercial viability and production of the gas and also submit proposals for an agreement relating to the development of the discovery. Such an agreement is to be based on terms and fiscal requirements that are no less favourable to the Contractor than those provided for the sharing of crude in Article 10 of the Petroleum Agreement, and the measurement and pricing of crude oil in Article 11. Because of the peculiar nature of gas and the fact that it is not always the Contractor's favourite choice, Ghana has made an effort to spell out clearly what the terms are and who owns the gas and how it expects gas to be treated, so that there are clear understandings as to the treatment of gas by the parties to the Petroleum Agreement.

The Work Programme

The Law also makes provision for the parties to agree on a work programme. Parties to the Petroleum Agreement agree to the minimum work and expenditure obligations of the Contractor during the initial exploration period and each subsequent extension period these terms are then negotiated and agreed on in the Petroleum Agreement.[17]

The Petroleum Agreement also provides for GNPC to take a participating interest in a discovery within a specific period after the discovery has been declared commercial and GNPC has the option to acquire such percentage of the interest. The rights and obligations of GNPC in respect of such a discovery are negotiated and such terms as are agreed between the Contractor and GNPC.

---

17 See Section 18 of PNDCL 84 and Article 4 of the Petroleum Agreement.

In practice this participating interest however is negotiated upfront when the fiscal terms are being negotiated by the parties, GNPC is allowed to take a certain minimum carried interest in the petroleum licence and this can be increased, but any increased interest taken is not carried and at that point GNPC has to bear all the obligations and acquire all the rights the Contractor is also responsible for. This applies when additional interest in the block is taken over and above the carried interest negotiated upfront.

Under the fiscal terms that are stipulated in the PNDCL 84 the Contractor is obliged to make annual rental payments to the Republic.[18] The rental payments may be stipulated by the Minister or negotiated and provided for per the terms of the Petroleum Agreement in respect of the area to which the Agreement relates. This implies that the rent to be paid can be negotiated and agreed on by the parties to a Petroleum Agreement. It is suggested however that it may be necessary in the future to leave the rental payments to be fixed by the Minister. So that all Contractors have a clear idea of the rent payable in the different petroleum blocks and the rent payable will be dependent on the proven resources of an area. Some figures are stipulated in the Petroleum Agreement Article 12. It is deemed that these figures allow for an upward adjustment in rent up but rent cannot go below them.

The Law makes provision for the payment of taxes; PNDCL 84 in Section 19 states that the Contractor shall pay income tax in accordance with the Income Tax Law of Ghana. The Petroleum Income Tax Law, PNDCL 188 of 1987 was put together solely to look at the tax regime pertaining to O&G exploration and production. The Law in conjunction with the Income Tax Act of Ghana regulates the taxation of petroleum revenue, Article 12 in the Petroleum Agreement states the specific tax breakdowns. Under the Petroleum Agreement Article 12 states that a Contractor will be subject to royalty, income tax, levied according to PNDCL 188, and Additional Entitlements. There is the Petroleum Income Tax Law, and the PRMA which was assented to on the 14 April, 2011. However, the Petroleum Revenue Management Law only deals with the management of petroleum revenues by Government and says nothing about petroleum taxation. With the discovery of oil in commercial quantities there may be the need to revise the Petroleum Income Tax Law to widen the tax net in the petroleum industry.

The Contractor is also expected to pay royalties. On petroleum produced, these royalties can also be negotiated and the rate of royalties to be paid

---

18   See Section 18 of PNDCL 84.

maybe specified in the agreement. GNPC is liable to collect and transmit such payments to the Commissioner of the National Revenue Authority.

Rights and Obligations of Subcontractors and Contractors

PNDCL 84 also has sections on the rights and obligations of Contractors and Subcontractors. These provisions begin from Section 22 of the Act.

The provision reiterate the non-assignability of the rights and obligations of the Petroleum contract and the fact that all data acquired by the Contractor as a result of petroleum operations, interpretations and analysis prepared for and on behalf of the Contractors, are deemed to be the property of Ghana held by GNPC.[19]

The Contractor cannot export any such data without the prior approval in writing of the Minister and any data acquired by a Contractor should not be exported. Where such data is exported it could constitute a breach of contract, and GNPC should write to Contractors to return the data and pay a penalty.

The Contractor also has an obligation to keep all data, found and processed by the Contractor, confidential. This data cannot be released by the Contractor without the permission of the Minister. The Act comprehensively looks at all the obligations a Contractor or Subcontractor has and these are all spelt out in the Act.[20]

Local Content

The Law is also very innovative and it makes an attempt to provide the use of local content by Contractors and Subcontractors in the industry.

> *A Contractor shall in accordance with the regulations ... ensure that opportunities are given as far as possible for the employment of Ghanaian having the requisite expertise or qualification in the various levels of operation.*[21]

---

19 See Section 23(2).
20 Sections 23 and 26.
21 See Section 23(10).

The Law goes on to extend the use of Local Content to the use of goods and service.[22] The Contractor however is not obliged to apply the section since the Law uses the words 'so far as practicable'. It is suggested that in any review of the Act., or in any regulations that will be made in respect of local content, a percentage should be applied and it should be made obligatory for Contractors or Subcontractors to adhere to the stipulated percentages for the use of local goods and services. It is only by doing so that local industries will grow to feed the petroleum industry in Ghana.

The Law also enjoins Contractors to register a Company not incorporated in Ghana under our Companies Code to carry out the petroleum operations under a petroleum agreement or a petroleum subcontract.[23] They are also expected to maintain an office in Ghana to carry out the petroleum operation and open a bank account. This office must have a resident representative who has the authority to enter into any binding commitments on behalf of the Contractor.[24]

The Law is also very clear on the transfer of shares in the Ghanaian corporate company. No share in such a Company can be transferred to a third party either directly or indirectly without the written consent of the Minister, more so if the said transfer either gives control to a third party or enables the third party to take over the interest of a shareholder who owns five percentum of the shares in the Ghanaian incorporated company.[25]

This in effect prevents a shareholder in a petroleum agreement from transferring their shares without the prior approval of the Minister. The section reiterates the principle that no interest in a petroleum block can be transferred to a third party without the Minister of Energy's consent. This emphasis on consent where there is a transfer of interest in a Petroleum Agreement and shares in a Company that has a Petroleum Agreement, shows just how sensitive Government is with respect to who its partners are.

There are no clear regulations on safety, pollution and the environment, but PNDCL 84 does have sections that enjoin a Contractor to maintain equipment, at the worksite, capable of dealing with fire oil spills, blow outs and accidents, to enable the Contractor control or prevent such situations.[26] With regard to pollution or damage resulting from petroleum operations, the Contractor is

---

22 See Section 23(12).
23 Section 23(15)(a).
24 Section 23(15)(b).
25 Section 23(16).
26 Section 23(18).

held responsible if this is caused by its employee or agent.[27] However, one must admit that these sections are far from comprehensive because these are areas where regulations and guidelines must be put in place to regulate these activities. The country must also have systems to deal with such situations since from experience blowouts and oil spills are not only the problem of the Contractor or Subcontractor[28] especially when they occur offshore. The country must have some systems in place to deal with the situation when a blowout or oil spill occurs especially where it is a major one. These regulations and systems are yet to be put in place.

The Law allows the GNPC to appoint an auditor or any person authorized by the Corporation at any time to inspect, test and audit where relevant, the equipment of the Contractor, and the works, operations, records and registers as well as the financial books of account relating to the Contractor's petroleum operations. It also allows for copies of any document pertaining to these operations to be made by the authorized representative of GNPC.[29] The Minister also has the power to authorize any person to inspect the petroleum operations of a Contractor, to ensure that the operations are being carried out in accordance with the provision of the law and applicable regulations.[30] These are powers that currently are exercised by the GNPC and the Minister, however, it is expected that these powers of auditing and inspection will be ceded to the new Petroleum Commission since they are basically powers that the regulator should exercise.

Offences and Penalties

PNDCL 84 makes room for offences and penalties under which it criminalizes certain activities.[31] It also makes every director of a corporate body that is involved in exploration and production of petroleum other than a partnership liable for any action that is deemed an offence under the law. In the case of a partnership every partner or officer of the partnership shall be deemed liable for the offence. However in both instances if there is proof that the offence was committed without the knowledge of the director or partner, or that there was exercised due care and diligence to prevent the Commission of the offence, then these officers will not be held liable.

---

27 Section 23(18).
28 The Macombo offshore oil spill in the Gulf of Mexico by BP.
29 Section 26.
30 Section 27(1) to (3).
31 See Section 31(1).

Regulations

The law specifies 25 areas for which regulations are to be made. This is specifically subsidiary legislation that is meant to regulate the petroleum industry in Ghana.[32] These include regulations to ensure there is safe construction and maintenance of installations used in petroleum operations. Others are regulations for health, safety and welfare of those employed in petroleum operations, prevention of pollution and actions to be taken in case pollution does occur. There are supposed to be regulations for the protection of fishing, navigation and other activities carried out within the vicinity of petroleum operations. Regulations for competitive bidding procedures and the conservation of natural resources and so on, the law has even stipulated regulations that should be made on the minimum conditions of service for workers engaged in petroleum operations. All these are to be formulated under the Act. There are also some regulations prescribed that will have to be amended for instance subsection 32(2)(o) states that there should be regulations that specify that

> … those involved in petroleum operations should submit to the National Energy Board, the Secretary and their investment programme.

Clearly there is no National Energy Board, presently in existence, what we have is the National Energy Commission, the Secretary is now the Minister. However, when the Petroleum Commission comes into being it will be the regulator and so submission of the investment programmes of an operator will have to be to the Commission.

The list of regulations to be made is very long. Unfortunately none of the regulations has been formulated and without them one can confidently say that Ghana does not have all the necessary legislation in place to regulate the industry efficiently and effectively and this situation needs to be rectified quickly.

The industry thrives on regulation and operators, oil companies and Contractors have more confidence in a system that is well regulated than one that is not. No regulation also comes at a cost to the country because it erodes investor confidence and prevents it from reaping the maximum benefit from the industry.

---

32 Section 32(20(a) – (w).

The Environmental Protection Agency

With respect to the environment, the Environmental Protection Agency (EPA) does have some regulations in place that are applicable to the O&G industry. Section 23(1) of PNDCL 84 deals with the Contractors Obligations and Section 24 spells out the terms for the restoration of areas affected by the petroleum operations after termination and states:

> *The Contractors shall restore the affected areas and remove all causes of damage or danger to the environment in accordance with regulations.*[33]

Unfortunately there are no regulations in place yet. The Environmental Assessment Regulations of 1999 LI 1652 is the main legislation on environment protection. It spells out the areas where an Environmental Impact Assessment (EIA) is required before any activity commences and is applicable to the upstream petroleum industry in Ghana. In covering the terms of issuing an environmental permit or certificate, these regulations have been enacted to define the role played by the EPA.

The regulations specify in Schedule one that:

> *... crude oil and natural gas production facilities require registration and an environmental permit.*[34]

Crude Oil and Natural Gas

The Legislative Instrument (LI) makes provisions for an EIA permit. This means that these operations require an EIA report before operations can begin. This is specified in schedule 2(12) of the Regulations. Schedule 1 of the LI 1652 is headed 'Undertakings Requiring Registration and Environmental Permit'.

The LI defines the word 'undertaking' as:

> *... any enterprise ... construction, project, demolition or decommission the implementation of which may have significant impact.*[35]

---

33   PNDCL 84, Section 24.
34   See Schedule I (6).
35   See Section 30(1), page 4, the interpretations section 'undertaking'.

It must be noted that this is the only time the word decommissioning is used in the LI.

The Environmental Protection Law and the subsequent regulations give the general requirements for the issuance of permits and EIA's permits but do not have specific guidelines for EIA's for petroleum operations and decommissioning of petroleum installations. The formulation of guidelines for the issuance of Environmental Permits for the petroleum industry is essential because the absence of these guidelines can lead to a misunderstanding between the Operator and the EPA on what the guiding principles are for the issuance of EIA permits in the industry. However, the EPA states that even though Ghana does not have EIA regulations for petroleum yet, its attitude to petroleum EIAs is very strict.

Decommissioning

Apart from reference to the schedules in LI 1652 the Petroleum Agreement does not require that a decommissioning plan be submitted together with the development plan of the operator to the GNPC and the Minister. This requirement however, has been incorporated into agreements negotiated between GNPC and some Contractors. The plan is to include the estimated cost for all facilities[36] to be decommissioned at the end of the production and the establishment of a decommissioning fund into which a defined amount of funds will be set aside for decommissioning. The Operator may be also required to take out insurance to cover any shortfalls that may arise when decommissioning is due. The law makes provision for the restoration of affected lands[37] and it is suggested that this also applies to the seabed, where both GNPC and an Operator are tasked to restore affected lands and remove anything that is of danger to the environment and plug or close off all abandoned wells and conserve and protect the natural resources in such areas.

It is clear that the industry in Ghana does not have clear and concise regulations or guidelines on decommissioning. This is an area that needs to be clearly spelt out so that Operators are made aware from the beginning of their operations what their liabilities in the area of decommissioning will be.

---

36 See the Unitization Agreement between Tullow, KOSMOS, GNPC, Anadarko and EO Group.
37 See Section 28 of PNDCL 84.

Taxation

All operations in the petroleum industry are subject to Company Income Tax.[38]

The Petroleum Model Agreement spells out the taxation and other imposts,[39] that Contractors, Subcontractors or affiliates are expected to pay in respect of activities related to Petroleum Operations and to the sale and export of petroleum. These include Royalties and Petroleum Income Tax

Payments for rental of Government property, public lands or for the provision of specific service requested by the Contractor,[40] are also spelt out in the model agreement. Other taxes include withholding tax at a rate of 10 per cent in specific circumstances. There are also some tax exemptions. Contractors are not liable to export tax and vessels exporting the Contractors' crude oil are not liable to any tax, duty or charge for that purpose and the Contractor may import into Ghana, void of all taxes, the plant, equipment and materials to be used solely for petroleum operations. This also extends to household and personal effects of Subcontractors, Contractors and their affiliates. The income tax laws however apply to individuals employed by Contractors, Subcontractors and Affiliates.[41]

Petroleum Income Tax Act 1987

This Law briefly spells out the processes for ascertaining the chargeable income of a Contractor or Subcontractor in the Petroleum Industry.[42] The Law spells out the deduction allowed in ascertaining the chargeable income[43] and those that are not allowed in the assessment of chargeable income. It also specifies the persons who are insurable for the chargeable tax, that is managers, partners and principle officers and agents. It also specifies the delivery time for the posting of annual returns for the Contractor or Operator.[44] The other areas the Act deals with are the modes of objections and appeals made available where there is a dispute as to how an assessment is made. The law allows for a review and a revision, by the Commissioner, of the assessment made on the application of

---

38 See Section 19 of PNDCL 84.
39 See Petroleum Agreement Article 12, page 42.
40 See MPA article 12.1 to 12.5.
41 See MPA article 12.6 to 12.8.
42 See Sections 1 and 2 of the PDNCL 188.
43 See Section 3.
44 See Sections 10 to 14 of PNDCL 188.

the assessed person who has an objection.[45] There is also a mechanism to deduct the withholding tax payable, by a Contractor or Subcontractor on the amount due to the Commissioner that is specified in the Petroleum Agreement,[46] it also makes provision for the payment of income tax and withholding tax by expatriate employees under the laws of Ghana.[47] There are offences and penalties stipulated in the Act, and failure to comply with the provisions of the Act carries sanctions. Finally, the Act makes room for regulations to be made to carry out its provisions

Government makes its income from petroleum production by imposing royalties, and petroleum income tax, it also negotiates a carried interest in the petroleum block and the possibility of taking an additional oil interest in the future that will be paid for.

The Petroleum Revenue Management Act

Even though it will be dealt with in more detail in other chapters in this book, it is necessary to briefly mention it here.

This is an Act that manages the petroleum funds and revenue that the Government of Ghana will derive from petroleum. This Act manages Government spending of petroleum revenues rather than the industry itself. The Act provides for various sovereign funds where percentages of oil revenues are to be placed as an investment for future generations, and also as a stabilization fund to cushion the economy in times of crisis.

The Act provides for a Ghana Stabilization Fund and Heritage Fund,[48] it spells out how petroleum revenues are divided between these funds and the Consolidated Fund out of which the Minister of Finance disburses funds for the running of government business and developments.[49] The Act also makes provision for the investment and management of Ghana's petroleum funds.[50]

The Act has clear provision to ensure accountability transparency and public oversight on the use and investment of the petroleum revenue. The Law

---

45 See Section 19 of Act 188.
46 See Section 27.
47 See Section 28 of Act 188.
48 See Sections 9 and 10 of Act 815.
49 See Section 13 to 20 of Act 815.
50 See Sections 25 to 28.

makes provision for the audit of the petroleum funds and the Bank of Ghana (Central Bank) is tasked under the Law to keep proper books of accounts on the Petroleum Holding Fund and the Petroleum Wealth Fund.[51] In addition to the audits prescribed in section 45 of the Law the Auditor-General may carry out special audits or reviews of the Petroleum Funds if he feels it is in the public interest to do so and he shall submit these reports and audits to Parliament. Transparency is a fundamental principle of the Act and so information on data on the funds, that is declared to be confidential by the Minister, subject to the approval of Parliament, shall not limit the access of that information to Parliament or the Public Interest Accountability Committee (PIAC) that is established under the Act.[52] This Committee has the role of monitoring and evaluating the compliance by Government and relevant institution in the management and use of the petroleum revenues and investments provided for under the Act.[53]

Ghana National Petroleum Corporation (GNPC)

It may be prudent to mention the institution which has played the role of the regulatory body in the upstream petroleum industry in Ghana since the early eighties. This is the GNPC, established by PNDCL 64 of 1984. This institution has been the torchbearer of our nascent petroleum industry. It was established in 1984 out of a unit in the Ministry of Fuel and Power, that begun by carrying out the procurement of crude oil and petroleum products. It was initially established to support the Government's aim of providing a reliable supply of crude oil and petroleum products by developing the country's own petroleum resources.

The GNPC has until very recently been the only organization responsible for the exploration, development and production of petroleum in Ghana. It engages in the exploration and production of Ghana's O&G fields in conjunction with International Oil Companies (IOCs), the promotion of these resources and data management of the geological and geographical information acquired in exploration. It is solely owned by the Government of Ghana and has exercised supervisory responsibility over upstream petroleum operations.

---

51 See Sections 43 to 45.
52 See Section 49(5) if Act 815.
53 See Sections 52 and 53 of Act 815.

However, that supervisory responsibility is being taken away from it by the establishment of the Petroleum Commission. The Act setting up this Commission was passed and assented to by the President on the 14 April, 2011. This new body that has not been fully set up is to take over the regulation of the upstream petroleum industry. GNPC has also been stripped off its exclusive right to the gas and its exploration and production of gas. Both associated and natural gas belonged to GNPC and by extension to the Government and people of Ghana,[54] except as may have been agreed upon by GNPC and the Contractor. However Government has formed a National Gas Company fully owned by Government. This Company is now to be responsible for the production and exploitation of natural gas and associated gas. This move therefore leaves GNPC to become the National Petroleum Company responsible for the exploration and production of crude oil. This means that the GNPC will no longer be a player and regulator in the industry as has hitherto been the case. This frees GNPC from the conflict of interest position of being a shareholder in a petroleum block and joint venture partner with an operator as well as being the regulator of the industry. GNPC cannot continue to be a player and regulator in the industry. This sends out wrong signals to prospective investors and so the establishment of the Petroleum Commission is in line with best practice in the industry. The problem however will be the expertise to man the Commission because currently, all of that is in GNPC. That will be Government's dilemma.

Conclusion

This in a nutshell is the regulatory and legal regime currently governing the petroleum industry in Ghana. The regime is not foolproof, there is still much more to be done, regulations in a lot of areas are still to be made. Areas such as decommissioning, the rate of recovery of petroleum by operators, regulations on health and safety of persons employed in petroleum operations, prevention of pollution and remedial action to be taken in respect of any pollution that may occur, the protection of fishing, navigation and other activities carried out in the vicinity of areas where petroleum operations are carried out, are but a few of the regulations needed to manage the industry successfully, but for now this is the regulatory framework in place. However Government policy is to review and add on to the regulatory regime to make sure the petroleum industry in Ghana is properly regulated for the benefit of all, to Government who is the regulator, as well as the Operators, Contractors and Subcontractors who are to be regulated.

---

54 See PNDCL 84, Section16.

10

Petroleum Economics – Ghana's Petroleum Tax Regime and its Strategic Implications

Francis Mensah Sasraku

Abstract

Rent extraction mechanisms form part of the core components of fiscal petroleum regimes. They have served as conduits for revenue generation and expression of sovereignty for most oil-producing countries. More importantly the dependency of these countries on oil revenues remains as real economic facts. There have been recent developments in the petroleum economics and taxation literature on principles of what developing countries like Ghana should consider in designing their fiscal regimes. Such principles recommend that these countries should analyse the discovery process, their disadvantaged position in terms of asymmetric information trade-off and the absorptive capacity of their economies in the design of their fiscal regimes. The consideration of these principles in the fiscal systems design is supposed to lead to a systematic generation of optimum economic rent for the oil-producing country in question. It is still unclear whether Ghana has deployed these strategies. This chapter seeks to answer the question: is the current fiscal design aimed at short-term economic rent or long-term revenue maximization given the liquidity constraint environment that Ghana finds itself in as an emerging oil-producing country? The chapter will investigate the effectiveness and adequacy of the various mechanisms in terms of flexibility, neutrality and stability. It will analyse further the upstream petroleum fiscal design structure to ascertain how it promotes rent-seeking objectives without undermining the long-term development of its petroleum resources.

Introduction

The right of people to use and exploit their natural wealth and resources is inherent in their sovereignty, a key aspect of which is the adoption of the fiscal system which determines the source revenue from the oil resource exploitation (Stickley, 2006). In line with its theme, this chapter focuses on the effectiveness and adequacy of the Ghanaian fiscal regime in areas of flexibility, neutrality and stability (Tordo, 2007) leading to the level of government take through its rent extraction mechanisms such as signature bonuses, royalties, state participation and profit-based element, against the backdrop of current petroleum economics and taxation literature which recommends that countries like Ghana should analyse the discovery process, their disadvantaged position in terms of asymmetric information trade-off and the absorptive capacity of their economies in the design of their fiscal regimes (Collier, 2010).

THE IMPORTANCE OF PETROLEUM ECONOMICS

This chapter contributes to how best emerging oil and gas (O&G)-producing countries like Ghana could reposition the objectives of introducing rent-seeking mechanisms to maximize its economic rent in future and the management of the trade-off between risk-taking and economic rent optimization in a liquidity-constrained environment. The first section of this chapter deals with the contextual economic and petroleum environment in which various developing countries attempt to develop their petroleum resources. The second section deals with the principles and concepts of economic rent and revenue maximization and how they apply to natural resources management such as petroleum. The third section attempts to critically and comparatively analyse the rent-seeking mechanisms in terms of time dimension by ascertaining how they conflict or synchronize with the fiscal design objectives and their possible impact on government take and future development of the sector.

METHODOLOGY AND FINDINGS

In answering the question, a theoretical–empirical analysis approach has been adopted by building on the theory of economic rent and the principles of revenue maximization in the natural resources. The use of models and theories served as the orienting lens that shaped the approaches to test the effectiveness of the Ghanaian fiscal regime. Although this is not a comparative study, examples from related fiscal systems of the UK, Canada, Norway and Nigeria were used as sources of identification of optional rent-seeking methods. Based on its findings, the chapter comments on the extent to which the rent-seeking mechanisms and their design enshrined in the Ghanaian Model Petroleum Agreement reflect the aspirations of Ghanaians and business interests of international oil companies (IOCs).

Fiscal Petroleum Design Environment

Ghana, like most emerging oil-producing countries, designed its fiscal petroleum regime under the circumstances of limited knowledge of its geological potential, lack of technology, limited skilled petroleum experts for administrative management to enforce petroleum regulation and possible measurement and monitoring of economic rent (Tordo, 2007).

Host Country Objectives for Imposing Petroleum Taxes Versus International Oil Company Investment Objectives

Governments have the responsibility to design a legal and fiscal regime which encourages responsible exploitation of the nation's resources, while at the same time seeking a fair distribution of the proceeds between the government and the companies (Andrews-Speed, 1998).

The design of the fiscal petroleum regime may have the objectives not limited to revenue for financing government expenditure; rent extraction or gaining a fair share of the petroleum resource; impact on the economic environment by removing 'Dutch Disease' to affect the competitiveness of the non-oil sectors; demand management to prevent or discourage wasteful energy as well as counteracting distortions in investment choices by pricing domestic market obligations (DMO) at world market prices (Model Petroleum Agreement of Ghana, 2000). These objectives may contrast that of the IOCs on the other hand with the following objectives of seeking O&G discoveries; obtaining a reasonable rate of return; securing crude oil supply; ensuring sufficient security on investment; retaining as much flexibility and control of the operation as possible (Gao, 1994).

PRINCIPLES OF PETROLEUM TAX DESIGN

Assessment criteria for a good tax system or design include:

- efficiency;

- neutrality;

- equity be it vertical or horizontal sense;

- stability;

- clarity meaning being transparent to allow taxpayer to know the true costs of transactions and less scope for manipulation and administrative discretion, a behaviour which is bound to increase industry's perception of risks;

- simplicity which refers to inexpensive to administer.

There is conflict between neutrality and simplicity as complexity in administration increases as each field rent and expected yields need to be calculated properly, subsequently imposing what is called a fully differentiated tax.

The next is neutrality and revenue generation. Neutrality promotes development of marginal fields but marginal fields do not generate resource rent (Nakhle, 2008). They do not generate revenue for the government. Under a neutral tax regime a company can exploit the resources without paying any tax.

Equity verses simplicity and efficiency

Incorporation of tax allowances and reliefs also impose additional tax burdens, thereby making the tax system complicated. Also these allowances can generate misallocation of resources, thereby creating inefficiencies. Moreover, the concept of fairness is subjective and has different meaning to different people. A simple tax may be unfair to some oil firms.

Stability verses fiscal risks

Stability cannot be fully achieved. Circumstances are constantly changing. Flexibility needs to be in any tax system, thereby increasing risk.

Given all these compromises between criteria and trade-offs between objectives, it is not surprising to find that the principal tax instruments fail to satisfy all the main criteria of optimal taxation. Different authors have accorded varying weights to the main criteria discussed. Heady (1993)[1] emphasized, the equity concept has to be added to the main consideration and it is certainly true that among most economists it has been widely discussed and certainly forms a major part of the evaluation of any tax policy.

---

1   Heady, see Nakhle, 2008.

By contrast Kemp and Rose (1983)[2] emphasized the importance of efficiency and risk sharing as well as a focus on efficiency/ neutrality and equity. Dickson (1999)[3] ignores the concept of risk sharing and focuses on efficiency/neutrality and equity. Raja (1999) concentrates on the concept of neutrality and Witkins (2001),[4] whilst respecting the majority of the key criteria, chooses to give most emphasis to the concept of risk sharing.

Despite such divergences in interest, the majority (if not all) of the work undertaken in the area of optimal taxation in the petroleum and energy sector follows a common theme, that of economic rent. In general, the studies contend that a tax based on economic rent is likely to be the ideal tax. To assist in understanding the validity of such views the concept of economic rent is discussed below.

IMPLICATIONS FOR PETROLEUM TAXATION DESIGN

In designing a fiscal petroleum regime, the conflicts inherent in the respective objectives of host countries and IOCs need to be taken into account. However recent work indicates that the use of flexible, neutral and stable regimes facilitates the reconciliation of these objectives (Tordo, 2007). A 'neutral' fiscal regime neither encourages over investment nor deters investments that would otherwise take place (Tordo, 2007). Further, is the conflict between neutrality and revenue generation objective? In the petroleum sector neutrality promotes development of marginal fields but marginal fields do not generate resource rent (Nakhle, 2008). The quest for neutrality does not imply the view that the market provides an ideal allocation. It does not exclude the use of special taxes to correct what are called 'externalities', that is to say, cases in which the market does not of itself tend to provide the best use of resources (Garnaut & Clunies-Ross, 1983). They do not generate revenue for the government. Under a neutral tax regime a company can exploit the resources without paying any tax. The next is stability and fiscal risk issues.

A 'stable' fiscal regime is one that does not change over a certain period of time, or one whose changes are predictable. Stability cannot be fully achieved. Circumstances are constantly changing. Stability is achieved through flexibility, and flexibility is achieved through the tax burden being dependent primarily on profit and only secondarily on revenue (Garnaut & Clunies-Ross, 1983). A 'flexible' fiscal regime is one that provides the government with adequate share of economic rent under varying conditions of profitability. This requires a

---

2   Kemp and Rose, see Nakhle, 2008.
3   Dickson, see Nakhle, 2008.
4   Witkins, see Nakhle, 2008.

progressive mechanism for rent extraction and its stability over time as market and project conditions change over time. A flexible fiscal system limits the need for renegotiation and targets the economic rent (Tordo, 2007).

Despite such divergences in interest, the majority (if not all) of the work undertaken in the area of optimal taxation in the petroleum industry follows a common theme, and contends that a tax based on economic rent is likely to be an ideal tax (Garnaut & Clunies-Ross, 1983). To assist in understanding the validity of such views the concept of economic rent is discussed below.

ECONOMIC RENT

Rent is generally a category of income paid to the owner of a property to allow access to the property. The economic rent for any non-renewable energy exploitation is 'the returns in excess of those required to sustain production, new field development and exploration' (Kemp, 1987). This manifests itself in the form of larger producer surplus. However, understanding the various types of rent provides insight into what type of rent has to be taxed in the fiscal petroleum design.

Scarcity rent, defined by Hotelling (Garnaut & Clunies-Ross, 1983) to mean a situation where the market price is not high enough to cover the production and user costs, means a firm is better off keeping the reserves in the ground for use in future. Therefore, for capital intensive industries, the differential rent or Ricardian rent which arises from differences in specific characteristics of production unit or factor input is relevant in the form of mining, technological, position and quality rent (Battacharyya, 2009). Timely and insightful access to information on differential rent is critical to the design of an effective fiscal design.

Quasi-rent and resource rent

Quasi-rent is the compensation or necessary expected reward for investment in what is unusually risky and it cannot be removed without reducing economic efficiency in future production (Garnaut & Clunies-Ross, 1983). It is apparent governments have to be careful not to tax away quasi-rent (Garnaut & Clunies-Ross, 1983).

Resource rent is the difference between the total revenues from the exploitation of a resource over a period of time and the total costs involved in the exploitation, including the minimum required rate of return for the investor. That is why it is resource rent that should be targeted as a source of long-term petroleum revenue from economic rent (Andrews-Speed, 2009) as it is neutral in effect.

Difficulties in governments estimating economic rent

Two key concepts that lie at the core of an effective tax regime and provide the basis for compromise or bargain are economic rent and discount rate (Andrews-Speed, 2009). Governments have to determine the acceptable rates of return for all companies especially oil companies as they do not reveal directly their required rate of return on investment (Andrews-Speed, 2009).The question is how to judge sensibly as different oil companies may well have varying views about what constitutes an acceptable rate of return. Measuring economic rent involves or requires knowledge of differing costs of individual factors of production as well as their opportunity costs. These costs can be complex to capture and controversial. Again, because the size of a given discovery and its related exploitation costs can vary substantially, economic rent will vary from field to field (Andrews-Speed, 2009). Although it can be overcome by progressive taxation, it is difficult to make conventional fiscal systems sufficiently flexible and focused on resource rent across a wide range of variables such as price and different costs structures. The challenge for the government is to design a fiscal regime which takes a large share of the economic rent without exceeding the amount of available rent.

DISCOUNT RATES

The discount rate used in cash flow projections in order to recalibrate future cash flow in terms of its value today (Andrews-Speed, 2009) in turn reflects the project risk and the investor's corporate profile (Tordo, 2007) coupled with the political risks they face. They have to make profits rapidly to satisfy shareholders and creditors. For these reasons the host government can afford to use a lower discount rate than private companies which impacts on the design through the level at which economic rent extraction has to be set in terms of rate, volume and timing.

Critical Analysis of the Ghanaian Rent-seeking Mechanisms

The Laffer curve illustrates the trade-off between rates and tax revenues and provides lessons on how high taxes do not always increase revenue and may not be competitive for both government and investors to benefit respectively from a fair share of revenues and appropriate profitability (Nakhle, 2008). Subsequent discussion considers the number of alternative instruments used to collect rents from hydrocarbon exploitation in Ghana.

THE GHANAIAN RENT-SEEKING MECHANISMS

The first is the use of taxes. These can be classified into three according to their target as follows:

- 'Presence-related' (Kemp, 1987) taxes are imposed on a company regardless of whether it has any revenue. There exists a surface rental charge depending on the phase of petroleum operations ranging from $30 per square kilometre at initial exploration to $100 per square kilometre at development and production phase.

- 'Revenue or production-related taxes' (Kemp, 1987) are imposed after production starts, but take no account of profitability. The IOCs are required to pay ad-valorem royalties fixed at 5% – 12% for crude with an American Petroleum Institute (API) gravity of less than 18°. The rate of royalty on gross production of natural gas it at 3%.

- 'Profit-related' (Kemp, 1987) taxes target accounting profit, but do not consider the time value of money. There is an income tax at 35 per cent in addition to oil entitlement depending on the level of output.

There are no 'NPV-related' taxes that are dependent on the Net Present Value (NPV) of the project exceeding zero such as resource rent tax as found in Australia (Kemp, 1987). Quasi-fiscal instruments mainly the state participation in production in the form of 10 per cent carried interest and regulations relating to ownership of enterprises set at 5 per cent share in every commercial discovery, foreign exchange regulations and requirements to use local services (Stephens, 2008). Their impact on the company's discounted cash flow may therefore be considerable.

GOVERNMENT TAKE

The key to an effective fiscal regime is to direct taxes at profits rather than at revenue (Andrews-Speed, 1998). Such progressiveness is determined through the analysis of government take illustrated opposite.

Table 10.1 Key indicators: Most favourable terms and assumed least cost scenario

Royalty – 5%		
Income Tax – 35%		
Cost Recovery Limit – NIL		
Carried Interest – 10%		
Assumed Cost per Barrel – $20		
Contractor take = Contractor net income after tax/Gross revenues – costs (Johnston, 1994)		
IOC – Tullow/Kosmos		Government Share/Take
	Gross Revenue $100 per barrel	
	Less Royalty 5% ($5.00)	$5.00
	$95.00	
Deductions		
Assumed Costs		Taxable Income
$20.00	$75.00	
$67.50	Less 10% carried interest	$7.50
($23.65)	Less Income Tax (35%)	$23.65
$43.85 + $20.00 =$63.85	Division of Gross Revenue	$36.15
$43.85	Division of Cash flow	$36.15
54.81%	Take	45.19%

Table 10.2 Key indicators: Most favourable terms and assumed highest cost scenario

Royalty – 5%		
Income Tax 35%		
Cost Recovery Limit – NIL		
Carried Interest 10%		
Assumed Cost per barrel – $20		
Contractor take = Contractor net income after tax/Gross revenues – costs (Johnston, 1994)		
IOC – Tullow/Kosmos		Government Share/Take
	Gross Revenue $100 per barrel	
	Less Royalty 5% ($5.00)	$5.00
	$95.00	
Deductions		
Assumed Costs		Taxable Income
$50.00	$45.00	
$40.50	Less 10% carried interest	$4.50
($14.18)	Less Income Tax (35%)	$14.18
$26.32 + $50.00 =$76.32	Division of Gross Revenue	$23.68
$26.32	Division of Cash flow	$23.68
52.64%	Take	47.36%

This indicates a regressive fiscal structure because the lower the profitability, the higher the effective tax rate. This is because of royalty. It is based on gross revenues (Johnston, 1994).

STABILITY, FLEXIBILITY AND NEUTRALITY OF THE RENT-SEEKING MECHANISMS

The varying government take with respect to the level of profitability reflects the design of the fiscal regime which impacts on the underlying characteristics of stability, flexibility and efficiency (Tordo, 2007).

The existence of 'presence–related' and 'revenue or production-related' taxes impact significantly on the IOCs (Andrews-Speed, 1998). Next is stability in terms of the taxes that are imposed on the IOC. The current regime lacks neutrality as it is regressive. Second, it lacks neutrality as critical issues of environment tax and bonds have not been considered. This is coupled with limited efficient administrative mechanism to monitor and control environmental effects as observed in neighbouring Nigeria. The fiscal regime only requires that the IOC undertakes to operate in accordance with petroleum industry practice (Model Petroleum Agreement of Ghana, 2000). Environmental cost can in future erode most of the short-run gains from the oil exploration. Flexibility and stability can be undermined by political risks even though the petroleum model recognizes the existence of force majeure. The IOCs may seek further protection in the form of stabilization clauses in the agreements in the form of 'freezing' type or the 'economic equilibrium' type depending on the circumstances. While a stabilization clause provides some level of comfort to the IOC, the clause is by no means a panacea, as meaningful enforcement may prove elusive (Duval et al., 2009).

Conclusion

Current huge commercial discoveries, environmental issues and world market prices have exposed the weaknesses in the fiscal design of the Ghanaian petroleum regime. A critical study of the fiscal regime indicates that it was designed for short-term rent extraction from IOCs on the surface. The fiscal design has no comprehension of strategy and tactics to promote domestication of petroleum revenues particularly through domestic supply of inputs and harnessing of key by products such as the associated gas.

Ghana's design replicates some aspects of fiscal designs of developed economies and is too simple; it thereby risks losing the full benefits of its hydrocarbon potential. The fiscal design should be broader and deeper to include the development of the domestic banking, insurance and capital markets which will serve as a conduit to provide the long-term financial capital to support an integrated approach to an effective local participation in the shortest possible time. The price has been the failure to exploit the associated gas from the Jubilee Fields. Moreover, Ghana remains capacity short in electricity generation while flaring of gas is continuing without environmental tax and bonds in the fiscal design.

Because of its capital intensive requirement and long-term nature, the tax framework should be linked to contractual savings to actualize Ghanaian participation which will translate into taxes on dividends, and value added taxes (VAT) on domestic firms. Furthermore, it will allow the government to borrow at near world market rate, during periods of low oil prices to meet budgetary expenditures and maximize revenue during periods of high prices. Increasing Ghanaian holding of shares will also reduce the discount rate used by the IOCs and on the whole cement the expected stability, flexibility and neutrality in the fiscal petroleum design.

Treatment of environmental obligations if introduced in future as being deductible as cost of environmental compliance will be of interest to Ghanaians (Tordo, 2007). Sliding royalty and income tax can be introduced to make the tax very progressive. However given the limited information on the Ghanaian geological potentials or information asymmetry, royalties appears to be the best option (Collier, 2010) but cannot support the development of marginal fields in future. In an attempt to optimize economic rent in the long run, the strategy should be to maximize revenue not only from the petroleum operations but the entire social rent by investing in knowing the geological prospects thereby separating the prospecting process from the extraction process to complement the tax design (Collier, 2010).

Future research should be focused on the process of internalization of economic rent through the strengthening of the domestic banking, insurance and capital markets in addition to how the National Oil Company's role can be expanded without undermining the flexibility, neutrality and stability.

References

Andrews-Speed, P. (1998). Fiscal systems for mining: the case of Brazil. *Journal of Mineral Policy, Business and Environment* 13(2), 13–21.

Bhattacharyya, S.C. (2009). *Energy Economics – The Tools*. CEPMLP: Dundee.

Collier, P. (2010) Principles of Resource Taxation for Low Income Countries in Daniel, P., Keen M., & McPherson C. (Eds), *The Taxation of Petroleum: Principles, Problems and Practices*. Abingdon: Routledge.

Duval, C., Le Leuch, H., Pertuzio, A., & Weaver, J.L. (2009). *International Petroleum Exploration and Exploitation Agreements: Legal, Economic and Policy Aspects* (2nd ed.). New York: Barrows Company Inc.

Gao, Z. (1994). International Petroleum Contracts: Current Trends And New Directions. London: Graham & Trotman.

Garnaut, R., & Clunies-Ross, A. (1983). *Taxation of Mineral Rents*. Oxford: Clarendon Press.

Johnston, D. (1994). International Petroleum Fiscal Systems and Production Sharing Contracts. Tulsa, OK: Penwell.

Kemp, A.G. (1987). Economic Considerations in the Taxation of Petroleum Exploitation. In Khan, K.I.F. (Ed.). Petroleum Resources and Development: Economic, Legal and Policy Issues for Developing Countries. London: Belhaven Press, pp. 121–145, Chapter 8, p. 122.

Model Petroleum Agreement of Ghana (2000). *Ghana National Petroleum Corporation*, retrieved 3 May, 2011 from http://www.gnpcghana.com/aboutus/newsevents.

Nakhle, C. (2008). *Petroleum Taxation: Sharing the Oil Wealth: A Study of Petroleum Taxation Yesterday, Today and Tomorrow*. New York: Routledge.

Stephens, P. (2008.) *Petroleum Policy and Economics Manual*. CEPMLP: Dundee.

Stickley, D.C. (2006). *A Framework for Negotiating & Documenting Petroleum Industry Transactions*. New Zealand: Wellington Publishers.

Tordo, S. (2007). Fiscal Systems for Hydrocarbons Design Issues. World Bank Working Paper No. 123.

11

Maximizing National Development From the Oil and Gas Sector Through Local Value-Add: Extracting From an Extractive Industry

Anthony E. Paul

Abstract

This chapter commences with a discussion of local content and participation (LC&P) aspirations. Next is a presentation of the mechanisms of value capture as well as the process of maximizing local value-add (LVA). This is followed by the development of policies and strategies for local content and private sector participation. Additionally, the building blocks of local content are discussed. Thereafter, government's role in creating a level playing field is addressed. In the context of local content in the petroleum sector, some pitfalls to be avoided by host countries are highlighted. Finally, pertinent learning lessons for Ghana and other African oil-producing countries are presented.

Aspiration of Local Content and Participation Policies

Typically, a developing country that is endowed with abundant natural resources of oil or gas recognizes that the country's development is enabled by a wasting asset which belongs to all its citizens and which, once removed, is not replenished. The government, as caretaker and manager of these assets, has an obligation to ensure that the exploitation of these resources is conducted in a manner that generates maximum benefit to all the people of the country.

The oil and gas (O&G) business is characterized as requiring high levels of skills, know-how, technology and capital. Developing countries, with their limited human and capital resources, will continue to engage foreign individuals, international businesses and organizations which have these capabilities, to explore for, exploit and commercialize their natural resources. In spite of this, countries have a right and governments have an obligation to ensure that their citizens get the maximum value from their natural resources. By recognizing that in depleting their natural resources, countries are simultaneously removing opportunities to capture future wealth, it might be argued that governments have a further obligation to ensure that they make the most of the current opportunity to create the capability to generate wealth in the future.

An Attitude for Success

Too often countries underestimate the value of their resource to the investors and, needing, as they often do, to present an attractive investment climate, they place their requirements as secondary to the investors'. This often reflects a lack of understanding of the value of the resource to the investor, its support companies and its home country.

Developed countries and the mature developing ones that have done better at extracting balanced terms tend to use an approach that positions them as owners and controllers of their resources and destiny, rather than recipients of reward or goodwill.

That is a very significant hurdle for poor, developing countries to cross and requires strong and courageous leadership, self-confidence, skilful analysis, procurement, negotiating, contracting and contract management at the operating levels, clearly articulated national objectives and consistently applied rules of engagement, across the board.

Recognizing that not all investors have strategies that align with their own or that the resource in a country may not fit ideally into every company's portfolio, countries would do well to deliberately seek out, attract and contract the partners who provide the 'right' fit for their national development goals.

The question of local content and value-add tends to be challenged on several grounds, particularly on cost and efficiency bases. Countries may note that similar concerns have been addressed in the practice of military procurement, where countries take the point of view that, for such large purchases, they are transferring major portions to their nation's wealth overseas. In return, they seek 'offsets' that return value, either directly or indirectly, to their country.

Offsets refer to 'the entire range of industrial and commercial benefits provided to foreign governments as an inducement or condition to purchase military goods or services, including benefits such as co-production, licensed production, subcontracting, technology transfer, in-country procurement, marketing and financial assistance, and joint ventures.' A discussion of the use of offsets is provided in Appendix 1.[1]

Mechanisms of Value Capture

Governments and countries with natural resources typically seek to maximize the value that is retained in country or locally through fiscal measures (taxation and royalty policies and government expenditure).

Other non-fiscal measures are available to support the local value capture and retention through the participation of local individuals and businesses. Getting the most out of these requires that local ownership and participation occur along as much of the value chain as is practical, both within and outside the host country/community and that local content seeks to maximize the level of usage of local goods, services, people, businesses and financing.

In addition, more and higher value can be captured through ongoing local capacity development. Local capacity, in individuals, institutions and businesses, can justifiably be built to support the sector's growth. Deliberate and considered decisions and approaches need to be taken for investment in developing the capacity which can provide access to local participation in more of the value chain and that which can be transferred to other sectors, so as to support wider national development.

The mechanisms for capacity development should therefore be carefully identified, secured and contracted for. A key approach is via transfer of

---

1   See also US Government Defence Offsets Disclosure Act of 1999, Pub. L. 106-113, Section 1243(3).

technology and know-how from international participants. Experience has shown that the alliances that have the best success at enhancing, deepening and broadening capability and international competitiveness of local people and businesses, come through partnerships that involve equity participation of locals (cf. Figure 11.1.)

In order to achieve the widest, cross-sector benefits possible, opportunities for creating and supporting cluster developments with other industries that have synergy with some aspect of the natural resource sector, need to be identified and pursued.

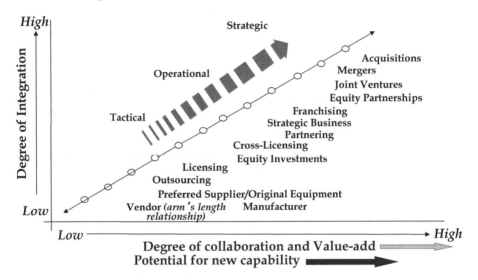

Figure 11.1   The Relationship between Transfer of Know-how and Technology and Degree of Integration

The Process of Maximizing Local Value-Add, First Things First

While countries and regions have done it differently and each needs to customize the approach to its own unique circumstances, a staged approach helps cover the bases and align the implementation strategy to national development goals.

The preliminary stage will require an analysis of the status quo and a mapping of the industry's requirements (inputs) and outputs against national development aspirations. To be effective, a detailed analysis of the industry value chain, including the country's capacity and the participating companies' strategies, will require expertise that may not be available to the host government, in the early stages of resource exploration and/or production.

This is the most critical time, however, as long-term contracts (up to 30 years, or more, in some cases) are put in place at this time and very significantly impact the quality of possible outcomes.

DEFINITION AND TARGET SETTING

Ideally, the entire question of defining local content, target setting and measurement are best addressed at the outset, so that there is clarity among all stakeholders. Operating companies, with a history of dealing in many places, often have their own experiences of what works and what does not. It is worthwhile to obtain their input, while keeping sight of the facts that their own objectives may be different from that of the host government and that the companies are ultimately charged with implementing much of the policy.

Local content policies often struggle with the definition of local content and the discourse with operating companies may become distorted in the search for 'simplicity'. This is not a simple matter, but that should not cause it to be abandoned. There have been several approaches to defining local content. The simple ones lend themselves to abuse. What should be sought is clarity.

Some of the methods used for defining a local company or service include:

1. Whether or not the company is registered to do business in host community.
    - This is sometimes augmented by a requirement of compliance with local tax laws. This is a very weak definition, as it usually does not address the use of affiliate companies to provide financing, goods and services and the cost of these, for instance.

2. A requirement of local ownership – usually 50 per cent or more of its shareholders have to be nationals or legal entities registered to do business locally.
    - Again, companies may abuse this through shareholder agreements that give decision-making or revenue/profit-sharing rights that are out of alignment with shareholding, often favouring a foreign partner.
    - In some instances, the foreign partner may have other rights that effectively give it majority control, such as the right to buy out the local partner, at any time, for a nominal sum.

Majority of staff are national – usually 50 per cent or more of its employees and contractors must be nationals/locals to be considered a local entity.

- This too is subject to abuse. When, for example, the actual expenditures associated with foreign workers, as compared to that for locals, is vastly disproportionate to the ratio of numbers of employees.

3. Goods and services substantively produced locally – for example 50 per cent or more of its employees and contractors are nationals/locals (for companies that use skills as an input), 50 per cent of its raw materials are of local origin or 50 per cent combined goods and people of local origin.

- The same issues of numbers of employees and source of origin and cost of goods, rather than numeric comparisons, arise.

DEFINING LOCAL CONTENT AND VALUE-ADD IN NATIONAL DEVELOPMENT CONTEXT

Best practice suggests that local content definition should carefully consider ownership, control and financing by citizens of the home country and be in conformity with internationally accepted norms and international conventions.

We can therefore consider a definition of local content as:

Local/National participation in the oil and gas industry with the objective of creating value and contributing to the economic and social development of the country.

Where contributions to local/national economic and social development can emerge from income to a variety of local *factors of production*:

- land;

- resources;

- labour (including entrepreneurial and non-manual skills); and

- capital.

Local content is, therefore the sum of:

- income received by locals/nationals;

- revenues accrued by owners of land and resources; and

- income streams to local/national shareholders and creditors.

The goal of local content initiatives must be to maximize the value added by the O&G industry to the local economy, by sustainable and efficient provision of internationally competitive local goods and services. In this case, success is defined as achieving a much higher proportion of the expenditure from the O&G sector being spent within the local economy.

There is a critical implication here in the range of factors that contribute to true local content. In particular, it is clear that local ownership of firms and assets is a contributing factor, but certainly not the only criterion for judging true value-added local content.

The difficulty in definition shows itself most when the question of setting targets arises. Again, companies can be great allies or can erode a lot of value by the effort they put into perverting the process. Companies, because of the engineering bent in projects and operations, seek clear, measurable and reportable targets. Governments often have more general requirements of measuring targets.

Instead of stating fixed, overarching targets on a project-by-project or activity-by-activity basis, the successful countries or regions pick selected activities, skills or clusters for focus and measure their achievements in ways specific to those targeted areas. The level of granularity is best worked out by those who are expert in the work processes and skills requirements involved. In time, as capacity and demand change, new or revised targets are introduced.

For consistency of application and clarity of monitoring and reporting, an independently auditable system is desirable.

THE CONCEPT OF LOCAL VALUE-ADD

While the concept of local content is well understood and dominates the host government/ company dialogue, a more meaningful outcome may be achieved if the local aspiration were to be cast in the frame of LVA. This brings to the table the concept of local ownership and participation in different parts of the value chain.

This is not to be confused with nationalization and does not imply 100 per cent local ownership of any aspect of the industry. The ability of locals to own some aspect of the industry, whether as shareholder or controller, whether through the state or as private individuals, or whether as a primary operator or supporting services provider, brings a greater level of local integration in the sector, allowing for profits to flow back into the local economy and for business skills to be developed, above and beyond the industry specific manual skills, in line with the requirements of the international partners.

LVA captures the inputs of local goods and services as well as the benefits of local ownership, participation and financing. This can in turn address issues of local capacity development to meet current and future needs. Taking this approach to local content policies and strategies might create better alignment with the aspiration of national development.

ROLE OF THE STATE

Aside from aggressively promoting and rigorously applying enabling policies wherever state-controlled resources are involved, the state has a role to:

- facilitate the development of local capability to enable LVA;

- remove barriers for local participation;

- set targets of LC&P that will be assigned to individual projects, operations and/or operators and supporting these targets with appropriate contract terms;

- ensure that the metrics for each target are appropriate to achieving the required objectives and consistent with the current and future states of the industry and country;

- put in place the required regulatory capacity and administrative systems;

- measure and report on the performance of operators in the sector;

- periodically compare the LC&P performance amongst operators, between projects and operations and with other countries, to establish benchmarks, targets and opportunities for improvement and for the transfer of best practices.

The approach used to describe the process of capturing maximum value from natural resources, through LVA can be summarized in Figure 11.2.

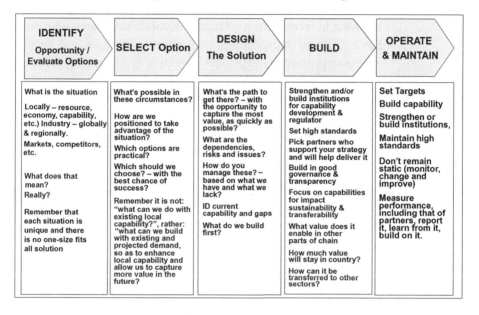

IDENTIFY Opportunity / Evaluate Options	SELECT Option	DESIGN The Solution	BUILD	OPERATE & MAINTAIN
What is the situation Locally – resource, economy, capability, etc.) Industry – globally & regionally. Markets, competitors, etc. What does that mean? Really? Remember that each situation is unique and there is no one-size fits all solution	What's possible in these circumstances? How are we positioned to take advantage of the situation? Which options are practical? Which should we choose? – with the best chance of success? Remember it is not: "what can we do with existing local capability?", rather: "what can we build with existing and projected demand, so as to enhance local capability and allow us to capture more value in the future?	What's the path to get there? – with the opportunity to capture the most value, as quickly as possible? What are the dependencies, risks and issues? How do you manage these? – based on what we have and what we lack? ID current capability and gaps What do we build first?	Strengthen and/or build institutions for capability development & regulator Set high standards Pick partners who support your strategy and will help deliver it Build in good governance & transparency Focus on capabilities for impact sustainability & transferability What value does it enable in other parts of chain How much value will stay in country? How can it be transferred to other sectors?	Set Targets Build capability Strengthen or build institutions, Maintain high standards Don't remain static (monitor, change and improve) Measure performance, including that of partners, report it, learn from it, build on it.

Figure 11.2   A Systematic Approach to Capturing Local Value-add

Developing the Policies and Strategies

The intent always is to implement strategies that ensure delivery of the stated goals. Pragmatism is therefore advised.

For maximum benefit, it is best to design the objectives, policies and strategies through:

- a deep analysis of the sector and country/region:
  - as this typically needs to happen before production and revenue to the state, the ability of governments to access good advice is often limited at this critical stage;

- taking a long-term view, with a clear understanding of the base line of local capacity and the building blocks/dependencies for each capacity targeted;

- focusing on the areas of maximum impact;

- transparency and the involvement of civil society:
  - given that developing countries have limited human resource and expertise in the areas of interest, there are huge benefits of working in consultation with other local stakeholders, who may have different perspectives, aspirations, priorities and so on. This is important, if the primary objective of addressing national and community priorities is kept in mind.
  - procurement in the natural resources sector, being the biggest areas of spend and occurring, as it does, frequently across national borders, is notorious for price/cost centre transfers and corruption. Transparency of procurement procedures, tender awards and contracts, where state resources are concerned is important for achieving the best results, in terms of national objectives.
  - the involvement of civil society as both a supporter to government and a check-valve is enabled by transparency;
  - benchmarking of contractors' costs and other performance indicators across different contract areas, different contractors and different countries in the region or across the world. International companies routinely share such information with benchmarking companies or agencies, so as to measure their performance and seek areas of improvement. Governments tend never to do similarly and would do well to adopt this practice, so as to gauge the performance of their contractors. Civil society should welcome these measures to ensure that the country/region is getting the best outcome for its citizens.

The national development vision, into which the LVA approach is cast, should have clearly defined national goals and objectives that allow for developing policies that guide the behaviour towards achieving those goals.

In designing and implementing legislation and regulation to give effect to the policies, it must be acknowledged that national objectives are not negotiable. While companies at a local level acknowledge and often support the LVA concept, head office and regional procurement considerations often militate against their supporting the initiatives. The presence of regulation makes it clear whose objectives have priority.

A policy framework should articulate the guiding principles that will determine:

- the major mechanisms for local content, participation and capability development;

- where, how and by whom these will be delivered, including some key areas for priority focus; and

- the performance measurement, assurance and reporting processes to be used.

In attempting to get the maximum multiplier effect, it is important to seek out and capture capacity that is transferable to other sectors of the economy. Building other sectors provides a road to sustainability.

With all the goodwill, well-crafted policies provide no guarantee of delivering the objectives unless the policies and strategies are adhered to. This only comes through regulating them and empowering the responsible institutions through:

- capacity for procurement, negotiating, contracting and contract, and project management;

- systems, tools and processes for metrics definition, target setting and data collection that are easy to implement and use;

- reporting for accountability, performance measurement, continuous improvement and updating;

- appropriate legislation, regulations, contracts and operating procedures.

Getting results depends on the right partner, who is typically the operator and who will be at the front line of delivering LVA, alongside the international contractors. In selecting that partner and in the projects and activities that are carried out in the operations, LVA experience and culture should be used as criteria for evaluation and selection of service providers and operator partners.

At a national level, beyond policy and regulation, delivery has to be contracted and monitored. This is only effective if rewards and penalties are attached to compliance or lack thereof.

Bidding should include a requirement for plans to use local content and building local capability. These can be weighted to reflect the importance to delivering the national/regional objectives, so that, for example, one criterion for evaluating bids might be the level of local content and/or capacity development involved in delivering the contract. Winning bidders should then be contracted to deliver on these promises.

Even as legislation is essential and has been/is being implemented (Timor Leste, Nigeria) conflict of interest may arise where a government or National Oil Company (NOC) works as regulator, while being a production sharing contract (PSC)/production sharing agreement (PSA) partner. In such cases an independent agency, charged with overseeing the local content policy, is required. This independent local content agency needs to have the power of law to be effective.

Another obstacle to local content initiatives may be presented in the form of bi-lateral trade and investment treaties that the home countries of International Oil Companies (IOCs) seek with the host country, so as to give preferential (to other countries) access to their own (foreign) people and companies. These often promise reciprocal access to the host country's market, which has proven extremely difficult for the developing countries to take up, due to other barriers or more competitive markets. Host countries are often intimidated by the spectre of violations of multilateral treaties and trade agreements, without clearly understanding their options and hence shy away from implementing the stringent controls that are required to enable their own people and companies to grow and thrive. This period of 'incubation' has been used by all successful countries and applies across the spectrum of developing and developed countries.

Getting Down to Work – the Local Content Building Blocks

Developing countries have some common history and situations. Typically, they have some natural resource (oil, gas, minerals, forestry, beaches, agricultural lands, water and so on). Historically, they lacked the capacity to move these from natural resource to revenue stream and have been conditioned to use the same model for resource development:

1. Find an advisor (usually foreign, usually supplied by some aid agency, donor government or multilateral agency), who will:
    a) evaluate the resource;
    b) conduct a market analysis;
    c) scope a development programme.

2. Having identified a potentially viable business opportunity, the government, alone or in concert with a development partner, will then choose a business partner to:
    a) design a detailed development plan;
    b) source and contract for markets and marketing support services including shipping, logistics, marketing, trading, distribution and so on;
    c) source and contract for financing, including possibly using the asset for equity and then raising some debt against this or future revenues;
    d) source and contract engineering, procurement and construction providers;
    e) oversee the design of infrastructure, plants and so on;
    f) oversee the selection of equipment and so on;
    g) procure goods and services to build out the infrastructure, plants and so on;
    h) manage the design and implementation of operations systems, procedures and so on;
    i) manage the construction and commissioning;
    j) hire and train staff to operate the facility;
    k) operate and maintain the facility.

It is only at the very last stages of this process that locals are typically involved, since all the initial work is done at head office, outside of the host country. As this 'head office' work is front end and is typically only required for 'new projects'; there is no opportunity for locals to participate or to capture the knowledge needed to do it. This viscous circle results in these always remaining as head-office skills, never transferred to locals and some developing countries stuck in a position where they are always dependent on external help to develop their resources.

To move forward, countries need, therefore, to develop the building blocks that have the potential to get them to the state where they too can possess those 'head-office' skills. A major deterrent in trying to go after these is the lack of continuity of demand for new projects. Trying to get all the capability and at once, therefore, may not be practical.

A far better approach is to put in place a system of building blocks, so that:

1. the basics are done in country and done well;

2. sustainable skills and services are targeted from the outset;

3. the highest-value capabilities that are immediately accessible are secured;

4. a plan to build on these to go after higher-value but sustainable capabilities is implemented;

5. decisions around what is high value and what is sustainable consider the multiplier effect on the national economy of that capacity;

6. cluster development, both among resource-related services and with non-resource-related sectors, should be sought, to ensure more benefit is captured;

7. collaboration and/or pooling of demand and supply among neighbouring states, perhaps building individual centres of excellence for those goods or services that have limited demand.

One way of thinking about the building blocks, as used in the Trinidad and Tobago (T&T) Framework for Local Value-add, is in terms of developing capacity in people, businesses and the capital markets (Figure 11.3). Moving up the pyramid enhances sustainability through the creation of transferable capability.

PEOPLE

T&T developed skills in support of their development needs, by focusing on the whole education system (curriculum, teacher development, systems, processes

Local Value-Add building blocks:

Human Capability –

- employment, training, development and internationalisation (making globally competitive) of nationals

Enterprise Capability –

- improving the value-add, know-how and innovation capability of local businesses and institutions

Capital markets –

- encouraging the growth and use of the local capital market

Moving up the pyramid enhances sustainability through the creation of transferable capability

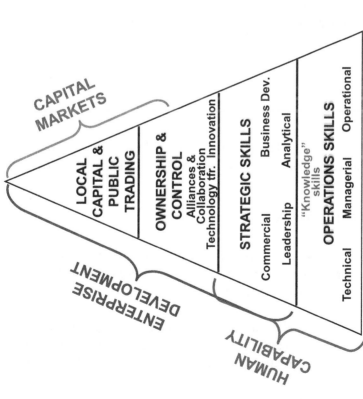

Figure 11.3   Increasing Local Value-add: The Trinidad and Tobago (T&T)Framework.

Source: A.E. Paul, 2003.

and so on) to meet industrial demand. But, not stopping there, the country leveraged the education infrastructure and systems to deliver training to other sectors and the broader community. This was augmented by development programmes that included on-the-job training and overseas assignments.

Recognizing that the technical skills programmes were paying dividends, new and more specialist training programmes were introduced over time. T&T became a leading exporter of technical experts in everything from drilling complex wells to operating sophisticated chemicals plants.

As the industry became more mature and sophisticated, the training moved to degree programmes initially, engineering and geo-sciences then to business/commercial skills. At this time, the focus is on postgraduate research and development, for getting higher value out of the resource.

For a long time though, the commercial skills were ignored. So also were the design engineering skills, even though there were superb operations and maintenance engineers being routinely produced. Some of these technical skills were in the realm of head-office skills – the ones that dealt with front-end planning, design, procurement and so on. Training programmes were augmented by, among other things, creating industry relationships with universities and technical schools, and on-the-job training as part of education programmes. Recognizing that engineering training was very theoretical and limited, changes have been made to get more front-end design capabilities in the engineering programmes.

Strategically, training programmes were dispersed around the country to give better access to the population, with specialized training, which needed on-the-job experience for completeness, being delivered nearer to O&G fields or industrial complexes.

ENTERPRISE DEVELOPMENT

The next step was therefore to raise the technical training to another level, while developing programmes for commercial skills development. These led, naturally, to business capacity development.

Aside from the commercial skills required to analyse, negotiate, procure, access finance, develop strategies, contract and project manage, another significant aspect missing from the local landscape was leadership development.

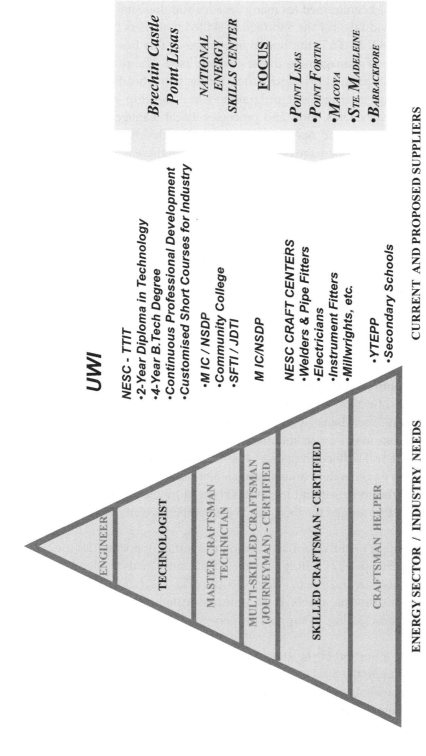

Figure 11.4   Energy Sector Skills Needs and Development – Note: Over time the focus shifts up (higher qualification) or down the pyramid, depending on activities. Note that more jobs are generally available nearer the bottom

Management has been trained for many decades and there has been no lack of competent individuals, yet the shortage of skilled managers is chronic in the developing world. In T&T, the underlying cause of this has been identified as the character of management in the country itself. The practice has been, through colonialism and the branch office, for the home/head office to design strategies, change management programmes and develop and deploy the supporting work systems, tools and processes. Local managers got involved after the management and operations systems were developed and about to be implemented and they were only required to learn these and oversee them.

The competent managers fell into two categories – those who managed the toolkits available to them well and those who can manage in the absence of structured tools and systems. The latter is a far smaller group and the former found their tools increasingly irrelevant as their world changed. This need to lead change applied across the entire spectrum of economic and social activities. Leadership development in the energy sector is able to provide a wider base of national leaders and leadership development systems.

CAPITAL MARKETS

In T&T, access to competitive financing has been a problem for companies trying to get into the O&G business. Even though this sector was generating huge amounts of capital for the local economy, the vast majority was going to the government. Local banks were awash in cash, but the cost of borrowing was very high. Banks took no risk and angel and venture financing were virtually non-existent. Local service companies had to rely on directors' or managers' private wealth to generate working capital. Not understanding the risk of the business, the risk assigned and high rates charged by the banks, resulted in a cost of capital that eroded the local supplier's competitive advantage.

Implementing venture capital schemes, providing opportunities for local investors to participate, including selected niche mature fields for development and small downstream plants, were identified as mechanisms to provide the kind of soft landing in which the unsophisticated investor class can feel comfortable participating, to support the very competent technical class.

Assigning a portion of the state's share in joint ventures of placing some state companies on the local stock market was seen as an effective mechanism for allowing the wealth generated by the industry to be more widely distributed, through the holdings of pension and mutual funds and individual investors.

LEVELING THE PLAYING FIELD

While governments can control the access of local companies to upstream and downstream opportunities, it is the operating companies who determine where expenditure on goods and services go. It is important to emphasize the services sector in O&G, as these represent around 80 per cent of all money spent by operating companies, often far exceeding the amount paid in taxes and royalties to the host government.

Governments often have more than one opportunity to impact how locals are given access to providing services. Aside from policy and legislation, government also contracts with companies to operate and often, in the case of PSAs, has oversight of budgets and the procurement process.

The traditional approach of 'giving preference to local suppliers if the cost, quality and timeliness of delivery of their goods and/or service are of equal quality to the international competitor' has not helped build local capability, as only those who are already globally competitive have a chance of succeeding. There is no opportunity to become competitive if the local is not given a chance to do, learn and improve. For this reason 'local capability development' must play an important part of any implementation strategy.

Companies may use the tendering process to give preference to local suppliers, for instance, by making local content and/or local capacity development a criterion for bid evaluation. The weight of this might be adjusted to reflect how important this capacity is to industry or national development. Foreign contractors are therefore not disadvantaged as they are typically the ones with the ability to build capacity locally.

None of the benefits of the capacity development will be secured unless locals have a fair chance to compete for services. Some companies can be very creative at subverting the intent of sound government policy or regulation. There are many examples of methods used to hinder locals, overstate the local content and so on. The onus is on the government to be alert and knowledgeable.

Some ways of levelling the playing field to support local suppliers include:

- Ensuring that they have access to opportunities in a timely manner (that is, at the same time in a project life cycle as other suppliers – companies doing work at head office, tend to engage home-based suppliers at the front-end stage and only invite local suppliers at the tendering stage, where they are disadvantaged, in terms of the time they have to respond.

• No special treatment – bid documents are often designed to target specific suppliers or groups of suppliers and to cause others to be excluded.

• Unbundling contracts – companies use the 'efficiency of managing less interfaces' as a reason for aggregating services, so that the ability to deliver far outweighs the competence of small, local suppliers. Often, locals are relegated to supplying labour and to competing on cost:
  – this leads to a situation where thin profit margins eliminate the potential for local companies to invest in growth and development, so the ability to compete becomes an illusion;
  – using a work breakdown structure, governments may get to a very granular level of the inputs used in delivering a good or service and cause the contracting to be broken up, so that the strategically important goods or services can be delivered locally and/or by locals; government can view any extra cost, which, through cost recovery, they pay for anyway, as an investment in the future;
  – the supporting capacity development institutions can then be shaped to deliver to the needs, while having a market to serve.

• Timely payment of invoices/reimbursement for goods and services actually provided. Small local businesses have a harder time collecting and, because of higher finance costs locally, end up with reduced profit margins, which stifles their ability to grow and improve.

• Addressing barriers that currently prevent this from happening, such as:
  – bilateral treaties;
  – the cost of local financing;
  – other procurement practices:
    ◦ access to project pipeline and front-end work,
    ◦ tendering and bid evaluation criteria may give credit to local content or capability development (where current local content is limited).

- Creating and maintaining databases of:
  - projects and operations work programmes, including their needs for the provision of goods and services and their scheduling;
  - local suppliers of goods and services;
  - people development programmes and initiatives of the operators and their international contractors, including work permits awarded and the related commitments;
  - business development programmes and initiatives that support the small and medium-sized enterprises (SMEs) in the sector;
  - the status of activities of in-country operators, state-owned companies and agencies and their contractors, including their:
    - LC&P policies, strategies and initiatives,
    - targets, benchmarks and performance metrics,
  - appropriate legislation, regulations and contracts.

- Selecting, from time to time, specific goods or services for focusing the local content, participation and supply capability development efforts. Recognizing that not all projects, activities, goods or services can be addressed immediately nor can they all be delivered or sustained locally, the strategy employed should identify areas of focus and special treatment.

- Implement policies to make specific opportunities or equity in projects available to local private sector companies and investors:
  - acreage management strategies that recognize the differences between land, shallow water and deep water exploration and production, to promote the development of local independent operators and suppliers:
    - local operators utilize and support local services companies and ensure their sustainability. They also continue to produce older fields with lower margins after internationals leave.
  - delineate midstream and downstream projects for favourable local treatment, so as to create and promote opportunities for local, private investment, perhaps alongside state participation in new ventures.

- Typically, the themes of LC&P have focused primarily on the aspects of in-country activity. The oil, gas and minerals industries generate tremendous value in downstream parts of the value chain, which multinational companies (MNCs)/IOCs tend to break up and place outside of the resource-rich country:

- skilful partnering can result in building local capabilities that are essential for the capture of further opportunities in the value chain that are outside of the country (shipping, processing, trading, distribution and so on);
- this potential is not achieved unless there are specific strategies to do so.

- To address the issues of limited capacity and demand, regional collaboration among neighbouring producers, may allow for creation of centres of excellence for training, fabrication, accounting services, maritime services, for example:
  - the countries of the Economic Community of West African states;

- Enshrine LC&P metrics and reporting in ongoing operations, via annual reporting to state company or Ministry, PSC Operating Committee meetings and so on.

- To understand how well they are doing and how they might improve, countries (through governments, civil society or both) can create and support a benchmarking database, into which they submit their local data and allow for analysis and comparison of different operators and subcontractors, in their own country, region or other parts of the world.

Some Pitfalls

Beware of bi-lateral treaties that promise trade and investment, in favour of an 'investment friendly' climate that eliminates local content and work permit requirements.

- companies convince their home governments to put these in place to support their investments.

- companies' home country governments set up treaties that promise more trade and investment, in return the host country agrees not to introduce 'investor unfriendly' legislation and to hold certain projects immune against local content and work permit requirements, for example:

- governments are convinced that these are essential for further, sometimes downstream investments;

- treaties can have the effect of diluting the intent of natural resources laws and/or contracts already in place, including local content and capacity development requirements;

- the state often uses other tools to assist in capacity development and/or local content (such as work permits). Bi-lateral treaties may remove the impact of these;

- a clear linkage must be articulated to those in other government agencies who manage these supporting tools/processes, so that the effective impact of LVA is not diminished;

- country self-confidence and capability to manage challenges with respect to the World Trade Organisation (WTO), bi-laterals, protectionism and internal corruption and so on are important disincentives to some countries aggressively pursuing LVA strategies.

- companies have capacity to either corrupt the process or improve it:
  - their initial requirement is that any provider of goods or services must be competitive in cost and quality. This is not likely to happen at the outset, since there has been no experience or opportunity to learn, far less become competitive. This should not be a reason to exclude local suppliers, rather one for local capacity development through incubation, which can be seen as an investment that is ultimately paid for by the host country, through cost recovery;
  - operating companies are very creative at finding ways around the reporting system, using a whole host of mechanisms and are able, for example, to shift costs around different (national or contract area) cost centres, which the local regulator or tax authority may not have the capacity to track;
  - by the same token, they can also be very good at finding ways to develop the local supply chain, which they do as a matter of routine in their home countries;

- typically, companies will invoke 'international best practice or standard' to ensure that locals are unable to compete, and bring in a preferred international partner;
- in one instance, from Trinidad and Tobago, a British company changed all the requirements for diving contractors to meet North Sea standards, in an environment where the conditions were nowhere near those of the North Sea. Local diving companies that had been operating for more than 30 years were immediately displaced by a British firm, who then promptly hired the local divers and recertified them with minimal training;
- in other instances, health, safety and environment (HSE) standards are applied without any attempt to get the local contractors up to speed. Here, as in the case above, the absence of local standards opens up the process to abuse, as governments are not likely to tell companies that their standards are too high;
- the response is to have the companies work with local training institutions and contractors to build their capacity to be able to participate. Again, the need for targets and penalties cannot be understated;
- companies, having better negotiators than some developing countries, can and do claw-back gains made by the state in upstream licences/contracts, in getting into new or downstream projects. Access to skilful and experienced business analysts is critical here too.

- corrupt government and state company officials and IOC personnel can significantly affect the procurement process and the impact of LVA:
  - governments are not likely to find out about internal company investigations of corrupt or unethical practices in IOCs, unless the joint venture or Operating Agreements are carefully crafted to allow for proper oversight;
  - transparency of contracts, procurement procedures, including tendering and bid awards is critical to mitigate against this impact;
  - lack of skills available to government at start up, when most needed to put ground rules and contracts in place, means that gaps may arise in contracts and procedures;
  - codes of practice for company and government personnel, with penalties for lack of compliance, can assist, if there is an effective policing system.

Some Lessons

Have a very high-level champion:

- Policies and objectives must be clear, consistent and connected to national development goals.

- National goals and objectives must not be negotiable.

Think strategically, act practically:

- Set up a fair and realistic local content policy:
  - adapting it to the existing skills base is a necessary, but not sufficient condition;
  - focus on services.

- Disaggregate service contracts to give locals a chance to compete and build capacity.

- Companies' global or regional procurement strategies mitigate against this (remember 'Offsets'):
  - be selective, based on strategic value to stakeholders.

- Engage early in the life cycle and contract for it (do not make it optional).

- Take a business-like and business-friendly approach:
  - it should be desirable, but achievable.

- Manage the programme of activities in the sector as a portfolio, so that project pace and scheduling enable the maximum opportunity for development of local capabilities and their sustainable utilization.

- Target local capability development by increasing the amount, depth and breadth of in-country activities, so as to enable fuller participation of nationals and enterprises in the value chain:
  - 'do it in country' first;
  - 'do it with locals', will come next.

- Give preference, firstly, to locally owned, controlled and financed enterprises, then to those that demonstrate a clear culture, commitment and capacity for maximizing LVA, participation and capability development, consistent with the country's aspirations and vision.

- Focus on improving local technical and management skills, business know-how, technology, financing, capital market development, and wealth capture and distribution.

- Pick partners who support your strategy and will help deliver it.

- Consider 'regional centres of excellence' to build up critical demand mass:
  - shared services, skills development, infrastructure, equipment.

- Regulate local content and knowledge and technology transfer:
  - it does not work if it's an option to the IOCs and international service companies;
  - with all the goodwill in the host country, head office often has different incentives to use outside contractors;
  - international companies will always seek to minimize their risk and so use suppliers who they know and trust, at the expense of the developing new or even using established local companies;
  - it is human nature for foreign personnel of international companies to have a self-interest in protecting their jobs and privileges as expatriates (these can be quite considerable). The downside may be that they:
    ◦ retain contacts and relationships with their overseas suppliers, keeping them outside the reach and influence of the local government's policies and aspirations, so local supplier use and development may be limited;
    ◦ retard the development of their 'understudy' so that the pace of development of locals, in-house to the IOCs and their major international contractors, may be retarded.

- Beware of bi-lateral treaties that promise trade and investment, in favour of 'investment friendly' climate that eliminates local content and work permit requirements.

- Don't remain static (monitor, change and improve):
  - measure performance, report it, learn from it, build on it;

- set targets based on practical capacity development or usage goals;
- use these targets to determine appropriate metrics and then develop systems and procedures for measuring and reporting that are simple and clear;
- metrics should always be under review, reflecting changing circumstances;
- metrics may be combined, for example, number of man-hours, with specific focus on some types of activities, plus cost of local man-hours vs. foreign.

Analyse, analyse, analyse:

- See Capacity Development as an investment.
  - The question to be asked:
    - is not: 'what can we do with existing local capability?';
    - rather: 'what can we build with existing and projected demand, so as to enhance local capability and allow us to capture more value in the future?
  - identify current capability and gaps;
  - identify areas for focused effort;
  - set targets;
  - build capability, in a strategic and holistic manner;
  - strengthen or build institutions;
  - set and maintain high standards;
  - don't remain static (monitor, change and improve).

CHATHAM HOUSE GOOD-GOVERNANCE IN NATIONAL PETROLEUM COMPANIES

Appendix 2 lists some of the Local Content Best Practice and Recommendations from this project. (http://www.chathamhouse.org.uk/research/eedp/current_projects/good_governance/).

Why All the Fuss and What Does This Mean to Ghana?

When the term LC&P is used, myths and misconceptions arise, causing many to fear the spectre of nationalization and socialism. After all, if we need foreign investment, how can we be speaking of local content? Doesn't this go against bilateral and multilateral trade treaties to which we are party? Won't we run the risk of alienating our trading partners and make Ghana less competitive for foreign investors? Surely, the industry is too risky and requires far too much capital for locals to participate. If we insist on local content, are we creating a type of state support programme that will only benefit some elite businessmen? Isn't this opening us up to corruption, as the selection of local partners can easily be manipulated and, in fact result in higher costs? Will Ghana become another Venezuela or Nigeria?

As is typical, this route seeks out reasons we will fail and focus on them, rather than pursue an approach that focuses on the objectives we are trying to achieve. Aside from avoiding the real meaning and benefit of LC&P, these sentiments play into some significant shortcomings of economic systems in the developing world – weak analytical, negotiating and administrative capability, poor communication with the people of the country and less than brave leadership.

During the period since 2007 Ghana has made significant discoveries of oil and natural gas, the development of which will result in some of the highest rates of growth and levels of activity, production and revenues ever experienced in the country. At the outset of this phase, it was recognized that the experiences of the past had to be drawn upon, such that the country could maximize the benefits from the industry and its activities, for sustainable economic development. It is clear that companies would, for many years, spend more on third-party goods and services than they would pay to the government and country in taxes and royalties. All of these expenditures, amounting to billions of US dollars every year, would, of course be recovered from the benefits of the sale of Ghana's oil, natural gas and derivatives, in the normal course of business operations. Put another way – the people of Ghana, through their resources, would eventually pay for these goods and services.

A major push is being undertaken to capture some of the benefits of these activities, so that the people of Ghana retain as much as possible of the value of their resources in the country. Understanding that the resources would eventually be depleted, the challenge for national development is to use the O&G industry to help create an economy that is self-sustaining. Driven by citizens who understood the industry and are taking the time and effort to analyse it and make suggestions as to how this might best be done, LC&P has become a buzzword associated with the massive oil and natural gas industry growth. Through, first, the Local Content and Participation Policy Framework and then the Policy Implementation Planning Framework, an approach is being devised, requiring the mapping of overlapping areas between national development goals and the industry's goals and activities and crafting strategies to ensure the benefits of these overlaps were realized and maximized. An approach has been suggested that would link LC&P to the wider national development by the creation of capacity to capture value from the sector, while fostering those capacities that support selected sectors that can sustain the local economy beyond O&G.

The model was derived, not from a theoretical, business-school-type approach, but rather from those practical experiences that had worked well for T&T, Norway, Brazil, the UK and other countries. Just as importantly, Ghana's own experiences, where it was recognized opportunities had been missed in the past, will have to be drawn upon. The approach must be rooted deeply in Ghana's own environment, in the existing and expected circumstances, which can be related to similar circumstances in other places and at different times.

Conclusion

For the benefits to be derived, the model has to be pragmatic and desirable to stakeholders, such that the development of the industries is not impaired; yet the model must be taken further by embedding it in legislation, sector policies and contracts. The laws that affect LC&P must be consistently applied. Local companies must be fostered and, once capable, not systematically replaced by foreign ones, in spite of there being no question of the quality or cost of their services or performance, just in the name of open trade! Ghana must see these services and the value they bring as strategic to its national development goals. Huge investments in capacity development by the taxpayers and citizens of Ghana are required and will go down the drain if the doors are opened without restriction, as bilateral and multilateral trade and investment treaties will require. While these are important and valuable, negotiating and implementing them must be thoughtful and consider fully the trade-offs involved. The worst-case scenario is that foreigners will carry out jobs for which these locals are fully capable, yet remain under-employed.

Past periods of natural resources growth have not resulted in the kind of benefit that we all know could have been derived by developing countries in Africa and other parts of the world. This current O&G growth in Ghana and other parts of Africa allows the greatest opportunity we have to make the most of LC&P for national wealth capture and development. Future generations will not judge us well if we do not learn from those failings and move quickly to restore the balance of benefits to give the owners of the resources at least an equal chance.

Appendix 1

OFFSETS

- Common in Military procurement contracts.

- 'Offset' means the entire range of industrial and commercial benefits provided to foreign governments as an inducement or condition to purchase military goods or services, including benefits such as:
  - co-production;
  - licensed production;
  - subcontracting;
  - technology transfer;
  - in-county procurement;
  - marketing and financial assistance; and
  - joint ventures.

(Defense Offsets Disclosure Act of 1999, Pub. L. 106-113, Section 1243(3)).

- There are two types of offsets: direct offsets and indirect offsets:
  - 'Direct offset' is a form of compensation to a purchaser involving goods or services that are directly related to the item being purchased.

- For example, as a condition of a US sale, the contractor may agree to permit the purchaser to produce in its country certain components or subsystems of the item being sold.

- Normally, direct offsets must be performed within a specified period:
  - 'Indirect offset' is a form of compensation to a purchaser involving goods or services that are unrelated to the item being purchased.

- For example, as a condition of a sale the contractor may agree to purchase certain of the customer's manufactured products, agricultural commodities, raw materials or services.

- Indirect offsets may be accomplished over an expected, open-ended period of time.

- Valuation of offsets is an arbitrary process resulting from:
  - the perceived needs of the importing nation; and
  - the negotiating skill of the US supplier.

Appendix 2

CHATHAM HOUSE GOOD-GOVERNANCE IN NATIONAL PETROLEUM COMPANIES – LOCAL CONTENT BEST PRACTICE AND RECOMMENDATIONS[2]

Distortion in the procurement process:

- The risk is that the distortion to the procurement process created by local content requirements could lead to delays and cost increases, and unnecessary tensions between the IOCs and NOC.

- For most countries, the rational solution should be to develop a local supply of some competitive goods and services required by the petroleum industry, but not to demand an indiscriminate use of local suppliers.

- In the case of minimum local content requirements, waivers will often be required because the local capacity is too limited. This may easily create a situation of bureaucratic delays as applications for exemptions are processed. It may also prepare the ground for increased corruption aiming at avoiding such delays.

A neutral and transparent local content policy:

- Some countries such as Norway and UK have neutral organizations (Achilles, Offshore Supplies Office) to facilitate efficiencies in the

---

2   Report On Good Governance of The National Petroleum Sector, April 2007. www. chathamhouse.org.uk/goodgovernance.

supply chain management, and to provide objective information to the oil companies on potential and actual capabilities of suppliers and contractors and to provide suppliers with consistent and up-to-date information on potential contracts and purchasers in the markets.

- In Nigeria, the oil industry has been arguing strongly for a similar system to ensure fairness and transparency, and the Nigerians have accepted the need for an independent body to register and pre-qualify the companies to avoid some of the pitfalls often linked to local content policies.

- Helpful processes may include:
  - the introduction of tools to monitor national content or adherence to labour standards of supplies related to such new developments; and
  - other measures to maximize local/national value creation from local/regional O&G developments.

- The local supply chain will be more successful if combined with exposing the local suppliers to the discipline of the market competition after a relatively short period of protection.

Key questions for local content and development policies:

- Are development requirements clearly specified?

- How is performance measured and by whom?

- Is there a process for adjusting obligations in light of changed circumstance?

- Are development requirements public?

Toolbox for local content (development) commitments:

- Public criteria for development commitments (for example, minimize discretionary support for individuals, competitive processes for gaining support).

- Benefits of development programmes should be public (not private deals for political favourites).

- Special agency (like UK OSO (Offshore Supplies Office) with knowledge of local development to:
  - advise on feasibility of requirements;
  - monitor performance;
  - adjust commitments;
  - report to government and companies involved.

12

Natural Gas as a Source for Downstream Industrial Development

Kerston Coombs

Abstract

This chapter discusses natural gas as a source for downstream industrial development. The significance of natural gas as an energy resource is highlighted. Next, the various activities that natural gas can cover are presented and a schematic diagram of products from natural gas is presented to provide a visual orientation of the multiplicity of benefits that can potentially accrue to a nation with gas as a natural resource. Also explored are gas-based petrochemical projects both in-country and for exports. Within this context, gas contract terms and their associated arrangements are clarified. Moreover, the concept of gas project finance is investigated where the need for a major petrochemical project to pass several tests in order to secure project financing is emphasized. In this regard, the importance of a sound, credible, feasibility report that indicates the viability of the project is underscored. In the same vein, various funding sources are presented against the backdrop of today's credit squeeze in the financial markets. Also discussed is project insurance, an interesting adjunct that can assist in facilitating project financing, and usually provided through multilateral insurance schemes. Finally, for all financed projects light is shed on provisions to guarantee specific performance criteria, covering areas such as managerial, operational and financial performance.

Introduction

Natural gas has for a considerable time been recognized and accepted as an important factor in global energy resources. Its importance has assumed greater prominence in recent years due to its cleaner burning characteristics in comparison with coal and oil. Add to this its role as a raw material for certain petrochemicals such as fertilizers and methanol, and it comes as no surprise that there has been rapid growth in gas-based developments worldwide.

In general, natural gas occurs either as associated gas during oil field operations, or as non-associated gas in gas fields which might also contain some oil condensates. This is an important distinction since a use must be found for the associated gas as soon as crude oil is produced from an oil field. If no immediate use is identified, the gas must either be re-injected into the well or flared resulting in environmental degradation and loss of economic value. With non-associated gas, a decision to produce can be delayed to a later date. Herein lies the major difference between the development of oil projects as against gas projects.

Crude oil is a globally traded commodity which can find a ready market depending on its cost of extraction and the prevailing price in the market. Gas development on the other hand, requires a pre-arranged and dedicated market to which the gas will be delivered be it a power station, petrochemical plant or other user, for example, a cement plant or steel mill. Indeed, the rapid build-up in liquefied natural gas (LNG) projects has only been possible because of long-term (20 years) marketing agreements with the receiving entities.

Project Development

As stated above, natural gas projects can cover a variety of activities. To some extent the type of project activity would depend on the characteristics of the gas. Most natural gas sources consist of methane (between 80 and 90 per cent) with small quantities of ethane, butane, propane and other higher hydrocarbons, as well as trace amounts of sulphur compounds, carbon dioxide, water and other impurities. Accordingly, a distinction can be made in the use of natural gas as a fuel for power generation, which would require minimal pre-treatment, as against its use in the manufacture of petrochemicals, which uses gas as feedstock which requires extensive pre-treatment to remove higher hydrocarbons, sulphur and other impurities.

Natural gas can be processed directly into a wide variety of products which can then be further processed into additional intermediate or final products. The most frequent first step is the production of 'synthesis gas' a mixture of hydrogen, carbon oxides and water which is the precursor of ammonia, methanol, hydrogen, oxo alcohols and other commodities. These intermediate compounds can then be processed further to other chemicals or final consumer products. Examples of these are fertilizers, resins, explosives and plastics.

An outline of examples of the scope and variety of derivatives that can be sourced from natural gas is shown in Figure 12.1 overleaf.

Gas-based Petrochemical Projects

A major concern of the authorities in countries endowed with natural gas resources is to find ways to monetize these resources. If there is a ready market in-country, the most viable options could be to use the gas for power generation and or to produce liquefied petroleum gas (LPG) for cooking. Gas can also be exported directly by pipeline or as liquefied natural gas (LNG). Alternatively, natural gas can be processed into various chemicals for local use or export.

Let us look specifically at the elements which are essential in the development of gas-based petrochemical projects. To begin with, it is assumed that gas is or will be available to the plant site from upstream activity either as associated or non-associated gas. As is usual with any project, the preliminary steps of pre-feasibility, feasibility and detailed market studies must be carried out. These studies must also take into account any comparative or competitive advantages or disadvantages the project might have because of its site location.

However, the most important aspects of the project development are the pricing and other arrangements between the gas supplier and the project company (gas buyer). Very often, these arrangements can determine whether or not the project will be executed and will be successful over time. Satisfactory gas supply arrangements are also vital towards securing adequate project financing on reasonable terms.

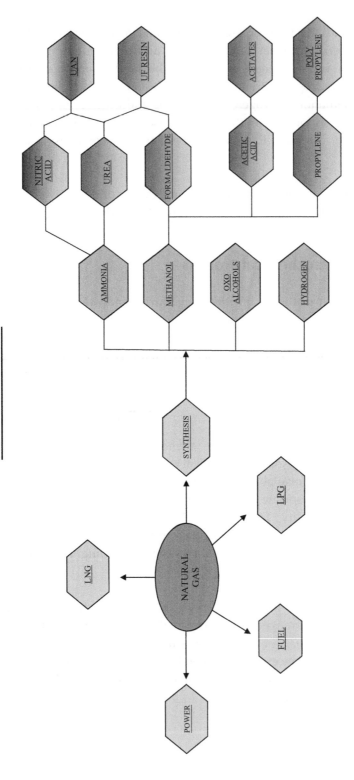

PRODUCTS FROM NATURAL GAS

SELECTED EXAMPLES

Figure 12.1   Products from Natural Gas – Selected Examples

Gas Contract Terms

These arrangements must cover the following items:

- length of contract term (usually 15 to 20 years but not less than duration of financing);

- whether renewable and on what basis;

- whether take or pay and provisions for recovery of unused gas;

- quality of gas and penalties for delivery of non-specification gas;

- contract quantity and provisions for variance in gas take;

- deliverability and equitable treatment during periods of rationing;

- pricing basis, flexibility (price cap and/or floor), price parity with similar projects, escalation provisions;

- reserves situation, whether or not allocated for life of project;

- treatment of previously unspecified charges such as state imposts (Value Added Tax (VAT), royalties and so on).

It is clear from this catalogue of requirements, as outlined previously, that a close and complex relationship exists between the gas supplier and the project company. The gas supplier would wish to see the project succeed since this secures its planned revenue stream. For the project company, a reliable gas supply of agreed quantity and quality is essential for the plant to operate efficiently at maximum output. It is of crucial importance therefore that the lines of communication between these two entities be free, open and frank.

Financing the Project

A major petrochemical project must pass several tests in order to secure project financing; financing in which the majority of the debt portion is based on the strength of the project itself. The starting point is a sound, credible, feasibility report that indicates the project will generate sufficient cash flow to meet the debt servicing obligations as they become due.

However other factors such as the proven reliability of the process technology, the financial strength and successful track record of the project constructor, the ability and experience of the plant management and operations staff, the track record, qualifications and integrity of senior company officials and board members, are also taken into account.

With respect to the gas supply, the potential financiers will critically review all terms of the proposed gas contract and comment on any aspects that they consider inimical to the interest of the project. Of particular interest would be the extent and adequacy of the gas reserves and its deliverability, the competitiveness of the gas price, any take or pay provisions and whether there are any unknown, uncertain or open-ended clauses.

In addition, the soundness and flexibility of the marketing arrangements must be demonstrated. Unless the financiers are fully satisfied with all these arrangements, the approval of the loans will not be forthcoming.

Sources of Financing

Generally, a petrochemical project will be financed by a combination of equity and debt. The debt portion will most likely be financed by a combination of bank loans, export credits, and/or loans from development banks and multilateral agencies. Depending on the robustness of the project, the state of the financial markets and the creditworthiness of the sponsors, a debt to equity ratio of 70:30 or 60:40 would be required.

Given the current state of global financial markets, project financing deals would be particularly challenging in the present environment. In addition, sources of equity funding apart from the sponsors, are now virtually non-existent. Nevertheless, some projects are being financed.

An important adjunct that can assist in facilitating a project financing is project insurance usually provided through multilateral insurance schemes such as provided by the Multilateral Investment Guarantee Agency (MIGA). These schemes provide coverage for political risks such as:

- expropriation;

- breach of contract;

- conflict and war;

- restriction of currency transfer.

The loan agreements will usually provide for payments during construction to be matched to agreed completion targets with time lines. Drawdown of loan payments will be strictly controlled according to an agreed protocol. In addition there will be proposals for dealing with cost overruns. Finally, the financiers will usually assign an engineer to monitor progress during the construction phase and to report the findings. Based on these findings, decisions would be made regarding the release of funds to meet construction costs in a timely manner.

Conclusion

PROJECT PERFORMANCE

All financed projects will usually include provisions to guarantee specific performance criteria. For example: the plant must be completed according to the agreed schedule, achieve its rated design capacity and the products must meet the design quality standards. In addition, the construction must conform to agreed international design requirements and the consumption of raw materials including feedstock and fuel and other utilities must satisfy the design specifications.

Penalties for inadequate performance can range from 'make good' provisions to heavy financial impositions. Finally there is a period, usually 12 to 18 months, during which the construction contractor is responsible for correcting any defects that may arise during the operation of the facility.

Providing everything goes according to plan with little or no obstruction or delays, the project should proceed relatively smoothly and deliver the financial returns expected by the project developers and financiers.

PART IV
Safeguarding Security and the Environment

13

Oil and Gas Issues: The Environment, Health and Safety, and Community Engagement

Samuel Aning

Abstract

Oil and gas (O&G) issues have attracted interest since Ghana discovered oil in 2007. The general discourse has centred on the use to which the oil revenues would be put, rather than on the standards and processes that would ensure a safe, healthy environment and peaceful coexistence with various communities. Ghana has had considerable experience designing the necessary environmental policies that are expected to guarantee safety from activities that may be dangerous to the environment. However, the current activities relating to the oil discovery go far beyond the environment. There are other issues of health and safety standards as well as community engagement and expectations and how to manage all of these in a manner that supports added benefits that petroleum brings to a developing country. In spite of Ghana's good approach to environmental management, there are challenges which results from inexperience in marine ecosystem management as well as enforcing standards of health and safety which are required as part of a growing petroleum industry.

Introduction

O&G is an interesting topic in Ghana. Since the discovery of oil in commercial quantities, many issues have come up for discussion relative to this subject. Issues of environmental concerns, health and relations with various communities dotted along the coast have been raised passionately. This feeling is a natural phenomenon given the challenges O&G activities have engendered whenever there are oil spills and such incidents. Furthermore, the relations with various communities have tended to be volatile depending on how relations are conducted and the impressions given as to benefits accruing to locals. Certainly health and safety issues also come to the fore. Standards of procedure, types of activities and their impacts on both staff and locals are issues of critical importance.

This chapter discusses the above issues relative to Ghana's oil find as a way of contributing to the general discourse on the subject. More importantly, it will help clear the air about some of the issues not often discussed, such as health, safety, environment and community engagement, but which are as equally critical as revenue sharing.

THE ENVIRONMENT: WHY IT IS IMPORTANT

Environmental issues are critical to the development and well-being of any country. However to gain an understanding of the likely effects of petroleum on the environment, it would be helpful to understand the various phases in the petroleum industry. Figure 13.1 below establishes general phases within the petroleum chain from exploration through to production and eventual marketing and distribution. Within each of the above phases, issues of environment are critical hence the need for Ghana to be extremely cautious relative to its O&G find.

Figure 13.1   General Phases within the Petroleum Chain

The oil industry comprises two main parts,[1] the upstream (which covers exploration and production) and downstream (dealing with refining, processing, marketing and distribution). The exploration phase is usually preceded by seismic activities that produce the necessary documents to be studied by the experts (geologists and geophysicists) to guide them in pinpointing the appropriate areas where there might be oil. This is followed by the exploration or prospecting phase where oil companies explore for oil.

---

1   There are references sometimes to mid-stream.

During this process, oil wells are dug to ascertain whether there is oil within the field. If there is no oil, the well is plugged and if there is, production begins.

Closely following production is the processing stage or the transportation stage based on the model that is adopted. In some instances, the oil that is extracted is transported through pipelines to the processing centres. In the case of Ghana, the crude goes into a Floating, Production, Storage and Offloading (FPSO) vessel, and is transported to the markets, where processing distribution and marketing occurs.

Decommissioning takes place after the useful life of an oil field is reached. During this process, the installations and other related equipment used for the production of oil are dismantled.

Environmental issues are important because the activities along the chain as described above can result in some form of environmental damage or degradation. Oil spills have resulted in severe damage to lands and aquatic resources, as well as emissions into the atmosphere that compromise the air quality of the immediate surroundings.

In petroleum operations, some form of emission would be experienced during the different phases of development. This situation occurs irrespective of the location of the activities, that is whether offshore or onshore. Given that Ghana's find is offshore the discussion is largely limited to offshore situations. Carbon dioxide and methane add to the greenhouse effect, a situation which contributes to global warming. Other gases such as nitrogen can lead to over-fertilization and acidification with the consequent negative impact on the marine environment.

Ghana's Environmental Protection Agency (EPA) has undertaken some work in preparation for oil exploration activities in order to be able to manage environmental issues relative to the sector. At the time of oil discovery, the EPA in our opinion did not have the requisite capacity and experience to manage offshore activities effectively. The experience of the Agency was excellent in relation to issues onshore. Although the agency had been using various management techniques to deal with environmental issues, it has activated the use of Strategic Environmental Assessment (SEA) for influencing policies and plans. Consequently, it entered into collaboration with the Norwegian Government and the Netherlands Commission for Environmental Assessment to build capacity for undertaking precautionary assessments for petroleum activities. Three phases have been developed to make the SEA active in Ghana. The phase that relates to current activities in Ghana is the low case, spanning the years 2010–2015. The medium case spans 2015–2020, with the high case beginning from 2020 onwards. It is expected that the EPA would have implemented the SEA over a period of time and would have gained considerable experience with managing environmental impacts of offshore O&G activities. Challenges remain however, given that the Agency still requires critical equipment to work effectively, and needs more practical hands-on experience within the offshore O&G sector.

As part of the requirements for undertaking O&G activities in the Jubilee Field, an Environmental Impact Assessment (EIA) was required of the Jubilee partners. This is a requirement by the EPA as per their guidelines for such activities. An EIA generally outlines the impacts likely to result from any given activity on the environment and assesses whether that activity would be harmful or not. Where the activity is harmful, specific mitigating activities would need to be undertaken, and this has to be documented otherwise the EPA would not grant a permit for that activity to take place.

In a paper presented at the International Network for Environmental Compliance and Enforcement Workshop on Environmental Compliance and Enforcement Indicators in 2003, Wilson Tamakloe, of Ghana's Environmental Protection Agency outlined the challenges facing the Ghanaian environment to include the increasing carbon dioxide emissions, depletion of biodiversity, over-logging of forest cover (it is estimated that 90 per cent has been logged), inadequate water management, coastal zone management and reduction in the availability of agricultural land. He concludes that for the issues of environment to be taken seriously, efforts must be made to *get the politicians to regard the environment as one of the national priority areas*, enact new legislation to reflect the current trend of events and support effective environmental regulation by making enough resources available for capacity building and environmental management.

The Challenge of Health and Safety

All over the world, the O&G industry has very high standards for health and safety. Since the discovery of oil in Ghana in 2007, the main discussions have centred on the use to which the oil revenues should be put without the consideration of other equally important aspects of the find. One of these aspects regarded as being critical is the challenge of health and safety. To begin with, Ghana as a country has had issues with the culture of maintenance that an effective health and safety regime requires. It is also a fact that, generally, health and safety is not treated as an issue of importance in many organizations, and it is easy to spot people working on different building sites without the requisite hard hats and safety equipment that are required as standard. Furthermore, the institutional mechanisms that should support the culture of health and safety tend to be weak. No wonder a series of serious accidents have occurred at various work sites within the country.[2] For most of these accidents, it was clear that the required safety precautions and standards were not adhered to.

The challenge of health and safety in Ghana is centred on the above issues, given the recognition that O&G activities have significant potential for health hazards. For a country such as Ghana that is new to the oil industry, ensuring the integrity of installations to be able to perform the activities that they are certified for, as well as ensuring their protection from encroachment, attack or any form of sabotage is important.

In order to do this and do so well, the necessary standards and guidelines would have to be developed and adhered to as well as the regular monitoring and evaluation by outside agencies to ensure compliance with the standards. It would mean that certain hazardous substances cannot be used because they would be injurious to health and the environment. These substances would have to be clearly listed and the operators within the industry informed to maintain standards relative to that.

The EPA in Ghana has already developed some guidelines to mainstream issues of health and safety into O&G operations. The key aim is to prevent people from being harmed, becoming ill or the environment being affected in an adverse manner. In the long term the idea is to take precautionary measures against all forms of injuries and provide an environment that does not affect Ghanaians in any adverse manner.

While all of the above if well implemented would be beneficial to the country, the difficulty is developing a culture that is supportive of health and safety and investing in institutions with the mandate to undertake effective implementation of the guidelines. While the EPA is working with a number of international institutions and agencies, it must be a matter of urgency that

---

2   Serious accidents have occurred at the Tema Oil Refinery (January 19, 2010) and well as the Tema Harbour because the required precautionary measures were not put in place.

it is adequately supported to meet the challenges that offshore O&G activities present. The right equipment to undertake regular and periodic sampling, and visits and inspections to see how the directives are being complied with is critical. The development of systems for emergency response and effective coordination are equally important.

At this early stage in the development of the industry, it is necessary to have a list of the risks that could be encountered to ensure effective preparation against any eventualities. In other countries, there are legislations that govern all identified risks relating to health and safety. Ghana's laws on this would need to be reviewed with the individual at the centre. Some of the key areas that a health and safety policy and legislation would need to cover in detail include:

- Slips, trips and falls: the main aim is to prevent injury due to slips and falls and the need to identify the hazards and control the risks they present.

- Hazardous substances: the idea is to ensure the control of substances which are hazardous to health. Workers would need to be given the right protective clothing, nose guards and other personal protective equipment where necessary.

- Falls from height: this would be a protective guideline to ensure that workers are given the necessary tools of the trade and training to work at certain heights, and in a manner that does not endanger them.

- Noise: this would ensure that workers work in an atmosphere that is congenial and where there is noise pollution it is controlled or that the workers are given the necessary ear guards to protect their ears from damage.

- Machinery and equipment: this would ensure that workers are trained to handle equipment they are expected to work with. This would minimize injury resulting from lack of experience.

However, with O&G activities there is much more required. Because O&G are highly combustible substances, there are standards that have to be maintained with respect to some of the following:

- flammable and combustible substances;

- storage and handling of liquefied petroleum gas;

- hazardous waste operations and emergency response;

- use of protective equipment;

- eye, face and respiratory protection;

- fire protection;

- pipeline safety.

The above are but a few of the areas for consideration with respect to safety for offshore O&G activities. In relation to this, the International Petroleum Industry Environmental Conservation Association (IPIECA) and the International Association of Oil and Gas Producers (IAOGP) are of the opinion that, apart from what national legislation might lay down, it is important for all companies within the petroleum industry to institute management systems to achieving continuous improvement in business performance. This is also related to health and safety, where the health status of employees is assessed on a continuing basis to ensure maximum output. Where possible, this should be extended to surrounding communities.

The two groups have recommended a traffic light system of assessment that supports continuing assessment and warns of issues to be taken into consideration. This is reproduced in Figure 13.2.

Clearly, where the system is not in place and under development, there is cause for worry and apprehension. Additionally, the two organizations give an outline of the issues to consider in the development of an effective health management system. These include:

- health risk assessment and planning;

- industrial hygiene and control of workplace exposures;

- medical emergency management;

Level 4	System to capture and report data is in place and implemented. System sustained and supported by an ongoing improvement process.

Level 3	System to capture and report data is in place and implemented. System functioning, system procedures documented and results being measured.

Level 2	System to capture and report data is in place but not fully implemented and embedded.

Level 1	System to capture data is under development.

Figure 13.2   Traffic Light System of Assessment

- management of ill-health in the workplace;

- fitness for task assessment and health surveillance;

- health impact assessment; and

- public health interface and promotion of good health.

In addition to the above performance indicators, there is the need to develop assessment indicators to tell an evaluator or the organization how well they are doing.

In the case of some of the major oil-producing companies, some standard approaches have been adopted that support their health and safety culture, such as Shell which has made extensive use of the Hazards and Effects Management Process (HEMP) consisting of four steps, mainly:

- identification of hazards within the operational process;

- assessment of how important the hazards are;

- management of the hazards; and

- recovery if hazards are released.

ExxonMobil has a safety structure that is hinged on 11 main elements with the employees, communities and those related to their operations at the centre. These include the following:

- management, leadership, commitment and accountability;

- risk assessment and management;

- facilities design and construction;

- information and documentation;

- personnel and training;

- operations and maintenance;

- management of change;

- third-party services;

- accident investigation and analysis;

- community awareness and emergency preparedness; and

- operations and integrity assessment and improvements.

Many organizations claim to believe in safety and commitment by management to identify hazards ensure their elimination and control and deal with unsafe work practices.

All of the above discussions have centred on the need for regulation not only to ensure that the individual, installations, processes and systems are safe, but also the need to institute a culture that supports the institution of safety systems and standards. It is important to hold organizations to the statements they make so that they do not become mere empty words but are effectively enforced.

COMMUNITY ENGAGEMENT

Community engagement is an important requirement for O&G activities if operations are to be conducted in a peaceful manner. Development planning is expected to be participatory in implementation. It is no longer possible to pay lip service to this concept, especially with the level of interest shown by communities.

The Western Region of Ghana, where the oil activities and operations are currently ongoing, was considered a peaceful place prior to the oil find. It is still considered peaceful although there are concerns that this may not remain so for long without some form of community intervention to make a difference.

Many challenges that the Western Region and the Sekondi-Takoradi metropolis have experienced in recent times have been attributed to the discovery of O&G. Some of the challenges residents in the metropolis list include:

- increasing traffic congestion and travel time;

- increasing crime and insecurity;

- lack of opportunity for jobs;

- high rents;

- increasing influx of people.

All of the above give a sense of insecurity to many residents of the Western Region. Within the smaller communities, there have been complaints about the influx of people adversely affecting community cohesion. Furthermore, the six coastal communities have expressed fears that in the event of any environmental disaster, their communities would be most affected and yet they have not been involved in any early warning mechanisms or systems, nor have they been adequately trained or integrated into the petroleum business.

The experience of the people of the Western Region since the discovery of oil has been one of promises that their youth would find jobs and would be trained without any concrete hopes or timeframe as to when this would materialize.

Since 2007, large tracts of land have been sold. Some people and companies have bought lands because owning large tracts has been seen as an issue of economic importance and also for long-term investment. The perception has been that since there would be jobs, new development and other related infrastructure, landowners would benefit greatly from land sales or partnerships in new business ventures. Under normal circumstances, this would be a good investment. However the reality of the size of the purchases gives cause for worry.

To begin with, the sizes of the lands sold are very large.[3] Some of the lands sold include villages and seafront areas that, when fully developed, would deprive natives of their lands and access to sea to engage in their economic activities. It is believed that there could be some agitations in communities with large youth populations who may come out of school within a short time of say two to three years and find that they have no lands for farming. If they are not integrated into any activity of economic importance, there could be problems with the safety of installations and personnel of companies who may become primary targets for their frustrations.

The Case for Community Engagement in the Western Region

The case for community engagement has been strengthened by the various calls by community groups for inclusion in issues concerning O&G and the direct request by the chiefs of the Western Region for a fair quantum of the proceeds to be given for development.

The increasing awareness and understanding by local communities of their needs, roles and capacities, interests and views relative to the O&G development is becoming prevalent in Ghana. The kind of awareness shown by the people of the Western Region has had to do with the realization that the region has had little benefit from the mining industry. They have complained that the conditions of their roads are deplorable, linkage within the region very poor and opportunities for their young people to integrate into the economy very slim. One of the traditional rulers of the region (Nana Abuna V) has complained that despite the resources of the region such as gold and diamonds, the region does not benefit proportionally when the national cake is shared. These fears are real

---

3   For example, an Accra based investment firm has acquired land in Princess Town that seems to
     be a source of conflict among the families that sold the land. There have been other purchases
     by government agencies and private energy firms.

for many communities. There is increasing concern about security, especially when Niger Delta boys were purported to have been brought to the region for training. Despite government assurances, these concerns remain.

Some of these concerns have been adequately addressed by the government agencies responsible for the environment for instance. The oil companies were asked to undertake an EIA prior to the commencement of activities. Discussions with residents have shown that although the EIA was undertaken, there was pressure to undertake the activities anyway because of the perceived benefits to the country should the activity take place. Besides, the EPA may not have had all the relevant expertise with respect to assessing impacts on the marine environment. For instance, it is unclear whether there were any questions raised regarding the use of a single hull FPSO for the Jubilee Field. It is interesting to note that within Europe, there was no single hull FPSO vessel at the time the EIA for the Jubilee Field was being developed for approval by EPA of Ghana. Communities have expressed concern that the same standard should have been applied.

While it is true that not all issues or concerns may have been addressed in the EIA, it is nevertheless an issue of significant importance to continue the engagement with a view to addressing new issues and concerns and finding solutions to them jointly.

Recommendations for Consideration

The recommendations for consideration in any community relations system have been made on the basis of the CASA Model.[4] The model places the community at the centre of the issues relative to oil and gas. The model has been reproduced in Figure 13.3.

The model operates on the basis that the community is at the centre of the engagement process and collaborates with local authorities on issues of health, safety, environment and incident reporting. This relationship is such that the community is allowed to contribute to early warning systems also with the oil companies through the joint committee that may be established for projects and other related development and corporate social projects.

---

4   The CASA Model was developed by two of the Fellows of the Centre for Advanced Strategic Analysis, Prof K. Appiah-Adu, a professor of Business Management at Central University, and Sam Aning, a Senior Lecturer in Contemporary Issues at the Methodist University, Ghana.

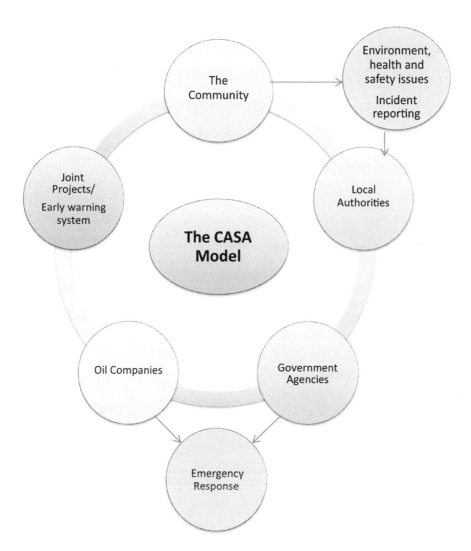

Figure 13.3   CASA Model

Where the issue is of a nature that relates to emergencies, the oil companies and the relevant government agencies are expected to work together to handle it. At all times, however, the community is kept apprised of what is happening because the people remain within the loop as outlined above.

It is believed that this model would foster harmonious relations between communities, local authorities and the O&G companies operating in the Western Region.

14

Oil and Gas Security Issues

Samuel Aning

Abstract

Ghana has been touted as a peaceful country within a region that has seen a lot of conflict. This notwithstanding, there are a number of security issues that must be taken into account where oil and gas (O&G) are concerned. Until the discovery of oil in 2007, Sekondi-Takoradi, the capital of the Western Region was considered a 'sleepy town'. It was largely seen as peaceful. However the dynamics are changing with increasing influx of people and growing crime that could give cause for worry. Furthermore, the Gulf of Guinea is registering increasing piracy activities, the use of the region as transit point for the transfer of cocaine and other harmful substances and other emerging threats. Aligned to this is the insecurity in some of the countries in the region and the likely spillover effects if the security agencies are unable to cope. The way forward is to engage all actors, design early warning systems and ensure that safety and security of personnel and installations of oil companies, safety of communities and engagement with fishermen who claim their fishing grounds have been taken over. More importantly, Ghana would need to develop excellent relations between the various security sector institutions and local communities for effective response to emergencies should they occur.

Introduction: Oil and Security

The discovery of O&G in Ghana in 2007 sparked a lot of interest, particularly in Parliament and in the media. This was occasioned partly by the fact that the Ghana National Petroleum Corporation (GNPC) had done so much in the past to find oil without success and partly because of the low number of barrels produced daily from the Saltpond offshore oil field.

These two factors notwithstanding, there was hope that this could be true, given attestations by the staff of the GNPC and its partners Tullow Oil and Kosmos Energy. The government of the day then established a team to work towards preparing the grounds for Ghana to maximize benefits from the oil find. One of the sub-teams that worked towards ensuring a right atmosphere was the security team.

O&G issues raise security concerns when discussed for obvious reasons. The dependence on oil the world over and its impact on the economy is an important factor. Ghana's oil happens to be offshore and given what has been seen in other countries, particularly Nigeria, it was prudent to begin to think about developing an environment that would engender the development of O&G in a manner that is safe and secure. Furthermore, it is a well-known fact that the West Africa region, having seen so much strife within the last 20 years, is awash with small arms and light weapons that could significantly endanger access to O&G in an environment that may not be secure. Additionally, the Government of Ghana has traditionally in the opinion of the writers not seen offshore activities as a serious threat to the security of the state. Consequently, the Ghana Armed Forces (particularly the Navy) had been severely starved of critical equipment for patrol and other duties in Ghana's Exclusive Economic Zone (EEZ). All of the above informed the work of the security committee towards working holistically to ensuring an environment in which O&G activities could be effectively pursued.

We believe, however, that in the aftermath of the oil find, there was more interest in how many jobs the O&G activities would create and how much revenue would accrue to the Government rather than the security of the resource in the first place. Discussions on security therefore seemed to have been downplayed and subordinated to other critical considerations. Unless the right thing is done, it would be difficult to maximize benefits if the security issues relative to O&G are not considered with the same importance given to transparency, revenue sharing and development issues that have formed the basis of the discussions in the country.

Additionally, the development partners have tended to focus on areas other than security as well helping to drive the interest and agenda away from this critical issue. This chapter discusses the security challenges relative to the O&G find and makes propositions as to issues for implementation, going forward. It is believed that the current emphasis on transparency, accountability and openness in revenue and expenditure while good, should also elicit similar interest in the security of O&G.

Security Issues within the Gulf of Guinea

The Gulf of Guinea is that part of the Atlantic Ocean, spanning a number of countries in West Africa including Nigeria, Cameroon, Angola, Ghana, Cote d'Ivoire, Liberia, and Sierra Leone among others. This area within the West Africa region is a major shipping lane, has significant economic resources in terms of fish and hydrocarbons and has also seen a lot of activity in terms of civil wars, drugs trafficking and other related crimes.

Although Africa does not produce cocaine, its western part has seen large quantities of drugs seizures lately.[1] The United Nations Office on Drugs and Crime is supportive of this view and has documented seizures of drugs that are indicative of this problem.[2] This is further supported by Gail Wannenburg (2005) when he states that West Africa is seen as an example of human tragedy, characterized by grand corruption, civil wars and leaders who have sunk their countries into the bottomless pit of poverty and underdevelopment.

Overall security within the Gulf of Guinea tends to be weak, thereby allowing illegal activities. Within the gulf, naval forces are not adequately resourced, making policing extremely difficult. Nigeria is estimated to be the only country within the region with the requisite logistics to police its territorial waters and EEZ with some measure of effectiveness. This is, however, undermined by the concentration of internal security challenges and activities within the Delta region.

Nicolas Cook and Liana Sun Wyler[3] believe that West African countries in particular have regional vulnerabilities that make cocaine trafficking attractive to criminal gangs owing to poor communications, porous borders, ineffective maritime, air and land surveillance, weak institutions, poverty and unemployment. While all of this is true, there are other indicators that make this region especially vulnerable. The civil wars and large unoccupied spaces as well as the inability to establish early warning systems, all add up to making the region especially vulnerable.

Other specific challenges that the region faces include:

---

1   See UNODC situation report 2007.which gives specifics for drug seizures within the region. www.unodc.org/pdf/research/wdr07/WDR_2007.pdf Last accessed June 13, 2011.
2   Ibid.
3   See http://www.fas.org/sgp/crs/row/R40838.pdf. Last accessed February 6, 2012.

ILLEGAL FISHING

The Gulf of Guinea is reputed to be the sixth largest fishing ground in the world with all kinds of fish stocks. It has however seen poaching and over-fishing in some areas because of poor policing. Pair trawling and fishing with lights are especially problematic within Ghanaian waters and have caused some measure of disaffection among fishermen.

It has been estimated that illegal fishing by Asian and European vessels costs the region an amount of about $350 million annually and seriously affects fishstocks, denies local populations of food supplies and thereby affects the local economies as they are forced to import fish at high cost to supplement protein needs.[4]

PIRACY

Piracy has become an issue of concern within the Gulf of Guinea. The region is suspected to have seen serious acts of piracy, which largely occur when ships are at anchorage within the harbours and territorial waters. Reported acts of piracy have been documented at the International Maritime Organisation sites. In fact, it is believed that 'piracy and robbery are now so well established as to represent a considerable issue for Nigeria, Cameroon and Angola. In 2009, the International Maritime Organisation (IMO) substantiated 28 attacks in their waters but believes the real figure to be twice that'.[5]

Given that the Gulf of Guinea is a major shipping lane and is seeing increasing activities in terms of fishing and oil exploration, such activities could significantly affect the maritime activities and overall economic development that is sea based. While Nigeria's waters are reputed to have the highest number of attacks, an otherwise peaceful Ghana has also seen some piracy activities as evidenced in the map of 2009 shown in Figure 14.1.

As is evidenced from the above map, the attack on the Nord Express was quite close to the Jubilee oil fields and should be a source of worry for Ghana which is a newcomer to the O&G business.

---

4   See http://www.nps.edu/Academics/centers/ccc/publications/OnlineJournal/2007/Jan/gilpin Jan07.html. Last accessed January 26, 2012.
5   See http://www.defenceiq.com/naval-and-maritime-defence/articles/piracy-storm-brews-in-west-africa-gulf-of-guinea-u. Last accessed January 26, 2012.

Figure 14.1   Nord Express

DRUG TRAFFICKING

The Gulf of Guinea is also seen as a major drugs trafficking route linking South America and Europe. The UK Serious Organised Crime Agency (SOCA) believes that source countries for cocaine such as Colombia, Venezuela and Brazil use West Africa's Gulf of Guinea as transit points. Key countries which are used by these criminal gangs include Guinea, Guinea Bissau, Togo and Ghana.[6]

SOCA further believes that an arrangement between the South American and West African criminal gangs[7] ensures that one-third of the drugs are used as payment for their protection and logistical support, culminating in a sophisticated system where air couriers and drops from airplanes are made as well as the use of fishing vessels. The difficulty for Gulf of Guinea states would be that in an era of declining fish stocks and greater regulation of fishing (including the banning of the use of lights for night fishing), fishermen may find that being couriers for drug lords tends to be more lucrative than fishing.

David Mudridge (2010) writes about a criminal super-highway that fuses Colombian cocaine with other illegal activities such as weapons and diamonds

---

6   P42 of UK Threat Assessment of Organised Crime (2009/10).
7   SOCA lists countries such as Ghana, Nigeria, Sierra Leone and Gambia as key countries where South American druglords have established links. Interestingly, all these countries are former colonies which still have strong business and other ties to UK.

smuggling through North and West Africa known as Highway 10. He believes that this super highway holds great usage for terror organizations and criminals.

OIL THEFT

The theft of oil is another security challenge that the Gulf of Guinea states would have to deal with. The country with the greatest challenge within the region is Nigeria which has been battling some of its citizens demanding resources from oil wealth. These organized groups have their own barges and sometimes puncture pipe lines to siphon oil to finance their activities. It is a source of worry for security agencies that such activities would find expression in the theft of oil on an even larger scale. It is estimated that oil theft costs the region about $3 billion each year, with Nigeria losing as much as 600,000 barrels of oil daily.[8]

Oil and Gas Security Challenges and Implications for Ghana

It has been established that petroleum presents, for any country, a number of security challenges which would need to be effectively managed if the resource is to be beneficial to the country. The key security challenges that are likely to face the country include the following:

ILLEGAL MIGRATION

This is concerned with the movement of people across national borders in a manner that is usually in breach of national laws. In Ghana's case, there would be influx of people who may believe, rightly or wrongly, that the oil find means lots of jobs. This would become the attractive factor for them to come into the country in the vain hope of finding work. Citizens of the Economic Community for West African States (ECOWAS) are allowed free movement within the region without the need for entry visas. What is likely to happen is that they would come in and refuse to go back to their countries and then become illegal migrants after the mandatory 90-day period to which they are entitled. After a period of time during which they become fluent in the local languages and assume Ghanaian names, they could then become permanent citizens.

8　See http://dailytimes.com.ng/article/n37tn-lost-yearly-illegal-bunkering-nigeria. Last accessed 12 September 2011.

Although this is likely to become more difficult to implement overtime because Ghana is implementing a national identification system, those illegal migrants who come in early enough would be able to beat the system due to the slow process of implementation. The bigger challenge though would come from persons not from ECOWAS. The likelihood of coming in without the necessary documentation would be high and an underground business could develop around illegal migration linked to jobs in the O&G industry. When these immigrants are especially low skilled and have no jobs whatsoever, the tendency to turn to crime would become high indeed.

HUMAN TRAFFICKING

Human trafficking is the movement of people by means of force, fraud or deception with the aim of exploiting them. Already there are incidents of such trafficking in the sub-region and Ghana. Businesses that develop within the precincts of the oil find and ancillary businesses that may develop would definitely require cheap labour.

ARMS TRAFFICKING

Arms trafficking is the illegal movement of arms and ammunition across national borders for profit. The West Africa sub-region is awash with small arms and light weapons given the civil wars and conflicts that have plagued the region in the past. The danger to Ghana is that it could be targeted as a destination for a number of these small arms where drug lords, attracted by the lure of oil money, would seek to consolidate their power or create new bases. Furthermore, these arms could support small groups of people who may wish to attack installations as an expression of their dissatisfaction with revenue management or their exclusion from participation in O&G activities.

DRUG TRAFFICKING

This is the transportation of illegal drugs across national borders with the aim of making profits in other countries. Where the O&G industries flourish, the drug lords target oil workers who are reputed to have ready income to expend when they come ashore from the oil rigs. The West Africa sub-region already has a reputation of being a haven for drug lords and this would be exacerbated when oil revenue starts pouring into the country.

POLLUTION

Pollution is the introduction of contaminants into a given environment that causes harm, instability or discomfort to the ecosystem and those that depend on it. Pollution can sometimes be trans-boundary in nature and affect the health of people. The oil industry makes use of processes and chemicals which have the capacity to pollute the environment and affect livelihood. In the case of Ghana, the oil is offshore and this makes the risk of pollution especially bad for the marine environment upon which many coastal communities are dependent. While the country has the necessary public institutions (Ministry of Environment, Science and Technology and EPA) to deal with pollution, the greatest fear is that they have a lot to learn about the O&G industry to be able to monitor the marine environment effectively.

CONFLICTS

O&G activities can lead to conflicts with different groups of people. In Ghana, conflicts are likely to arise from misunderstanding with local people, especially fishermen. Locals at a point in time may complain when they are not trained to have opportunities within the industry. The reference to local content and the media attention it has generated has been with respect to opportunities for locals. Discussions with fishermen and civil society organisations in the Western Region in February 2011 showed their disaffection with the petroleum sector, as they complained that they were not allowed to fish in areas that they would ordinarily have fished because of the O&G business. Conflicts over fishing grounds have occurred, with fishermen fishing close to the oil rigs in spite of warnings to them not to do so. The fishermen contend that the areas where O&G activities are taking place are their best fishing grounds. With the ban on the use of light fishing, their catch has been reduced and has affected business within the industry with fishmongers and other personalities within the chain becoming virtually unemployed.

LAND

There have been instances of seeming conflict and youth radicalization with reference to jobs and large-scale land acquisitions which have the capacity to affect access to land in future for young people. The Western Region has seen large-scale land sales to individuals and organizations, with locals not having direct access. While this may not seem to be a problem now, it could become a major security issue if not controlled.

PIRACY

This has been discussed already within the context of regional security within the Gulf of Guinea. However, for Ghana, this is especially worrying given that such incidents occur within the port vicinity. Discussions with the security services indicate that the practice is on the ascendancy with most of the attacks being made in the dead of the night during periods when ships and supply vessels are at anchor or at berth.[9]

Security Challenges for the Western Region of Ghana

The discovery of oil offshore in Ghana's Western Region naturally led to great expectations of wealth, jobs and opportunities led by locals. More importantly, prominent chiefs leading significant numbers of ethnic Ghanaians emerged to lay claim to the oil seeing that it had the potential to bring in some financial benefits.

An assessment of the security of the region in the course of this study indicated that the region has a very calm outlook. Discussions with residents and key personalities indicate that beneath the calm veneer, there are undercurrents that have the capacity to affect the overall security of the region if not effectively handled.

Various articles have identified the key risks to include the porosity of the borders, smuggling, illegal mining and fishing, drugs, prostitution and petty crime. While no evidence of direct youth radicalization was found, many residents alluded to this and there have been reports of youth organizing to make demands for inclusion in the sector. There have also been reports of Niger Delta Youth activities within the region.

The above notwithstanding, the Western Region is seen as a place with low crime rates. This is, however, likely to change given the influx of all manner of persons and the proximity of the region to Ivory Coast, which has experienced rebel activity with the resultant impact being faced in the Western Region of Ghana. Writing on O&G in Ghana, Stephen Yeboah (2010)

---

9 A July 6, 2011 *Daily Graphic* front page story on robbers raiding a ship centred on theft of paints from a supply vessel meant for offshore maintenance work. The story alluded to an earlier attack and stated that weapons were used in this attack and was supported by small canoes powered by motors.

has indicated that Ghana needs to be more pro-active than merely wasting money on equipping security agencies in fighting rebel movements and groups. Security should not be mistaken only to be the provision of training for the security agencies to contain attacks in offshore and onshore regions. Neither is it the acquisition of speed boats for the Navy to operate on the Continental Shelf and sophisticated weapons for the police and military for enforcement. Ideally, it is what calls for these actions that need urgent attention. There is the need to consider first the factors that fuel discords in oil-producing regions and countries before engaging the services of the security agencies.

Challenges facing the region would include the following:

CRIME

The statistics on crime for the region since 2003 is presented in Table 14.1 opposite.

It is believed that, even though the crimes shown in the table above are representative of what has plagued the region all these years, there are new security challenges that would emerge within the region to confront the police and other security agencies for which they must be adequately prepared.

The Western Region is endowed with a variety of natural resources, including timber, gold and diamonds, among others. As a result the region has always been a place of attraction to all sorts of migrants seeking a better life. In early 2011, there were reports of Chinese illegal miners in the country, working with Ghanaian collaborators.[10] Further reports of this nature are just a matter of time if the issue is not recognized and steps taken to curb their recurrence. Trends in other countries are that when people come into a region and cannot get jobs they turn to crime. Although the Western Region is largely cosmopolitan in many ways, it is likely that there would be a clash of cultures in areas where the people have lived in smaller communities without much interaction with those from outside of their region.

---

10 See http://af.reuters.com/article/investingNews/idAFJOE72D0DS20110314 and http://www. ghanaweb.com/GhanaHomePage/NewsArchive/artikel.php?ID=199666. Last accessed January 24, 2012.

Table 14.1   Crime Statistics in the Western Region of Ghana

Offences	2003	2004	2005	2006	2007	2008	2009	2010
Murder	47	32	48	47	49	60	58	42
Attempted Murder	5	7	12	9	10	3	9	10
Manslaughter	0	0	0	1	0	0	0	0
Threatening	1425	1440	1641	1936	1886	1928	2354	2318
Causing Harm	249	221	322	251	280	310	396	421
Assault	5737	6042	6570	6579	6313	6710	7459	7732
Robbery	28	22	25	39	31	40	25	25
Stealing	3706	3641	4652	4580	4728	5112	5537	4720
Fraud	679	865	1160	1107	1109	1311	1556	1825
Unlawful Entry	35	29	45	40	76	55	44	188
Causing Damage	597	549	582	615	687	677	867	836
Dishonestly Receiving	7	2	2	1	4	0	0	72
Abortion	26	19	21	42	49	43	54	42
Rape	63	22	37	51	91	49	48	41
Defilement	189	145	181	273	261	229	282	271
Possessing Dangerous Drugs	5	0	4	0	17	0	0	0
Possessing Indian Hemp	54	30	14	37	62	103	64	40
Abduction	67	85	88	115	117	108	78	0
Extortion	0	1	0	0	2	0	0	0
Forgery	5	9	19	16	4	14	9	60
Falsification of Accounts	2	0	0	0	0	0	0	0
Smuggling	0	0	0	1	0	0	0	23
Possessing Cocaine	0	7	8	14	8	6	0	0
Possessing Heroin	0	7	4	10	6	2	0	2
Counterfeiting	0	1	1	7	19	19	19	23
Issuing False Cheques	2	11	3	18	25	30	92	58
Child Stealing	3	3	1	12	31	4	1	2
Illegal Gold Mining	0	2	0	0	1	3	19	44
Other Offences	1581	1956	1603	2525	2568	2543	3542	2256
Total	**14,512**	**15,148**	**17,043**	**18,326**	**18,434**	**19,359**	**22,513**	**21053**

Source: Ghana Police Service (June, 2011).

LAND SALES/LAND USE

Land ownership in Ghana has always been an issue of great concern often finding expression in the use of landguards[11] to protect land and violence. Land is not readily sold but is passed on from generation to generation. Consequently, the sale of large tracts of land in a manner that is not managed (since oil discovery) has been a source of worry to many citizens. The expectations of massive wealth accruing to the region have fuelled this action. Some representatives of families who hold these lands in trust for and on behalf of communities sometimes sell off large tracts for private gain. When that happens, it leads to problems as members of the family who have other uses of the areas sold make demands and threaten those who have already purchased the land. Where the pressure on the land is great, there are multiple sales of the same parcel of land leading to conflict. The Western Region is likely to face this phenomenon given the rush to purchase land and the large tracts of land already sold to private organizations.

The potential danger that this is likely to create is that the younger generation will not have access to land for use, either as collateral for investment or development of a primary home. Without work and without land, they would turn militant, making demands that cannot be met. The installations relative to the sector would then become targets of their anger.

RISING MILITANCY AMONG THE YOUTH

There have been a number of reports of militancy within the Western Region, some of which have been documented with others being dismissed as merely speculative. However, Ampah[12] writing on these issues makes reference to a group calling itself the Cape Militia which is active in the coastal towns of Cape Three Points, Busua, Dixcove, Princess Town, Miema, Axim, through to Alomatuope.

There is a greater source of worry for residents who have come to know that former Niger Delta fighters from Nigeria are active within the region. Given that the maritime coastline of Ghana has seen some action with respect to piracy, this is adding to the fears of locals that security should be handled

---

11 Land guards are private persons hired to protect purchased land from being encroached upon, or securing it for one party in the case of multiple sale.

12 http://www.theghanaianjournal.com/2010/10/20/oil-war-looms-in-ghana/. Last accessed May 12, 2012.

properly to avert recurrence of experiences common to other oil-producing nations in Africa.

Influx of Refugees

Ghana as a country is not new to hosting refugees. However, the current situation in La Cote d'Ivoire has and continues to remain a security problem for Ghana and the Western Region. It is estimated that about 5,000 refugees from La Cote d'Ivoire crossed into Ghana during the initial inflows into the country. A number of the refugees were housed in camps although some have chosen to settle in the metropolitan capital, Sekondi-Takoradi. As at April 2011, there were over 5,000 refugees from Ivory Coast in Ghana.[13] The challenge for Ghana and overall security within the oil region has been that a number of these refugees are former combatants who have continued to hold on to their weapons. There have been incidents of violence within the camps and murder which the police service is currently investigating. The propensity for former combatants with access to arms to continue to foment trouble across borders is real and this should also be assessed in the light of the overall effect on Ghana.

Towards ensuring overall security for the Oil and Gas Sector

The discussions and issues raised above call for concerted efforts to ensure security for the region and protection for O&G activities in Ghana. To this end, a number of activities are critical to securing the peace and stability of the region and the country as a whole. Given the experience of neighbouring countries and the challenges encountered, it is only prudent that the country takes a serious view and learns lessons from those who have had this resource well ahead of Ghana.

A number of recommendations are therefore being made for consideration which include the following:

Engagement with local communities and fishermen

The issue of local community engagement is important to securing the safety of installations and persons working with the petroleum sector. First of all, local

---

13 http://www.myradiogoldlive.com/index.php?option=com_content&view=article&id=3567: ivory-coast-over-5000-refugees-arrive-in-ghana-&catid=44:world&Itemid=122. Last accessed August 15, 2012.

communities need to be assured that their needs would be taken care of in a manner that is satisfactory and participatory. It is important to let their leaders know that their people would share in the benefits of the sector, and regular consultation and public education would alleviate their fears and engender trust and support.

Furthermore, discussions with the fishermen, who have settled along the coast and have until now had a thriving business is also important. As soon as practicable, engagement with the fishermen should be undertaken on a regular basis that allows for exchange of ideas and their inclusion in an early warning system that informs the security of events offshore that are inimical to overall security.

Employment for the youth

Lack of employment for young people remains the single most significant threat to security in the Western Region. Owing to the lack of job openings, especially for the young and unskilled, there is a tendency to resort to illegal mining, logging and other fraudulent activities. Given the large-scale sale of land which would otherwise have been used as farmlands for those willing to work, there is real danger that the youth would be left on the fringes of society with nothing to do. When this happens, they would turn radical in their demands and find work through threats on the installations and personnel in exchange for money.

As a matter of urgency, the youth should be organised and trained to provide targeted support for the industry in areas where their skills may be required. A long-term strategy should be in place to train and fit them into the sector over time.

Activation of the police unit for oil and gas

The Ghana Police Service has a clear mandate of ensuring security within the country in order that all persons within Ghana can go about their work in peace. When oil was discovered, the police developed a strategy to contribute to ensuring peace and security within the region and provide patrols in support of the Navy within Ghana's territorial waters.

The Armed Forces and other security agencies also did the same with a view to providing a coordinated action against all forms of crime. It is important for the services to be supported to implement. It is more expensive to take reactive measures than preventive, and the police must be fully supported in this drive.

Undertake a risk assessment and develop a register detailing these risks

The battle to ensure security in the sector would require intelligence gathering and effective documentation of high risk areas, the types of risk and outline what needs to be done to mitigate the risks. Furthermore, it would support effective deployment of resources to handle the risks appropriately. To do this effectively, it would be necessary to have a risk register that is intelligence-led and details all known and perceived threats and outlines specific actions and resources for handling them.

References

Mudgridge, D. (2010). *Piracy Storm Brews in West Africa: Gulf of Guinea under Maritime Siege*, retrieved 3 October, 2011 from www.defenceiq.com.

Wannenburg, G. (2005). Organised Crime in West Africa. *Africa Security Review* 14(4).

Yeboah, S. (2010). *Oil and War: Using Security to Manage Ghana's Oil Find*, retrieved 30 November, 2011 from www.ghanaweb.com/ghanahomepage/features/artikel.php?ID=177580.

Further Reading

Aning, K., & Bah, A.S. (2009). *ECOWAS and Conflict Prevention in West Africa: Confronting the Triple Threats.* New York: Center on International Cooperation.

Aning K., & Lartey, E. (2009). *Parliamentary Oversight of the Security Sector: Lessons from Ghana.* New York: Centre on International Cooperation.

Birikorang, E. (2004). *Human Security in Ghana & West Africa*. African Security Dialogue & Research, retrieved 13 January, 2011 from http://centreforforeignpolicystudies.dal.ca/pdf/fff-birikorang.pdf.

Daily Graphic (2011). 8000 Homos in Two Regions. Tuesday 31 May, p. 1.

Ghanaweb (2011). Retrieved 2 July, 2011 from http://www.ghanaweb.com/GhanaHomePage/NewsArchive/artikel.php?ID=183484.

McCaskie, T.C. (2008). The United States, Ghana and Oil: Global and Local Perspectives. *African Affairs* 107(428), 313–332.

PART V

Country-specific Models and Lessons for Ghana and Other African Oil-producing Nations

15

The Trinidad and Tobago Model: Learnings for Ghana and Africa

Anthony E. Paul

Abstract

This chapter presents the Trinidad and Tobago (T&T) Model of value addition from natural gas, its characteristics and the lessons Ghana and other African countries can learn from it. It undertakes a critique of the policy-making and decision-making system of T&T's energy sector, including implementation of programmes. Moreover, investment strategies in using oil revenues for gas development and gas revenue for human resource development are illustrated. Also addressed are T&T's effective analyses of the industry's value chain as well as supply and demand factors to achieve optimal benefits. In this context, T&T's state sector participation in the oil and gas (O&G) value chain is highlighted. Furthermore, T&T's use of innovative strategies through local value-added building blocks and in natural gas development to meet changing market requirements, and sustain a competitive advantage in the industry are discussed. The chapter concludes with how T&T is leveraging its strengths for sustainability by becoming an energy services exporter, among other strategies.

Introduction

T&T's approach to monetizing its natural gas resources is widely recognized as a success story. The much touted T&T Model is derived almost entirely from the approaches that T&T has taken, from time to time, in making decisions and executing plans that involve the choices and approaches in using natural gas, assembling the pieces of technology, investor and the market, determining prices, both to the producer and the off-taker, and building the required local institutional and human capacity.

In the absence of a natural market, much of T&T's gas would have been defined as 'stranded'. The Government and people of T&T, working hard and smart to break out of that situation, defined and chose their own approach, which moved away from that of most extractives-rich developing countries, where the upstream producers (whether oil, gas or minerals) determined the timing and pace of development and markets and hence the price and usage of the country's resources. In so doing, T&T took deliberate steps towards downstream value addition and industrialization, choosing first to use natural gas for national development via power and fertilizers and servicing domestic needs, manufacturing and industrialization.

Surplus oil revenues were reinvested in the infrastructure and support services required for natural gas development in the absence of external investors; surplus revenues from natural gas is now being invested in human development, including training and services.

Another success factor in the T&T Model has been the continuity of policy over time and across governments. This single-mindedness reflects the purpose

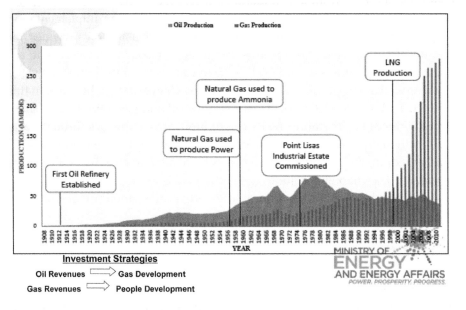

Figure 15.1   Investment Strategies

Source: Trinidad and Tobago's Oil & Gas Production, Natural Gas Development in National Development (T&T Ministry of Energy & Energy Affairs (MEEA) and A.E. Paul).

of the people of T&T that their resources will work, first and foremost, in their best interests.

Other key components/characteristics of the Model are:

- a clear, shared vision and aspirations;

- consistency of purpose – sticking to it/in spite of adversity and doubt;

- developing and empowering a tightly-knit team of committed, capable, purpose-driven leaders;

- listening carefully to others, but making their own decisions, based on analysis of the options available, including those that they put on the table;

- selecting and partnering investors who bring the required experience, technology and commitment to their vision;

- developing a deep and wide pool of skillful and experienced people in all fields and at all operational, management and leadership levels;

- providing supporting infrastructure, utilities services and fiscal and other incentives to facilitate business development and growth.

Today, with well-developed and functioning infrastructure and support services, the industry is 'mature' but not in the sense of one that is driven by competition. We still have limited producers and limited off-takers. The irony is that, even in the face of the success of the T&T Model, there is immense pressure on T&T to revert to the conventional model of producer determining market and price; to behave as if we were 'mature' in the sense of a developed country or market.

If one were to learn the lessons of the T&T Model, then one needs also to examine those aspects of its implementation that can be improved upon. Facing the challenges that we do today, one of the biggest failings becomes clear. If we are to be honest, T&T could have done a lot better at succession planning, so as one generation of innovators and leaders retires, there should have been a clear leadership path behind them.

Not only were the skills and experiences not developed in the breadth of people needed to take the model forward, decision making was notable for its opacity. Although the general premise is articulated above, only a small handful of citizens understand or know why decisions were made and the criteria used, in most cases. Lack of transparency has led to a lack of trust, not only of decision makers, but also of the decisions made and the investors and/ or projects chosen. This is not very helpful to the longevity of contracts and/or projects.

Decision-making criteria, as they were, gave little, if any, consideration, in a structured or consultative manner, of the needs, desires or aspirations of affected communities and the citizens at large. Lack of consultation bolstered the lack of trust and cynicism that followed new projects. In turn, this led to somewhat of an unraveling of one of the major planks of the T&T Model, when decision making around the aluminium smelter in the past few years became such a divisive issue, stopping the project became a major election campaign issue in 2010. Even-though the incumbent government lost and the new government kept good on their promise, they discarded the age-old policy of continuing with preceding government projects. The consequence is lowered investor confidence in a country that has a strong democratic tradition, with governments changing as they lose favour.

With projects that have a long gestation period and are more likely than not to extend beyond one electoral term, before all contracts and licenses are approved and signed off, as almost all major investments in energy are, there needs to be some national consensus around project selection criteria. By extension, there needs to be a mechanism for public engagement that is underpinned by clear policies and decision-making criteria that are generally approved by an informed public, with access to lucid, comprehensible and trusted information.

To be fair, this failing of the T&T state sector in engaging its citizens is not unique to T&T, nor is it necessarily deliberate or malicious. In fact, all over the world and in all aspects of major commercial dealings with multinationals, governments were convinced of the need for confidentiality and the 'commercial sensitivity' of deals. They responded in a manner that bred lack

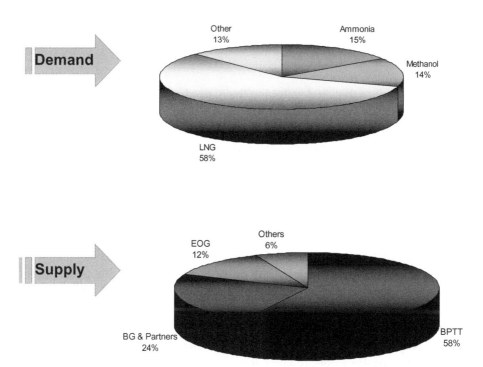

Figure 15.2   Trinidad and Tobago's 4bcfd Demand & Supply Diagram
Source: MEEA, 2010

of trust and, in many cases, corruption. The changing tide of citizen awareness and involvement seems harder for the 'old guard' to come to terms with, as it represents both a threat to the way they know and to their own 'comfort zone.' In the latter case, many choices, good or bad, were made with best judgment and often with all good intentions, but with significant compromises. In hindsight and with the benefit of experience, some of these decisions are very difficult to defend and, human nature being what it is, critics will tend to focus on mistakes, rather than achievements.

As we carried on our experiments, we made mistakes and often paid a high price. As we learnt from these, and as circumstances changed, we have managed to weather the storm and turn the tide in our fortunes. As we go forward, the choices that face us are either to:

• continue with the model;

- adopt and adjust it based on our experiences and the way forward that we choose; or

- abandon it.

T&T acknowledges that, in developing the natural gas industry, a large amount of the people's and nation's resources were invested and put at risk. Where other potential investors considered primarily the commercial aspects, the people of T&T saw the commercial and strategic value and were driven by what it meant to us as a people to take charge of our destiny.

We suffered losses, as the industries took a severe hit from the 1980s to 1990s. As profitability has returned, there are those who suggest that it is time for the state (and hence the people) to move away and give it over to private sector ownership. In the absence of a well-capitalized local financial market, this translates, largely, to putting it in the hands of foreign owners. There are others who suggest that the people of T&T retain ownership, continue to reap the benefits, so as to offset past losses and continue to learn and grow, even beyond our boundaries. Others yet suggest a widening and broadening of the portfolio, to make way for all types of investors, which in turn means that decisions about the project portfolio carefully consider the financing and ownership options that allow for the benefits of foreign direct investment to cohabitate with those of local capital working at the height of the local economy.

Successful innovators create new markets, work their way to the top of their industry and then retain that status by building on their leading position while remaining innovative. It is the initial risk that allowed them to get into this position. Like any leading company, there is no reason for the National Gas Company (NGC), for instance, to think of any strategy that will see it surrender its position as one of the world's leading natural gas companies.

Handing over to a local private sector requires the nurturing of the local capital market, which this industry has the standing to facilitate, if deliberately set in this direction. Whatever path we choose, the key elements of implementation still need to be present and, given the age and stage of our industry leaders and managers a key challenge is the 'Big Crew Change' as it is called in the industry – changing out our current set of leaders and managers with a new crew that is ready and capable to take us forward. A leadership development and management succession plan is critical for future success in the industry, particularly as it applies to the state sector, for managing investments and operations and for regulating the industry.

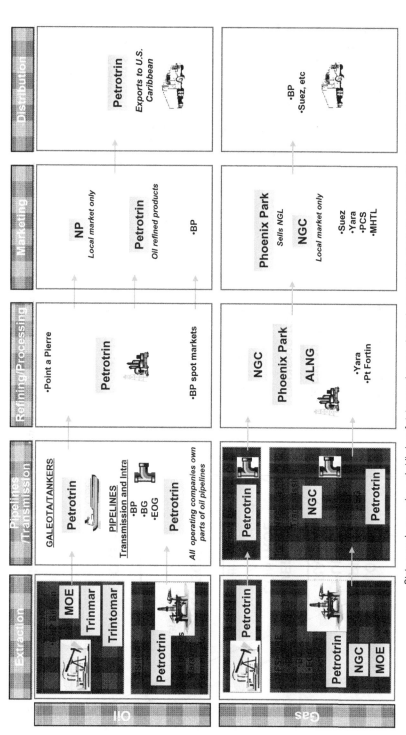

State owned companies, subsidiaries of state owned companies and companies in which the state are a/the major shareholder

Figure 15.3   Trinidad and Tobago's State Sector Participation in the Oil and Gas Value Chain
Source: A.E. Paul, 2003

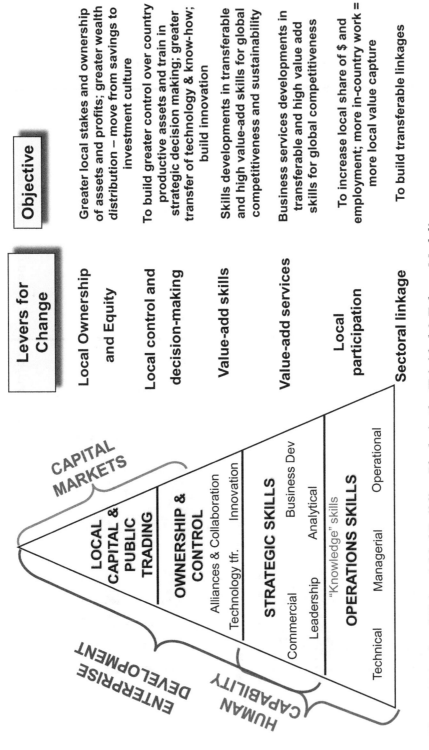

Objective

Greater local stakes and ownership of assets and profits; greater wealth distribution – move from savings to investment culture

To build greater control over country productive assets and train in strategic decision making; greater transfer of technology & know-how; build innovation

Skills developments in transferable and high value-add skills for global competitiveness and sustainability

Business services developments in transferable and high value add skills for global competitiveness

To increase local share of $ and employment; more in-country work = more local value capture

To build transferable linkages

Levers for Change

Local Ownership and Equity

Local control and decision-making

Value-add skills

Value-add services

Local participation

Sectoral linkage

CAPITAL MARKETS

LOCAL CAPITAL & PUBLIC TRADING

OWNERSHIP & CONTROL

Alliances & Collaboration
Technology tfr.   Innovation

STRATEGIC SKILLS

Commercial   Business Dev
Leadership   Analytical

"Knowledge" skills

OPERATIONS SKILLS

Technical   Managerial   Operational

ENTERPRISE DEVELOPMENT

HUMAN CAPABILITY

Figure 15.4   Local Value-Added Building Blocks in the 'Trinidad & Tobago Model'
Source: A.E. Paul, 2003.

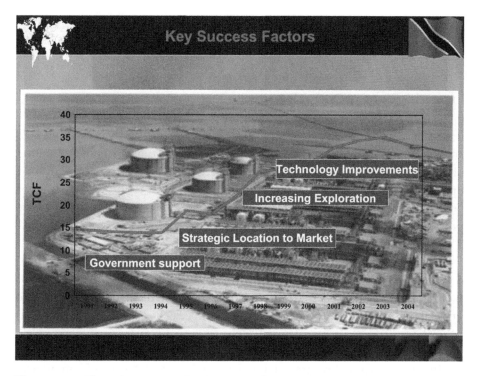

Figure 15.5 Changing Strategies in Natural Gas Development
Source: MEEA

As a small country, the value of the learning experiences we have had in the past 50 years was magnified by virtue of there being only a relatively small pool of people who have been involved. As they worked in close contact and were forced to multitask, they covered a wide range of activities, gaining wide and deep experiences. This is an experience we can replicate and improve upon as we implement a leadership succession and knowledge management programme.

As T&T changed its strategy to meet changing circumstances and grow the gas business, so it must change its strategy around human capacity development and investment, to meet the new challenges and position itself to take advantage of the upcoming opportunities. In the 1970s, a deliberate decision was made to convert some of the windfall from oil production and high prices to development of the natural gas industry and Point Lisas. As the gas industry grew and prospered in the 1990s and beyond, another deliberate strategy was implemented to build human capacity, this time extending the earlier human capacity drives that were always built to meet our needs and used as the indigenous demand as a facilitator.

Exporting Energy Expertise

In the history of mankind, the last century has probably seen more change and certainly has been the period of the most rapid rate of change than any other. The economic, social and cultural upheavals of that period have thrown up experiences that have previously not been available to the vast majority of people, governments or businesses. Even so, all of the hyperbole of the century probably pales against the changes of the last 50 years.

What is remarkable about the experiences of these past 50 years is that there are many among us who have lived through, been part of or created some of the changes that have shaped this world. In T&T, we have a disproportionate (in relation to our population) share of these experiences in the world of oil and natural gas.

In our 100 years of commercial oil production and 50 years of commercial natural gas production, we have experienced almost every imaginable scenario that a country can find itself in, relative to these two industries – the whole spectrum, from high to low, good to bad of every factor that affects the industries: status of the world economy; war and peace; commodity prices; exploration, production and construction costs; reserves; investment climate; activities; tax regimes; institutional, legal and administrative frameworks and capability; local services and ownership; capital availability; skills. You name it, we have either been through the best of times or the worst of times.

At every time though, we (T&T) have had to get on with it. We made decisions and took actions. Most of these we have had to live with for a long time. We have made good choices and bad ones. Many of the latter we could not turn back; some we addressed when we had the skill, know-how and/or courage to so do. We have learnt valuable lessons from all of these experiences. Looking at us today what is seen is a function of the viewer's perspective. Through the eyes of T&T nationals, we often focus on the failings, the problems. We all know how we could have done better. Hindsight is indeed perfect vision.

Not so through the eyes of many an outsider; especially if that is someone who walked with us through colonialism and independence; who shared our sufferings, our struggles and our hopes. Someone, who like us, has worked hard to extract the wealth of their nation – resources above and below the ground and the skills and labour of their people, in the expectation that it would lead to a better quality of life for their new nations. They look at us and find it remarkable what we have achieved; how we have done so by standing on our own feet; by having the self-confidence to do the things that we were always told we did not have the experience to do.

They walk or drive through Point Lisas, Point Fortin, Port of Spain, Scarborough or La Romain and marvel at the progress we have made – in their own lifetimes. If T&T can do it, surely they can too! That is what the T&T O&G story inspires in visitors from Africa and other countries as far away and diverse as Timor-Leste – the self-confidence that we can achieve bigger things than we are given credit for. But more than that, they recognize, as few T&T nationals do, that whatever we did and learnt was done by only a handful of people; men and women of immense capability, national pride and conviction – working together with a common mission – to get this industry to work for us. They recognize that, as they do, we faced adversity and self-doubt and yet we persevered and overcame. They look at us and see people like them doing all the things that are required to run the industry – operating and managing and even owning billion-dollar plants, oil fields, service companies – all by ourselves.

Conclusion

To a large extent, what the world sees in the T&T Model and wants from it is the outcome. But not just that – how did we do it? What are the pieces of the energy eco-system that we built? What did we do right and what did we do wrong? What did we learn from those experiences? How can they avoid them? Can we hold their hands in this process? And therein lies the advantage T&T has above other countries. We are small, non-threatening and we have walked the path on which African and other developing countries now find themselves.

The help required is in many areas – as investors, sometimes to hold the hands of state companies as they engage other foreign partners in a venture that is new to them; as strategy advisors; for operational and administrative support (you do not get experience in a classroom, only by doing it); as business partners to transfer technology and know-how; and in education – because of its small size, the interconnectedness of people and systems, and the relationships between institutions, T&T presents an ideal learning eco-system, where classroom and plant or oilfield are geographically close and otherwise interlinked, allowing for education, on-the-job training, coaching and mentoring to be easily facilitated.

Given our size and reach, T&T is recognized around the world for performing well above our 'weight class'. As T&T seeks to offer support outside its shores, we are stepping into new territory, wanting to assist, being summoned with open arms, but fully aware that the 'usual suspects' and some new ones are set on transferring the wealth of the developing world and the fruits of the labour of our citizens to the benefit of their own citizens, as disproportionately in relationship to their inputs as we allow them to get away with. They are seasoned and capable adversaries, against whom we are not always capable of competing.

References

Paul, A.E (2003), Sustainability – Local content and Diversification: Trinidad and Tobago Case Study, Centre for Energy Enterprise Development. Also presented at the Good Governance of the National Petroleum Sector Workshop at the British Academy, London, 2005.

16

The Main Attributes of the Norwegian Approach

Farouk Al-Kasim[1]

Abstract

Over the years Norway's governance of its petroleum sector has been exemplary. This chapter explores the main attributes of the highly extolled Norwegian Model (Approach). It systematically highlights the tenets of the Model that have made the administration of Norway's petroleum resources the envy of many oil-producing countries and a role model for several host nations to emulate. Commencing with governance of the sector, features discussed include legislation, national steering, host nation participation and petroleum administration. Also addressed are licensing rounds, diversity in licensing, joint venture agreements, the fiscal regime, openness, integrity and transparency and the development of national expertise. The final set of issues discussed are health, safety and environmental protection (HSE), internal control, improved oil recovery (IOR), regional optimization, gas issues as well as joint cooperation between Norway and licensees.

Introduction

Norway's highly developed system of governance is perhaps the prime factor behind its success in petroleum resource management. It explains the efficiency with which Norway has been able to agree on and implement national policies that are in full harmony with long-term objectives for the development of its

---

1   This chapter is identical to the first part of Chapter 13 of Farouk Al-Kasim's book entitled *Managing Petroleum Resources – The Norwegian Model in a Broad Perspective*, The Oxford Institute for Energy, (2006).

national economy and society. The slogan of developing petroleum resources 'for the benefit of all the people' has been seriously adhered to throughout. The Petroleum Fund has helped in achieving this objective.

At the beginning of petroleum operations, Norway wisely avoided elaborate and comprehensive legislation. Early legislation was thus confined to the fundamental principles of governing the sector. Since petroleum operations in North Sea environments were novel to both Norway and the oil industry, a gradual approach to legislation was justified. It left detailed legislation to be dealt with by regulations and guidelines as and when the need arose, and as the authorities became sufficiently familiar with the challenges and implications.

The first comprehensive petroleum law was enacted in 1985. Until then a series of royal decrees and regulations covered the basic needs for legislation. It was not until 1998 that the 1985 law was revised.

Main Features of the Norwegian Model

A distinct feature of the Norwegian Model has been the political consensus on the fundamental principles of petroleum policy. Foremost among these was the principle of 'national steering'. This meant that the conditions for, and tempo of, petroleum operations were to be closely monitored and ultimately decided by the national authorities. The systems, policies and strategies that were introduced to govern the sector reflected that basic resolve.

Throughout the 1970s, the country adhered to a policy of 'accelerating slowly'. The policy meant careful balance between the desire to accelerate petroleum operations on the one hand and the prudence to avoid shocks to the economy and way of life as a consequence of excessive stimulation by petroleum operations.

As the country became reconciled to its role as a major petroleum producer, petroleum activities were allowed to develop more freely but with at least 50 per cent Norwegian participation (that is, state participation + participation by Norwegian companies). The main objective of national participation was to help the authorities maintain close control on the direction, tempo and impact of petroleum activities.

The allocation of roles within the petroleum administration of 1972 has proved to be prudent. In many petroleum nations at that time, the state's petroleum administration was built around national companies that combined the state's administrative, regulatory and commercial interests. In contrast to that trend, Norway insisted on full and clear separation between the three different functions of government within the petroleum sector. Accordingly, the Ministry of Industry (later the Ministry of Oil and Energy) was to concentrate on legislation, petroleum policy, planning and licensing. All technical and regulatory functions were organized under the Norwegian Petroleum Directorate (NPD) while the commercial interests related to state participation were allocated to a specially created company (Statoil) which was 100 per cent owned by the Government. Although the NPD has been subsequently split into two directorates and Statoil has partly been privatized, separation between the three functions in different organizations has prevailed. It is this clear separation that has been admired by other petroleum countries and is often referred to as the Norwegian Model.

Norway's licensing policies have undergone a remarkable evolution. Back at the beginning in 1965, the licensing rounds were largely market oriented, but nevertheless based on optimizing work programme commitments rather than monetary bidding. Starting from the Second Allocation Round, state participation and joint venture agreements became permanent features of the licensing policy. Following discoveries in the 1970s, two trends became predominant; a deliberately restrictive allocation tempo and an insistence on a large national share in the operations.

Following the relaxation on tempo restrictions in the mid-1980s, licensing rounds became more frequent and more geographically widespread. The objective was to maintain a steady level of investment thus sustaining development operations and securing future levels of production.

Diversity in licensees has always been a major principle in Norway's licensing policy. Originally, diversity was considered necessary in order to cope with the various technological and operational challenges presented by the harsh environments of the North Sea.

In order to achieve diversity within individual licences, Norway resorted to the formation of licence groups, typically with three to five co-licensees in each group. Until recently, the Ministry had full discretion in selecting the co-licensees in the groups including the national companies. More importantly, Norway has insisted on appointing, or at least approving, the nomination of the operator.

Positive competition among licensees has made it possible not only to attain optimal terms for licensing but also to improve overall performance through benchmarking. Differences in interpretation among oil companies have helped achieve more comprehensive evaluation of prospects and hence to higher discovery rates. The authorities have benefited greatly from this variety of interpretation when formulating licensing strategies.

Similarly, the presence of selected co-licensees in licence groups has served to improve performance by bringing together a variety of operational experience and expertise. From the authorities' point of view, this variety has provided a better and more nuanced basis for approving the plans submitted by licence groups.

The licensees within a licence group are required in Norway to enter into a joint venture agreement. Each of the co-licensees is considered to be a separate legal entity with direct ownership to its share of the petroleum production entitlement from the licence. The co-licensee can thus book its share of the reserves in the license.

Individual co-licensees are taxed separately and on the basis of their overall portfolio in Norway. The intention of the fiscal regime is to provide adequate reward to each licensee by allowing it to write off losses against revenues for all licences on the Norwegian Continental Shelf. The licensees are thus assured of a reasonable rate of return on their total investment and are therefore encouraged to undertake reasonable risks.

The fiscal regime has however been the subject of some controversy. While providing comfort against potential losses, the system is criticized by some licensees for denying them an adequate upside reward to compensate for undertaking high investment risks. The criticism has been particularly topical for mature North Sea operations where a majority of the remaining resources are in so-called marginal discoveries.

Norway has long traditions in openness, integrity and transparency. The Civil Service Code of behaviour guarantees all users of government services full access to the process leading to decisions on their cases. Moreover, the office of the Public Auditor watches over all civil servants to ensure their adherence to the Civil Service Code. In addition, the press enjoys free access to almost all public documents on decisions made by the Government with only few exceptions related to national security. All documents submitted by the Government to the national assemblies are made public and are thus available for research by public institutions that constantly monitor government performance. All these democratic features provide confidence to oil companies that the government exercises discretion in a forthright and objective manner that is open to scrutiny if and when required.

Norway's approach to managing its petroleum resources also included the policy of optimizing the local content of deliveries to petroleum operations. Towards the mid-1970s, Norway invited oil companies to contribute to the development of national expertise, particularly within the petroleum sector. They made it clear that the performance of oil companies in this regard would be monitored and taken into account when selecting licensees in forthcoming allocation rounds. The positive response by oil companies made it possible for Norway to achieve accelerated technological development within a rather short period of time. The oil companies were pleasantly surprised to discover that not only was research in Norway relatively inexpensive but it also was of high quality. It did not take long therefore before the Norwegian academic and industrial environment was operating at the very front of offshore and petroleum technologies.

HSE has always been a top priority for Norway and a prerequisite for allowing petroleum operations to take place. The fact that Norway is a fishing and shipping nation has further underlined the focus on HSE. The oil companies have not only respected the Norwegian objectives in HSE but have also fully embraced them as their own. There has therefore been continual cooperation between the authorities and oil companies on how to pursue HSE objectives so as to make petroleum operations viable within reasonable sets of norms and standards. In many cases, joint research projects were initiated to help achieve these objectives.

A special feature of the Norwegian Model is the so-called 'Internal Control Principle' which simply means that the licensees are responsible for maintaining the Government's standards for HSE by developing their own codes and procedures. The authorities' role is to ensure (1) that the companies' codes and procedures are adequate to meeting the HSE objectives and (2) ensuring through audits that the company adheres to its own codes and procedures.

One of the most spectacular features of the Norwegian Model is without doubt the achievements in the field of IOR. The term means improvements in both production profiles and ultimate recovery of oil compared to conventional methods of production. Success in applying IOR technologies and practices has resulted in increasing the average oil recovery for the whole Norwegian Continental Shelf from 25 per cent to 42 per cent. This remarkable achievement was only possible through active cooperation between the authorities and the oil companies involving joint research projects, pilot production schemes and consultations on how to make such schemes technically and commercially feasible.

Another feature of the Norwegian Model is active central planning by the petroleum authorities. One part of petroleum resource management that has greatly benefited from such planning is that of regional optimization. Once large discoveries have been made and developed, the challenge for the authorities is to try and utilize the infrastructure that is established in connection with these discoveries in order to promote the discovery and development of smaller structures in the vicinity (satellite fields). To achieve this objective, the licensing and development policies within major production regions must be synchronized and optimized so as to reduce cost and thus enhance the development of satellite fields that may otherwise be permanently marginalized.

Conclusion

Norway had to deal with a considerable gas challenge. The planning, optimization and development of an infrastructure for gas over the long coastline of Norway is one major feature of the Norwegian Model. Since gas constitutes around two-thirds of all petroleum resources in Norway, its value is entirely dependent on bringing it to the European and other markets at minimum cost. To achieve this, a planned and optimized approach to developing a transport network was vital. Equally vital for gas development however was the challenge of negotiating contracts that provided sufficiently high prices to warrant the development of the infrastructural investments. Since gas flaring is strictly forbidden by law, it was equally important for Norway to negotiate flexible gas contracts that allowed the sale of associated gas from oilfields at comparable prices to free gas that guaranteed the uninterrupted delivery of the associated gas. The development of an extensive gas infrastructure in Norway is proof of the reciprocal interests between Norway as producer and the Continent as a purchaser of Norwegian gas.

The most distinctive and important feature of the Norwegian Model is perhaps its success in creating a working mechanism for joint cooperation between licensees and the authorities. By participating as investor in petroleum operations, the Government not only understood the commercial challenges but also sympathized with them. As administrator, the Government was objective in its dealing with all commercial interests and could recognize where technological challenges required joint efforts between the authorities and the industry. This led to joint cooperation projects with oil companies in order to investigate or promote common operational objectives. There are several examples of such cooperation ranging from projects on IOR/enhanced oil recovery (EOR), deep water operations, HSE, cost efficiency, drilling breakthrough technologies and so on. Another example of such cooperation is the jointly-owned database system where the authorities and several oil companies keep their data and access them in accordance with agreed confidentiality rules.

Through working together to meet common challenges, both the Government and the licensees increase their in-depth understanding of the issues they faced as well as of each other's attitude towards these problems. By enhancing this mutual understanding, the two sides have a much better chance of reaching mutually agreeable solutions.

The Norwegian regulatory practices are designed to reflect the petroleum policies of the country at least in two major aspects. Firstly, they are intended to provide the authorities full access to data from petroleum operations so as to satisfy the national desire to be in the driver's seat. However, with time the practices have been somewhat softened in the sense that progressively less operations now require approvals by the authorities without affecting the requirement for information and data. Secondly, the emphasis on HSE and IOR have been maintained but more and more in cooperation with the licensees.

References

Al-Kasim, F. (2006). *Managing Petroleum Resources: The Norwegian Model in a Broad Perspective*. Oxford: Oxford Institute for Energy Studies.

Further Reading

Anderson, M. (1995). *Petroleum Research in North Sea Chalk*. Stavanger: RF Rogaland Research.
Annual Reports by the Norwegian Petroleum Directorate, Stavanger.

Fact Sheets prepared and published by the Royal Ministry of Petroleum and Energy, Oslo.

Hanisch, T.J., & Nerheim, G. (1992). *Norsk Olje Historie – Bind 1 (Norwegian Petroleum History – Volume I)*, sponsored by Norsk Petroleumsforening. Oslo: Leseselskapet.

Hossain, K. (1979). *Law and Policy in Petroleum Development*. London: Frances Pinter Ltd, New York: Nichols Publishing Company.

Kindingstad, T., & Hageman, F. (Eds) (2002). *Norges Oljehistorie (Norwegian Petroleum History)*. Wigerstrand Forlag.

Kvendseth, S.S. (1988). *Funn (Findings)*. Oklahoma: Phillips Petroleum Company.

Legislation concerning the Norwegian Continental Shelf, 1977, published by the Royal Ministry of Industry and Handicraft, Norway.

Lemen, V. (1996), *Gas for Generations*. Stavanger: A/S Norske Shell and Statoil on behalf of the licensee group for Troll.

Ministry of Oil and Energy. (1990). *Petroleumsindustrien mot 2000 (Petroleum Industry to 2000)* . Norway: Ministry of Oil and Energy.

Olsen, J., Olausen, S., Jensen, T.B., Landa, G.H., & Hinderaker, L. (Eds) (1995). *PROFIT 1990–1994*, Project Summary Reports, Reservoir Characterisation near Wellbore, 1995. Norwegian Petroleum Directorate, Stavanger.

Skjzeveland, S., & Kleppe, J. (1992). *SPOR Monograph, Recent Advances in Improved Oil Recovery Methods for North Sea Sandstone Reservoirs*. Norwegian Petroleum Directorate, Stavanger.

Skzeveland, S.M., Skauge, A., Hinderaker, L., & Sisk, C.D. (1996). *RUTH, A Norwegian Research Program on Improved Oil Recovery – Program Summary, 1996*. Norwegian Petroleum Directorate, Stavanger.

Storting and Odelting reports and proposals related to petroleum operations, 1965 to 1998, prepared mainly by the Royal Ministry of Petroleum and Energy but also by other ministries.

Young, T. Ekofisk (1997). *Looking Beyond the Year 2000*, UK SPE Review Articles 1995–1997, September.

17

The Norwegian Experience: Potential Lessons for Ghana and Other African Countries

Kwaku Appiah-Adu

Abstract

This contribution draws upon the previous chapter on the Norwegian Model by Farouk Al-Kasim (2006) which was written to discuss what other countries could learn from the Norwegian experience. It discusses lessons that Ghana and other African countries (Ghana et al.) could learn from the Norwegian Approach. The chapter highlights areas where Ghana et al. would do well to apply specific lessons in their quest to ensure that petroleum resources become a blessing and not a curse. A variety of subjects are covered include legislation, national participation, petroleum administration, licensing, petroleum agreements, the fiscal regime, transparency and accountability, national skills development, health, safety and environment, community relations, oil recovery and natural gas utilization.

Introduction

In the context of developed countries, Norway's governance system is arguably second to none. However, this does not mean Ghana et al. should not aspire to develop their systems along those lines. Particularly critical for sound petroleum resource management is to endeavour to incorporate decisions into a national blueprint for growing the overall economy in order to ensure that petroleum income benefits the society. Strong emphasis should be placed on developing systems for managing petroleum proceeds in a way that avoids misuse and guarantees sustainable gains to the country concerned. Short-range benefits to the economy should be designed such that they are consistent with and contribute exponentially to the realization of the long-term benefits anticipated. Above all, the administration of such systems must be transparent in a way that enhances accountability.

Legislation

The Norwegian approach of 'gradual legislation' may not be seamlessly transferable to most host nations where the requirement for legislation is obvious from the outset. In several instances it would be disastrous to allocate licences devoid of appropriate legislation as this would open the floodgates to manipulation and conjecture. Nevertheless, the initial priority should be to establish the cardinal principles of petroleum governance in a petroleum law. The law should ideally be succinct and then regulations can concentrate on details.

Host nations should not be in a haste to develop detailed legislation. Ideally, regulations should be instituted just before or only when they are needed and if possible after the host nation has understood better the phase of operation under consideration. In reality, a balance must be struck between waiting too long and rushing to cover a growing need. Provisional regulations may be a useful way of evaluating before ultimately enacting them.

Only a few nations can view the potential of petroleum wealth in the same laid-back and incredulous way that Norway did in the mid-1960s. Most host nations are harried to access their petroleum resources or petroleum income so as to fix their economy. Thus, they would be willing to agree to less optimal terms and conditions so as to commence activities or keep them at a certain level. The goal of full-blown national steering would in reality differ greatly from country to country in relation to the necessity to commence petroleum operations.

National Participation

One point must be stressed – *national participation* is not necessarily a precondition for profitable resource management. It should be considered as an alternative that requires prudent analysis in the context of the realities, prospects and capacity of the specific host nation. To invest a country's scant funds into risky cooperative projects can indeed be a weighty load on the host nation if the investment cannot be safeguarded by proficient and robust business management, technical expertise and practical experience. Some of the issues to take into account are the risks involving exploration and development (E&D) in the host nation, accessibility to business and industry expertise, experience in international ventures, and optional requirements in the nation for public or private investments, among others. Besides, the nation could contemplate settling for a decision to participate commercially when the licensees make a commercial discovery. Using this approach the nation would not be exposed in the most uncertain stage of the venture while earning a chance to understand the industry via hands-on involvement though at a nominal percentage stake.

Petroleum Administration

It is recommended that host nations such as Ghana study the Norwegian *Petroleum Administration*. The expression Norwegian Model (Approach) was originally introduced to mean the strict organizational distinction between Ministry, Norwegian Petroleum Directorate and Statoil. The key significance of the Approach is rooted in its capacity to produce conditions of impartial and healthy competition among different national and international players. Moreover, by creating a relationship built on trust and mutual appreciation between government and the oil companies the Approach facilitates effective collaboration in spheres of shared interest.

Nevertheless, it is reasonable to caution that the organizational paradigm per se does not ensure the required effect. Just as vital is the way in which business is carried out by the various institutional authorities, their degree of competence, their integrity and ability to dialogue and collaborate.

Licensing

In several host nations, including Ghana, the planning of licensing rounds is yet to be instituted, non-existent, feeble or not really linked to the effect on overall economic development. Thus, generally, not much importance is given to prudently scheduling and factoring allocation rounds to complement a required economic growth blueprint. Norway's experience reveals that allocation rounds are formidable means for regulating the pace of operations.

While the host country has authentic alternatives to prepare its allocation series, this should be done to guarantee increase in reserves that would consequently sustain the desired levels of operations and income. Host nations need to make strenuous efforts to ensure that only competent oil companies are permitted to conduct business in their country. Meticulous choice of partners is a valuable investment in profitable and enduring relationships.

Additionally, host nations such as Ghana should not take lightly the issue of variety in licensees, not merely a small group of early-birds. Norway's experience shows that diversity in licensees, via constructive competition, will make it easier for the host nation to strike deals with better terms. Above all, diversity would result in more proficient exploration as regards better resource growth and minimal unit discovery and not least development cost. It also enhances the likelihood for developing discovered reserves. In development operations, an array of skills exhibited by the various licence groups would help compare the performance of individual players, hence helping to enhance the general efficiency in operations.

Nevertheless, if the system is to work effectively, host nations such as Ghana need to present enabling conditions characterized by healthy competition that is perceived to be impartial in recompensing ingenuity and healthy collaboration. These goals will drive the host nation's petroleum governance to exhibit even-handedness, proficiency and integrity.

Norway's experience suggests that a diversity of licensees can effectively be established in licence clusters. The extent to which this practice would be beneficial to Ghana and other host nations would depend on the particular conditions. The practice is hard to justify where the geological potential is comparatively limited, but if it is extensive there should be no difficulty in requesting consortia of reputable companies to apply. The licensees may be granted the liberty to choose their co-licensees themselves conditional on the approval of host nation's government.

Production Agreements

Undoubtedly, currently the most prevalent mode of contract is the production sharing agreement (PSA). Other frequently used contracts include the Service Contract and the Buy-back Contract. Norway's mode of contract; the Joint Venture Agreement (JVA) is not particularly common; neither is there any specifically noble rationale for advocating it for use by Ghana and other host nations except if the particular conditions justify it in their own right.

A great deal of debate has focused on the advantages and disadvantages of PSAs from the host nation's perspective. PSAs are favoured by oil companies because it permits them to sign up (book) the reserves when they are discovered. This may or may not be in accordance with the nation's laws. Nonetheless, the main anxiety involves the propensity of oil companies to be adamant that detailed provisions be included in the contract to augment the law or offset for the lack of it. Consequently, there is a risk that several types and editions of PSAs would render forthcoming laws worthless, especially because virtually all of them have purported stability provisions that safeguard the contract from consequent amendments in the law. Host nations (including Ghana) that consider PSAs would do well to insist on ascertaining that they are discussed on the basis of ample legislation.

Fiscal Regime

In many host nations, adaptability in managing the potential of different size, unit cost and risk are all a critical component of the fiscal regime that can make the difference between success and failure. Norway's fiscal regime does not proffer any attribute that could be of specific interest to Ghana or other host African nations. It appears to be devised to contend with huge profits flowing from comparatively sizeable fields. The fact that it is an issue of repeated deliberation between oil companies and government suggests that the system is possibly not sufficiently adaptable to promote the development of relatively smaller deposits of petroleum.

Arguably, the most significant instruction from the Norwegian Approach is the great level of *integrity, openness and transparency* with which it has been implemented. Many host nations are yet to anchor these traits in their petroleum principles and procedures. For Ghana, this is where all efforts have to be made to surmount real challenges, knowing that success will result in huge gains.

Accountability and Transparency

The achievement of other host countries in fostering the *enhancement of national skills* so that it may offer services to petroleum operations is somewhat mixed but in actual fact not as remarkable as Norway's. While most host nations cannot match Norway's enhanced position in technology coupled with its commercial and industrial practices, Ghana et al. should be spurred by Norway's experience to do everything possible to promote participation by institutions in the technological and contracting sectors.

Currently in several host nations, the interest in health, safety and environmental (HSE) protection appears to be eclipsed by other concerns. Nevertheless, responsible oil companies today are very much keen on upholding robust HSE standards worldwide. In this regard they are their own trail blazers in the area of maintaining standards.

Internal Control

Norway's *internal control* approach continues to captivate attention globally primarily since it assigns responsibility to the appropriate quarters, that is with the oil companies, while Government's role is that of auditing the companies' observation of their own codes and standards. For host nations that are short of expertise to undertake these audits, there are a number of international consultants who can be engaged for such assignments.

Oil Recovery

Additionally, Norway's improved oil recovery (IOR) experience has attracted much attention among other oil-producing nations. Specifically, the concept of joint reservoir studies and exploratory IOR arrangements with the licensees is indeed promising because it attempts to connect the two parties to engage in win–win goals. Most of the IOR technologies and field practices used in Norway's offshore are reckoned to be even simpler to employ on land. Contemporary research affirms that the IOR prospects worldwide constitute a primary source for alleviating the scarcity of oil supplies in the near term. Collaboration between oil companies and governments in oil-producing nations is a precondition for realizing that potential in reality.

Gas Challenge

In several host nations, the *gas challenge* is initially and fundamentally to avert the squandering of gas as a derivative of oil production. Norway's case provides answers that may assist in this context, for instance, gas injection and gas storage. Nevertheless, in host countries with only gas potential, the challenge is to determine sound projects for gas utilization in-country. In many nations it has been feasible to utilize gas reserves for power generation. These projects nonetheless presuppose that the collection of power charges is sorted out so as to guarantee a cash flow for the project. In most instances the dynamics of the venture would require cooperation with bordering nations to reach the requisite scale economies. In almost all cases, the participation of the authorities in promoting the development of gas is expected. Consequently, it is conceivably a plus that government is also a commercial participant.

Joint Cooperation

In many oil-producing nations collaboration between oil companies and government (*joint cooperation*) leaves a lot to be desired. If Norway's lessons are examined critically by Ghana et al., they could provide useful pointers as to how a healthy relationship could be developed.

An essential foundation for constructive relations between government and the oil companies is the presence of mutual respect for each other's goals and skills. The other precondition is open sharing of information based on a sincere willingness to collaborate to identify, unearth and implement win–win solutions.

Data gathering and storage is a test that all host nations encounter. In many instances, the test constitutes building a system that meets the needs of all parties and is also cost-effective to government. In this regard, Ghana et al. can learn from Norway's case since it embodies a solution that can be used as a basis for a shared data system between government and the licensees. The benefits are clear; readily exchangeable data, minimal cost to all parties as well as sound communication with government.

Will the Norwegian Approach be of Use in the Future?

Given that the petroleum era is likely to continue for several decades, it is worth considering whether the experience of Norway will continue to be useful to other nations, particularly Ghana and new oil producers in Africa.

A retrospective examination of the petroleum sector provides a noteworthy development in the association between the host nation and oil companies. From private ownership in America during the nascent period, the association in other nations grew into major concessions where oil companies were awarded rights over extensive acreage for lengthy time periods. These concessions continued till the end of the 1960s when the Organization of the Petroleum Exporting Countries (OPEC) initiated a new development in which commercial participation by the host nation became a critical goal for most OPEC members. During its embryonic stage the Norwegian Approach was influenced by this development. The international oil companies (IOCs) attempted to fight it but ultimately had to embrace a high level of state participation.

The Supply and Demand Equilibrium

At the time of writing, it was widely held that production capacity is not adequate to meet the increasing global demand for oil. This view has resulted in a relatively high price of oil of at least $100/bbl.

Generally, there are a number of explanations for the high prices. Firstly, examining issues related to demand side, economic growth in China, India and other populous emerging economies such as Brazil coupled with developments of mega infrastructural projects in thriving economies has spawned a steady increase in the demand for energy as a whole and for oil in particular. A corresponding slow expansion on the supply side has heightened the view of looming scarcity. In the 1980s and 1990s, the petroleum sector experienced a long period of low oil prices and was reluctant to rush into high levels of investment. The comparatively high costs and challenges presented by the petroleum resources yet to be tapped did not inspire the oil companies to invest greatly in new production capacities.

From the early 1980s, several leading geologists have cautioned that the outstanding oil reserves are not adequate to support the estimated rise in global petroleum output. They asserted that global capacity for conventional oil production had either peaked, or nearly peaked, beyond which global oil output would start waning.

As a result of the escalating rise in world population and the quest for economic advancement, fulfilling future needs for energy is expected to pose profound challenges to the petroleum sector. To address these challenges, players in the sector will need to sharpen efforts in all phases of petroleum activities so as to operate more productively. The challenges will linger irrespective of whether we depend completely on traditional resources or employ non-orthodox oil resources. Both the oil companies and host nations need to work together in order to achieve success.

Challenges in Development

In order to meet their own energy needs over the next few years, Ghana and other new host nations will need to step up petroleum output from existing active fields or from discoveries that are set for prompt development.

Starting with the producing fields, the prospect for greater production from such fields will be based on enhanced production schemes via IOR or enhanced oil recovery (EOR) processes. The impact of such schemes on world oil production is highest in the case of giant fields. Several large fields are located in the Middle East, and do require IOR/EOR measures, and hence, it is vital to the international community that such projects are commenced within the shortest possible time based on the best possible technical/economic terms. Initiating such ventures will in many cases demand modern world-class technology and the operational know-how developed by IOCs. In this context, some political, institutional and contractual issues need to be addressed. Given that the physical processes linked to fluid flow in reservoirs are irreversible, these challenges need to be faced without delay.

In an effort to meet the need for oil promptly, extra output can be realized from commercially viable finds that are yet to be developed. Aside from the Middle East and very few other exceptions which are now emerging as oil producers, many petroleum regions are mature or maturing. This suggests that new finds will be smaller and/or more expensive than the producing fields in the specific petroleum province. Mostly the commercial development of these finds will be based on success in discovering innovative solutions, for instance by developing discoveries in groups, or as satellite fields to enormous fields, or by sequencing them to take advantage of present infrastructure. The North Sea is an example of a maturing region that demonstrates these challenges.

Challenges in Exploration

With the escalating rise in the demand for oil in the years that lie ahead, there will be a need for additional discoveries. Since several of the world's well-known petroleum fields are quite well explored, the possibility of making huge finds is reducing. Future discoveries are likely to be smaller and more daunting to make. Hence, the petroleum industry will have to develop more advanced tools in an effort to identify and evaluate the residual resources before drilling. This also means that the licence conditions will have to become more appealing in order to attract investment in exploration.

Aside from the Middle East, huge discoveries are likely to be made in inadequately explored or virgin reservoirs. Nevertheless, there are many sound reasons why these reservoirs have not yet been explored; these may be political, climatic, topographic, geological, technical, economic or a combination of these factors. If the prevailing high oil prices do not abate, the industry may be influenced to shift its exploration endeavours to regions where the investments in E&D are expected to be high. The contractual conditions will have to be highly appealing to get such exploration to commence. Expectations that comparatively high oil prices will persist in the future will also be a precondition.

If the high oil prices continue, the heavy burden of oil imports will intensify the pressure on developing countries to discover and develop their own petroleum resources quickly. Not all such countries are adequately endowed by nature to provide attractive acreage to the oil industry. Most developing nations are likely to compete with each other in an effort to appeal to oil companies and maintain their interest by providing them with attractive contractual conditions.

Considering the environmental requirements involving non-conventional oil resources, the challenges of exploitation are expected to be greater than those involving conventional oil.

Natural Gas Challenge

During the 1980s it was forecast that gas would emerge as the major energy source replacing oil. This prediction was especially applicable to North America and Europe where the societal pattern and industrial development are suitable. While the forecast has been realized to some degree, the extent and rate of replacement has been lower than anticipated. Nevertheless, given the prevailing relatively high oil prices, interest in natural gas is being rekindled.

Substituting oil with natural gas in developing countries has proved to be a much harder test. Nevertheless, some exciting and pioneering gas projects have been achieved in Africa (for example, the West Africa Gas Pipeline) and Southeast Asia. These ventures are particularly significant to the economies of the host countries to the extent that they would reduce the oil import costs which are at alarming proportions in developing nations such as Ghana.

From the perspective of the oil companies, which have been principally keen on exploration for oil, a commodity that is easier to trade on the global markets, exploration in gas-dominated territories is still not very appealing. If the capacity is not extremely huge, natural gas can only be sold at the national and/or regional level. Clearly, the effective participation of the producing nation is critical to consummate the sophisticated and essential series of contracts on gas sales. It is also vital for establishing the appropriate incentives for investment in the gas sector.

Oil-producing nations such as Ghana et al. typically grapple with gas issues and government involvement is certainly needed to plot the methodical removal of associated natural gas from various gas-producing oilfields. As a derivative of oil production, associated natural gas is usually emitted at uneven rates that suit the former. Because purchasers of gas insist on stable deliveries as the challenge is to attempt to trade associated gas at attractive prices in spite of fluctuation in the rate of delivery. Nonetheless, a vast gas pipeline system can interconnect gas production from numerous oil and gas (O&G) field sources, thus enhancing the general robustness of the gas output. This last point is particularly critical for the economics of associated gas projects.

Conclusion – The Institutional Challenge

With some potential future prospects analysed let us consider how applicable the Norwegian Approach will be in the years that lie ahead.

In keeping with international law, host nations such as Ghana et al. own natural resources. It is inconceivable that this stance will alter in the predictable future. Nonetheless, the likelihood is that the international community will exert pressure on host nations that are bestowed with petroleum reserves to avail them for exploration, development and production, as part of a global strategy to meet energy needs. Consequently, resource-endowed nations such as Ghana et al. will maintain a key position in administering petroleum activities within their jurisdiction but will be influenced to contribute to the increasing global need for energy. In leading petroleum-producing nations, national oil companies are likely to maintain a pivotal role, but it may be advisable to work alongside IOCs so as to benefit from a rising need for operational management and financial resources as well as world-class technology.

Prospective operational and technological requirements regarding petroleum E&D will heighten the need to involve IOCs. The solution to achieving efficient exploration, development, extraction and utilization of the remaining petroleum resources lies in having a number of such organizations engaged in constructive competition with each other. Through constructive competition, host nations such as Ghana et al. will be able to optimize the universal gains that stem from these non-renewable resources.

Host nation responsibilities will differ based on the nation, the petroleum resource reserves, the market environment and the detailed needs of the projects under consideration. Where government behaviour is consistent, it will engender trust among potential investors. Nevertheless, consistency needs to be displayed alongside a readiness to be adaptable in responding to the specific conditions experienced by the industry, be it country or project related. In certain instances, development may entail the amalgamation of various concerns into a shared effort or project. It may also call for support from neighbouring nations (for example, West Africa Pipeline Project). Irrespective of who makes the first move, host governments assume a cardinal role in promoting and facilitating such projects. In some cases the project may have to be initiated by the host government.

Within this context of anticipated challenges it is expected that the Norwegian Approach will still serve as a source of inspiration to host nations. While precise Norwegian propositions may not be exactly germane, the lessons learnt in finding the appropriate answers will be beneficial in helping to discover custom-made solutions. In particular, profitable collaboration between host nations and the IOCs will remain a critical success factor.

References

Al-Kasim, F. (2006). *Managing Petroleum Resources: The Norwegian Model in a Broad Perspective*. Oxford: Institute for Energy Studies

Further Reading

Andersen, M. (1995). *Petroleum Research in North Sea Chalk*. Stavanger: RF Rogaland Research.

Hossain, K. (1979). *Law and Policy in Petroleum Development*. London: Frances Pinter Ltd, New York: Nichols Publishing Company.

Kvendseth, S.S. (1988). *Funn (Findings)*. Norway: Phillips Petroleum Company.

Olsen, J., Olausen, S., Jensen, T.B., Landa, G.H., & Hinderaker, L. (Eds) (1995). *PROFIT 1990–1994*, Project Summary Reports, Reservoir Characterisation near Wellbore, 1995. Norwegian Petroleum Directorate, Stavanger.

Skjzeveland, S., & Kleppe, J. (1992). *SPOR Monograph, Recent Advances in Improved Oil Recovery Methods for North Sea Sandstone Reservoirs*. Norwegian Petroleum Directorate, Stavanger.

Skzeveland, S.M., Skauge, A., Hinderaker, L., & Sisk, C.D. (1996). *RUTH, A Norwegian Research Program on Improved Oil Recovery – Program Summary, 1996*. Norwegian Petroleum Directorate, Stavanger.

The Royal Ministry of Industry and Handicraft (1977). Legislation concerning the Norwegian Continental Shelf.

Young, T. Ekofisk (1997): *Looking Beyond the Year 2000*, UK SPE Review Articles 1995–1997, September.

18

Conclusion

Kwaku Appiah-Adu

Although Ghana is replete with natural resources, these treasures have not been able to transform its economy, a situation that may be attributed to the lack of proper and prudent management of its resources in the past. With the recent discovery of oil in commercial quantities and with Ghana's status as a new petroleum oil producer, this is the time to put in place robust measures that would provide the platform to turn it into a resource-blessed country, a model that would be emulated by other host nations in the developing world. Indeed for the extractive sector as a whole, host nations need to evolve effective resource management approaches which can be a guide to the effective management of their rich and abundant resources. Revenues that accrue from the exploitation of Ghana's natural resources should be channelled to providing amenities required for socio-economic advancement. In this regard, civil society groups as well as research and advocacy organizations have a responsibility to shed light on revenues and overall operations of both extractive industry companies and government in order to set the stage for accountability and prudent management of the people's money. A comprehensive publication of revenue flows will ensure a level playing field that would extirpate unwarranted contentions and suspicions.

In order for Ghana to maximize the benefits of its petroleum resources to the people, the Petroleum Revenue Management Act (PRMA) broadly responds to public preferences and public choices. The basic revenue management strategy is investment led. The law lays down the key parameters for the accounting and collecting of petroleum revenues due the Government. It establishes the limits on the amount of revenues that shall be directed into the annual budget and into savings. The underlying fiscal rule is simple and logical. It provides for cautious spending. Flexibility is part of the fiscal guideline by allowing for the exact spending percentage to be determined on year-to-year basis. A fixed percentage is a straight jacket likely to be stripped off under political pressures.

At the same time, for the fiscal guidelines to be credible, there are limits to the flexibility: limits that are to be revisited every three years. It provides for the operation and management of the savings and that the assets of the savings shall be prudently managed.

By providing for clear assignment of institutional responsibilities for the assessment, collection and management of petroleum revenues; by establishing processes and standards for reporting, accountability and auditing; by setting out the clear guidelines for the management of savings and investment policy; by entrenching transparency as a fundamental principle in how Ghana intends to collect, account for and manage its good fortunes from petroleum; and by providing a platform for public interest and accountability, Ghana has taken a step to assure all its stakeholders that the petroleum revenues will be managed wisely for the benefit of the current and future generations.

The clear provisions notwithstanding, there are challenges, not least of them being the enforcement of the provisions of the law. For the Act to be effective, much depends on the collective vigilance of citizens and on the ability of the Public Interest and Accountability Committee (PIAC) in carrying out its mandate as provided for in the law. The absence of fiscal responsibility rules or laws can easily undermine any restrictions in the law against borrowing. To be effective, the law needs strong complementary provisions that enforce comprehensive government accountability and disclosures in public financial management.

It must be appreciated that managing oil revenues is a combination of art and science, and as such, policy makers should understand the dynamics of project financing as a driving mechanism to achieve the harnessing of the oil resources. It is advisable to use the funds to finance initial engineering, procurement and construction than to keep them in monetary assets. Additionally, it is considered that whereas there is little correlation between keeping oil money in financial assets and economic development, developing the gas sector which can translate into electricity trading, fertilizer, plastics, and construction sectors leads to higher economic advancement. More challenging, yet a strategic issue, is how the potential in aluminium, which Ghana has huge deposits of, can effectively be harnessed depending on cheap and reliable power supply. The gas–aluminium development strategy can provide a sound basis to eliminate the potential 'Dutch disease' syndrome.

What this approach implies is that a concrete strategic export-driven plan needs to be formulated based on the initial concentration of the oil money into the energy sector itself. The oil out of which these fund management concepts are being developed demands intensive capital injection to optimize its usefulness to the country with sovereign rights over its existence. Therefore short-term management of funds should be distinguished from long-term management because resource availability and usage would be different depending on the time horizon under consideration. Creating sustainable assets with both forward and backward linkages should be the guiding principle.

On the fiscal regime, Ghana's design has to be re-examined with time in order to harness the full benefits of the country's hydrocarbon potential. The fiscal design should be broader and deeper to include the development of the domestic banking, insurance and capital markets which will serve as a conduit to provide the long-term financial capital to support an integrated approach to an effective local participation in the shortest possible time. There is a need to exploit the associated gas from the Jubilee Fields and ensure that Ghana does not experience capacity shortage in electricity generation while flaring of gas is continuing without environmental tax and bonds in the fiscal design. Treatment of environmental obligations, if introduced in future as being deductible as a cost of environmental compliance, will be of interest to Ghanaians.

The legal and regulatory framework to support the generation of the wealth to be managed should be the focus of the initial allocation of the oil wealth so that the financial packages and commercial structures underlying the oil wealth generation processes are strategically, structurally and continually tilted towards Ghanaian ownership and control. Institutional and comprehensively thought through energy-wide legal and regulatory frameworks should provide the orienting lens in the dynamics of managing the funds.

Using experiences in Peru, and project successes and failures in the UK, the impact of specific Laws on Infrastructural Development and Gas Laws in terms of promoting transparency, accountability and project bankability cannot be underestimated. Further deregulation in the energy sector, coupled with the incorporation of project finance legal framework into the banking and financial services laws and practices, is necessary to deepen and improve the liquidity of the Ghanaian power markets. Should Ghana implement these changes, it should, through project financing, be able to realize the benefits of its gas reserves, speed up its economic transformation and possibly become a major exporter of power in the next decade.

On the issue of accountancy and governance, it goes without saying that society would want to see Ghana disclose its financial agreements with international oil companies (IOCs). Ghana's civil society, particularly those based outside of Accra, need to develop their capacity to conduct advocacy around complex technical issues. Though Ghana has made some impressive strides vis-à-vis transparency, key pieces of information about how the oil sector is managed remain shrouded in secrecy, limiting the ability of citizen groups to influence policy. And as the thrill of first oil fades, it will be imperative for civil society to maintain a tight focus on oil sector accountability. In many countries once the obvious, concrete tasks such as the passage of legislation have been completed, civil society attention can be distracted to other issues, leaving a void in terms of rigorous monitoring of the conduct of exploration and production and the management by the state of oil revenues. If Ghana is to build on the promise that has developed during the build-up to oil production, civil society must remain vigilant, and government must work to ensure that open dialogue is ongoing.

Institutionalization and democratization are decisive factors addressing whether abundant resources will be a curse or a blessing for a developing country like Ghana, and that the country will be cursed *only* when the discovery of petroleum resources, for instance, is made before accountable and democratic state institutions are established and consolidated. Ghana has held four free and fair competitive, multiparty elections since 1996, and the incumbent ruling party and president have stepped down peacefully, twice, as a result of the popular will as expressed in the elections. Furthermore, the country's institutions have *not been* destroyed by civil war and conflict and it has not gone into petroleum production shortly after independence, with an authoritarian government as is the case in other resource-endowed African countries. Combining the above with data on institutionalization in Ghana, it seems fair to conclude that Ghana has reached a sufficiently high level of democratization and institutionalization to avoid the trappings of a resource curse, and perhaps even be blessed by its newly found petroleum resources.

The regulatory and legal regime currently governing the petroleum industry in Ghana is not foolproof and there is still much more to be done; regulations still need to be established in many areas. Areas such as decommissioning, the rate of recovery of petroleum by operators, regulations on health and safety of persons employed in petroleum operations, prevention of pollution and remedial action to be taken in respect of any pollution that may occur, the protection of fishing, navigation and other activities carried out in the vicinity of areas where petroleum operations are carried out, are but a few of the regulations needed to manage the industry successfully, but for now there is a regulatory framework in place. However, Government needs to speed up and implement its policy to review and add on to the regulatory regime to make sure the petroleum industry in Ghana is properly regulated for the benefit of all, to Government who is the regulator, as well as the operators, contractors and subcontractors who are to be regulated.

Concerning local content and private sector participation, the approach must be rooted deeply in Ghana's own environment, in the existing and expected circumstances, which can be related to similar circumstances in other places and at different times. For the benefits to be derived, the model has to be pragmatic and desirable to stakeholders, such that the development of the industries will not be impaired; yet the model must be taken further by embedding it in legislation, sector policies and contracts. The laws that affect local content and participation must be consistently applied. Local companies must be fostered, and, once capable, be protected from systematic replacement by foreign ones, if there is no question of the quality or cost of their services or performance, or, worse, if such a replacement is being made simply in the name of open trade! Ghana must see these services and the value they bring as strategic to its national development goals. Huge investments in capacity development, by the taxpayers and citizens of Ghana, are required and will go down the drain if the doors are opened without restriction, as bilateral and multilateral trade and investment treaties will require. While these are important and valuable, negotiating and implementing them must be thoughtful and the trade-offs involved must be fully considered. The worst-case scenario is that foreigners will carry out jobs for which these locals are fully capable, yet remain under-employed. Past periods of natural resources growth have not resulted in the kind of benefit that we all know could have been derived by developing countries in Africa and other parts of the world. This current oil and gas (O&G) growth in Ghana and other parts of Africa allows the greatest opportunity we have to make the most of local content and participation for national wealth capture and development. Future generations will not judge the current generation well if lessons are not learnt from earlier failings and efforts made quickly to restore the balance of benefits to give the owners of the resources at least an equal chance.

In relation to financed projects, Ghana needs to usually include provisions to guarantee specific performance criteria. For example: projects have to be completed according to agreed schedules, achieve their rated design capacities and the products must meet the design quality standards. In addition, the construction must conform to agreed international design requirements and the consumption of raw materials including feedstock and fuel and other utilities must satisfy the design specifications. Penalties for inadequate performance can range from 'make good' provisions to heavy financial impositions. Defect liability provisions must be enforced, and construction contractors must correct any defects that may arise during the operation of the facility. Provided everything goes according to plan with little or no obstruction or delays, the project should proceed relatively smoothly and deliver the financial returns expected by the project developers and financiers.

Recommendations of the health, safety, environment and community relations system have been made on the basis of the CASA Model which places the community at the heart of the issues relative to O&G. The Model operates on the basis that the community is central to the engagement process and collaborates with local authorities on issues of health, safety, environment and incident reporting. The pertinent communities need to be included in contributing to early warning systems also with the oil companies through the joint committee that may be established for projects and other related development and corporate social projects. Where the issue is of a nature that relates to emergencies, the oil companies and the relevant government agencies are expected to work together to handle the issue. At all times however, the community is kept apprised of what is happening because the people remain within the loop as outlined above. It is believed that this model would foster harmonious relations between communities, local authorities and the O&G companies operating in the Western Region.

Security for the region and protection for petroleum activities in Ghana cannot be overemphasized. To this end, a number of activities are critical to securing the peace and stability of the region and the country as a whole. Given the experience of neighbouring countries and the challenges encountered, it is only prudent that the country takes a serious view and learns lessons from those who have had this resource well ahead of Ghana. Recommendations for consideration in the area of security include: *engagement with local communities and fishermen* to secure the safety of installations and persons working with the petroleum sector; *employment for the youth* by organizing and training them to provide targeted support for the industry in areas where their skills may be required; *activation of the Police Unit for Oil and Gas* to support the other security agencies with a view to providing a coordinated action against all forms of crime; *undertake a risk assessment and develop a register* detailing high-risk areas, the types of risk and outline what needs to be done to mitigate the risks.

Regarding lessons that Ghana and other host nations can learn from model petroleum-producing countries, the first point is that, in keeping with international law, host nations own their natural resources. It is inconceivable that this stance will alter in the predictable future. Nonetheless, the likelihood is that the international community will exert pressure on host nations that are endowed with petroleum reserves to avail them for exploration, development and production, as part of a global strategy to meet energy needs. Consequently, resource-endowed nations such as Ghana et al. will maintain a key position in administering petroleum activities within their jurisdiction but will be influenced to contribute to the increasing global need for energy. In leading petroleum-producing countries, national oil companies are likely to maintain a pivotal role, but it may be advisable to work alongside IOCs so as to benefit from a rising need for operational management, financial resources and world-class technology.

Prospective operational and technological requirements regarding petroleum exploration and development will heighten the need to involve IOCs. The solution to achieving efficient exploration, development, extraction and utilization of the remaining petroleum resources lies in having a number of such organizations engaged in constructive competition with each other. Through constructive competition host nations such as Ghana et al. we will be able to optimize the universal gains that stem from these non-renewable resources.

The responsibilities of host nations such as Ghana and other new petroleum producers will differ based on the nation, the petroleum resource reserves, the market environment and the detailed needs of the projects under consideration. Where government behaviour is consistent, it will engender trust among potential investors. Nevertheless, consistency needs to be displayed alongside a readiness to be adaptable in responding to the specific conditions experienced by the industry, be it country or project related. In certain instances, development may entail the amalgamation of various concerns into a shared effort or project. It may also call for support from neighbouring nations. Irrespective of who makes the first move, host governments assume a cardinal role in promoting and facilitating such projects. In some cases the project may have to be initiated by the host government.

Within this context of anticipated challenges it is expected that the success of resource-blessed countries will still serve as a source of inspiration to new oil-producing nations. While precise propositions of these model countries may not be exactly germane, the lessons learnt in finding the appropriate answers will be beneficial in helping to discover custom-made solutions. In particular, profitable collaboration between host nations and the IOCs will remain a critical success factor in the long term.

In this book, it has been argued that natural resources can be a source of blessing or curse and in Ghana and other new host countries, there is a general consensus that the O&G can be a blessing if managed properly. Involvement of all the various stakeholders as well as transparent and efficient use of the income would guarantee development for all. This would also ensure public confidence in the management of the sector, on the basis of the sound equitable distribution of resources for current and future generations.

Index